C000001270

Isaa
A Life in Poetry

Chris Searle

To my old friend Siva,
who urged me to write it.

From the *Guardian*,
March 10, 1972

Isaac and I:
A Life in Poetry

Chris Searle

Five Leaves Publications
www.fiveleaves.co.uk

Isaac and I
A Life in Poetry
by Chris Searle

Published in 2017
by Five Leaves,

14a Long Row,
Nottingham NG1 2DH

Revised Edition 2021

www.fiveleaves.co.uk
www.fiveleavesbookshop.co.uk

ISBN 978-1-910170-80-9

Typeset by 4 Sheets Design and Print

Printed in Great Britain

Acknowledgements

I would like to thank all the poets and writers whose words I have quoted in this book, and the power and beauty of language that they have created. They have been my teachers during a lifetime of teaching.

My thanks too to Amanda Kitchen, for the skill of her word processing, Alan Dein, Tony Harcup, Joyce Hidden, Pedro Fuentes, Jenny Bourne, Liz Fekete, Harmit Athwal, Hazel Waters, Danny Reilly, Frances Webber, Jon Burnett and Colin Prescod for their encouragement, and to Ross Bradshaw and Five Leaves Publications for their publishing prowess. Also to Michael Rosen for his introduction and the everlasting educational spirit of his father Harold. My friend Dan Jones, truly a William Morris of our generation, generously painted the cover picture, and the book contains illustrations and photographs by other dear friends: Ron McCormick, Mel Robinson and Alan Gilbey. My thanks go to them all.

If this book makes author's royalties, they will be paid to UNICEF, for the benefit of the children of the world.

Forward ever,
Chris Searle,
March, 2017

Contents

Introduction

This is not just a book about Chris Searle. It's about a vision of poetry: poetry in education, poetry in a fight for a better world and poetry in life.

I have known Chris since the early 1970s. He drew me into publications and performances he was organising in schools, community centres and theatres, where people of all ages and many backgrounds, performed, declaimed and acted. Apart from being fantastic fun, deeply moving and uplifting, there was an important politics going on here: Chris resolutely and practically resisting a notion about people and art: that art is supposedly something that only arty people can do; and linked to all that: that people whose lives have been spent in doing non-arty jobs — or their children — supposedly can't do arty things. Right here, with the children, working people, and retired people who Chris brought together, such ideas were defied.

Anyone who came near to Chris, then or now, immediately gets a sense of him as someone with a motor inside him. It's not just the energy, though. It's the direction and the commitment. There were times when I wondered where this came from. How had he arrived at a point where he was so devoted to poetry, politics, education and progress? How had he arrived at a point where this devotion could enthuse others? On the odd occasions we chatted between sending each other poems, or waiting for shows to start, we swapped anecdotes about our backgrounds. One time, we did a gig together at Pimlico School, and a part of his life appeared in his performance that I hadn't even known about. One of the poems that he read was his translation of of a Mozambican poem about changing the image of the Land Rover from being the instrument of colonial armies into a friend of the people. He talked of 'decolonising the Land Rover'. I thought, how

9

surprising, how free, how defiant is that: to come into a London secondary school and make poetry out of Land Rovers![1]

Needless to say, this is the sort of thing that gets you into trouble — not that day, I hasten to add, because there was and still is a commitment amongst many teachers to see literature as something that stirs, awakens, changes and makes problems. It is never written for the purpose of streaming and segregating. It's not a matter of agreeing with it. It's a matter of accepting its power to provoke. But there have been times in Chris's life he's been in the headlines, in serious bother. He tells the story of one of these in this book. I remember reading about it in the papers. I have the booklets that kicked the whole thing off; I have Chris's great books *Classrooms of Resistance* and *The World in a Classroom* which lay out how he worked with school students. Yet neither of these nor his books of poems join the dots: how did he evolve, how did his life engage with his times?

Now we have it.

But we have more than that. In this book we aren't viewing the world solely through Chris's eyes. Chris shows us scores of writers, young and old, reflecting on the changes going on around them, thinking about the past, having 'conversations' with long dead writers. And these many conversations are folded within a longer conversation that Chris is having with Isaac Rosenberg.

So the book tells one story and many stories; anyone reading it will find crossovers, sometimes with Chris, but just as likely with any of the writers he puts in front of us. One example (you'll find others): Chris shares a conversation he has with Joseph Leftwich. Leftwich talks of the Stepney branch of the Young Socialist League from before the First World War. It brought out goose pimples on me: I owe my existence to that branch! It's exactly

---

[1] see Appendix for poem

where and how my father's parents: Morris Rosen and Rose Hyams met, Morris from Poland, Rose from Newcastle. It was a surprise to read, but shouldn't have been. It's what the book is about: people moving, changing and meeting to make a better world. In this process there can be no barriers on the basis that you belong to 'that lot'. We can be proud of who we are and where we came from, without that being a reason to keep myself apart from you.

This book spells this idea out in many, many different ways, through the beautiful words, dreams, hopes and images of the people Chris has encouraged and brought together. And, behind that, we can see why Chris did these things.

Michael Rosen

Preface

This book begins, continues and ends in poetry, in my life and in the life and inspiration of the young Jewish working class poet Isaac Rosenberg, who, at the age of twenty-eight, was killed in a war which killed millions like him of many nationalities, races and religions, a war made and managed by the powerful and the rich who controlled all the levers and economies of the societies in which their underlings lived and struggled.

In 2013, when I was sixty-nine, I went to my local hospital in Sheffield for a colonoscopy. Five years earlier I had been screened for and diagnosed with bowel cancer, and through the blessings of the National Health Service, within two weeks of diagnosis I had surgery at the same hospital to remove the tumour. The colonoscopy was a key part of my post-operative care to determine whether the cancer had returned.

As I lay back in the surgery for the camera to pass through my gut, its passage revealed to me on a small screen directly above the table where five years before I had seen the contours of the tumour inside me, a nurse — a man in his fifties, I should think — sat next to me for care and reassurance, while the consultant colonoscopist pursued his task with skill and acuity. The nurse asked me about myself as the images of the inside of my intestine flickered across the screen above me. I told him that I was a recently retired English teacher. He told me that he read a lot of poetry and we began to talk about the poets we both loved most.

For him it was the poetry of Wilfred Owen, one of my beloved poets too, and we exchanged lines from his *Strange Meeting* as if they were our own words. I told him about the East Londoner Rosenberg, killed in the same war as Wilfred, and quoted lines from some of his great trench poems like, *Returning, We Hear the Larks* and *Dead Man's Dump*.

'Did you say his name was Isaac?' said my nurse and new-found friend. 'Do you know Owen's poem about Abraham and Isaac called *The Parable of the Old Men and the Young*?' he asked me as my eyes searched the screen for threatening images. 'No, I don't know it,' I said, 'Tell me about it.' He quoted lines from it verbatim while he grasped my hand, this wonderful nurse, like his predecessors, those who had held the living and dying hands of thousands of young soldiers like Wilfred and Isaac. The poem begins to re-tell the narrative of Jehovah's test of Abraham's faith. But this Abraham does not hearken to Jehovah's messenger, the angel, to tell him that he must not kill his son after he has bound the youth 'with belts and straps/And builded parapets and trenches there', and like the Kaiser, the King and his whisky friend Lord Haig, he does not listen and he 'slew his son/And half the seed of Europe, one by one.'

The poem had such an effect upon me as I lay in that theatre that it had made me forget the camera inside me, and I had remained unaware of its removal, as the consultant turned to me and said to me simply: 'You're fine.'

I thought to myself of my friends Isaac and Wilfred and all the others and I knew how it was never fine for them. Yet the consultant's brilliance, the nurse's humanity and the words of two loving poets had taken me through these moments nearly a century later and I thanked the power, insight and healing of poets and their poetry and doctors and their medicine. As for the nurse, I had never met him before and have never met him since and I don't know his name. And yet for a few minutes poetry made us brothers and I will never forget him.

Chapter One
Divide and School Blues

I was born in February 1944 in the Essex outskirts of London, in the market town of Romford. During my first months of life the Nazi doodlebugs, the flying bombs aimed at the capital from their occupied French launching pads, fell on and all around our town. There were no blue suburban skies over Romford that year. My parents had a black spaniel, Tessie, who would hear the drone of the doodlebug's engines a good half a minute before my parents, and when she heard them she would howl and cavort crazily around the bungalow, giving us priceless extra time to reach the Anderson shelter at the bottom of our small back garden. There were many direct hits close by, and my mother would always say that it was Tessie that had saved our lives — hers, my sister's and mine — when the doodlebugs fell. My father, a fireman in the Auxiliary Fire Service, was dousing fires and rescuing those injured in the Blitz. The school I was to go to was badly bombed, streets I would later walk down were savaged and pubs I would drink in during my teenage years were wrecked and torn apart. Growing up in the shadow of the Blitz is, I believe, why I hate war and have always campaigned against it, like many of my generation who may have similar conscious or subconscious memories.

My father was the son of a country pub landlord, first in Great Waltham, Essex, and then closer into London at Lambourne End on the edge of Epping Forest. His mother had grown up in the northern Essex village of Coggleshall, and had been the daughter of a very singular union. Her mother's father was a prosperous Norfolk country squire. He employed a gamekeeper who crossed class lines and fell

The rocking horse came to the surface when a large house at the corner of Heath Drive and Main Road, Gidea Park, was completely demolished on November 1st 1940. One person in the house was killed.

Photograph from:
Ordeal in Romford
(Romford Mutual Help
Association, 1945)

for the squire's daughter. Her love for him was also rebelliously strong, and when their relationship was exposed, he was dismissed and she was disinherited. They moved to Essex where they both became agricultural labourers. There were few prospects for their daughter — my grandmother — and she migrated during the 1890s to East London to work in service for a wealthy Jewish family in Stoke Newington. She would always say that they treated her more like a daughter than a servant, and would never tolerate any anti-Jewish comments, always repudiating them powerfully with an instant riposte. She passed this on to my father who had many Jewish clients in London and Germany, and took me to meet them often in brushmaking factories and pubs in Hackney. And then, a salt beef sandwich in Bloom's kosher restaurant in Aldgate East, just up from Whitechapel Library, the meat carved straight from the steaming boiled joint in the window and piled between thick slices of rye bread — it was heaven for an ever-hungry gentile boy like me. My father would tell me about his own life as an East London boy growing up in Leyton and his vivid memories of the war before the one which bore me. He lived through the Zeppelin raids and remembered hundreds of local families piling into the basement of Leyton Town Hall for refuge. He also had a distant view of the first Zeppelin to be shot down, by the Royal Flying Corps pilot Leefe Robinson over the Essex countryside. He told me of the hellish ball of flame in the sky as the Zeppelin dived towards the earth.

My father's mother was a powerful woman who carried the heartsblood of history inside her like a living page. She used to speak of her childhood prime ministers, 'Mr Gladstone and Mr Disraeli' as if they were still the denizens of Downing Street. Every Sunday morning, when I used to visit her with my father, after I filled up her scuttles with coal from the backyard bunker, she would ask me to address the air mail envelopes for the weekly letters that she sent to her daughter, my Auntie Connie, who had emigrated to Australia in 1919 after she married an Anzac soldier. She never saw her again, and I never met her. Travel to and from Australia was both rare and expensive in those days, but the weekly letters were sent faithfully every Monday for over half a century to the address still imprinted on my memory: Mrs C. Linklater, 4 Nicklin Street, Coorparoo, Brisbane, Australia. As a boy I built fantasies about this place, which to me was as far away as it was possible to reach, even though, as my father insisted, they played tough cricket there.

As for my mother, she came from a very different background. She was the thirteenth child of a Welsh toymaker named Herbert Rees from Abergavenny who had become rich in the years prior to the 1914–18 war, and an Irish immigrant mother. She had grown up with a nanny and a horse and carriage in a very stylish street near Clapham Common, but her father's wealth dissolved in the years after the war, largely, it was whispered by her sisters (for all the family affairs were spoken in whispers) because of their elder brothers' spendthrift ways. Her father became a Tory councillor in Battersea, and he was sent to France in the beginning of the war to urge on the troops. I once read a newspaper report about this, and I remember how shocked and ashamed I felt. After her father's ruin turned to family crisis, my mother was sent to live with her very stern married elder sister in Romford in her large house overlooking the Gallows Corner County Cricket ground. She would go into the long back garden to watch the cricket at the weekends, and my father, when his side was batting, would stroll around the boundary and meet her, talking over the fence. It was a cricket idyll, and my sister and I had been born out of it. So without a doubt, cricket was in my blood too.

I don't know how old I was, perhaps three or four, but this was one of the first things I can remember, even now. I was standing by our front gate with Tessie, as I used to almost every day, when a man started talking to me, and led me away to a grassy field at the end of our road. I can't remember what he did beyond laying me down and lying

18

next to me, but I remember my mother racing towards me, screaming and waving her arms as if she were possessed. As she was, of course, with anger, fear and love. The man saw her hurtling towards him, and small as she was, she was enough to make him rise and run away towards the hedge that separated the field from the park, and beyond. I can remember my mother picking me up, weeping and enraged, and carrying me back home, sitting me down while she shook, giving me juice and biscuits and holding me tight, crying while I ate them. How dear, how blessed are mothers and their love.

My mother's family never escaped their rigidly Tory upbringing, with the exception of one of her sisters, Ruby — or Auntie Rue, as I knew her. Of all my aunts, I loved her the most. She was full of laughter, friendliness and generosity and I could tell that my mother loved to be with her. Then one day in my teens, I heard my mother whispering over the phone to another of her sisters. They were talking about Auntie Rue, I could hear that, but when I asked my mother about her, she embarrassedly said nothing. A couple of years later Auntie Rue died and the whispers spoke of suicide and my dear Auntie being a lesbian. Such were the secretive and repressed ways of middle-class families, and my rebellious Auntie Rue became another hero.

My father told me a story of the Blitz which I shall always remember. He played centre-forward for a local football team, and one morning he was called out when a doodlebug had hit a house in a Romford street. The house had been obliterated, and within the wreckage there were two bodies, two brothers. He recognised them as the inside left and inside right of his team, and now he was between them again. And in his bookcase I found a book, published in the year after the war, called *Ordeal in Romford,* with reminiscences and photographs about the Blitz. In one photograph, a fireman struggles to put out a fire engulfing a blazing building. He told me that was him. And in another, a child's undamaged rocking horse swings over the debris of a totally devastated house. I used to think, where are the children that used to ride it and the mother and father who would push it? I thanked my lucky stars that we had survived.

My post-war memories of primary school were almost entirely happy: times of friendships, learning, drama and cricket. But I was outlandishly huge for my years — tall, fat and very clumsy, and I would react angrily to anyone who ridiculed me because of it. I once took a much older boy's bike and put it up a tree because he was laughing at my size. And another time, feeling irate and frustrated at another boy who called me names in the playground, vexed and desperate, I sought to gain revenge by taking my penis from my short trousers and shouting at him: 'That's a picture of you!' A dinner lady saw me, reported me to the head teacher who didn't want to know any reasons and simply gave me the cane. Then there was the 'country dancing' class that filled me with embarrassment. There was a prancing dance we had to do with our partners called *Little Man in a Fix,* but I could only feel like a big fat boy in a fix. But these were rare negative moments. I played the black king of Ethiopia, Balthazar, in the nativity play, and the teachers wiped deep black Cherry Blossom shoe polish all over my face, my neck and hands, and it took two weeks to come off and I was sore and chapped all through January. And in the play written by the drama-mad art teacher, Mr Rudd, called *Bats in Begonia,* about a mythical kingdom enduring a plague of bats, I played the King's Lord Chancellor, who bossed around the palace cleaning ladies as they sang out to me:

> We are the girls of the mop brigade
> And we do our best to keep the palace clean.
> We scrub and rub at the marble floors
> And wipe the sticky finger marks from all the doors.

Sixteen years later after I was sacked from my teaching job in East London for publishing the anthology of my students' work, *Stepney Words,* the children came out on strike and wrote their slogans and messages over the school walls. Although the school cleaners, all local women, were commanded by the head to wipe them away, they refused. And I remembered that play and the 'girls of the mop brigade'.

Every day as I walked to school and sucked penny chews from the papershop called 'The Gem' or chewed on their bubblegum, entranced by the footballers' cards of Stan Matthews, Billy Wright or Tom Finney, I passed hundreds of besuited men striding and clipping to Gidea Park Station to catch their trains at an exact time. And I wondered, where are they all going, and why, to do what? My own father was one of them and yet I had no idea about their magnet of the City of London, the centre of 'work' and the city of capital, and how much huge power and leverage it had in the commerce, finances and control in our post-war world. When I went with him once to his office buildings in Creechurch Lane, in the heart of the still bomb-scarred city near Houndsditch, I couldn't believe that this was the mysterious place that these thousands disappeared to every morning, a place so wounded and smashed, but still the apex of wealth. They were an army with their rolled-up umbrellas, their *Daily Telegraphs* and *Daily Expresses* under their arms, and I wondered, who did they serve — for they dressed as if they were servants. Who were their masters who summoned them to catch the same train, every day, to a place called Liverpool Street? And I had this aching feeling that whatever happened to me in the future, I could never be like them.

Then Saturday morning and it was the Romford Odeon for Saturday Morning Pictures. The films and serials were all American, full of comic book heroes, Americans saving the world, good cowboys and very bad Indians, and Laurel and Hardy escaping every week from astonishing scrapes. And yet if the screen lauded and praised America, the songs we sang before them, with an organ rising from the pit in front of the stage and the cinema manager in evening suit and bow tie introducing and conducting them with their words behind him on the screen, were very, very English. The organist piped out *There'll Always Be an England, Take Me Back to Dear Old Blighty, Lambeth*

Walk, Roll Out the Barrel or *The White Cliffs of Dover,* and as we all heartily sang 'Red, white and blue,/What does it mean to you?', we knew it meant that we were English; absolutely and undoubtedly English — for always, forever.

Halfway home from school I would stand on the embankment overlooking Gidea Park station and wait for the Britannia Class engines that pulled the express trains between Liverpool Street and Norwich. What a sight and what a sound as they roared and rampaged through the station without stopping! I could just make out their nameplates as they stormed through in a hissing cloud of steam. Imperial icons like Sir Walter Raleigh and Clive of India; rebels like Boadicea — the only woman — Hereward the Wake, Owen Glendower or Oliver Cromwell; writers and poets like Geoffrey Chaucer, William Shakespeare, John Milton, William Wordsworth and Lord Byron — it was the first time I had ever known of these names that were to feature in my life and knowledge, and I learned them, sunken deep in my consciousness, from the side of seething and speeding steam engines as their iron wheels hurtled past me going northwards.

Then the main event was upon me and like all my classmates I took the eleven-plus scholarship examination. I was a boy from a local and very ordinary middle- class family — my father had worked for the same commodity brokers' firm in the city since he left school at fourteen in 1922 (his 'commodity' was bristles, from the backs of Chinese pigs) — and it was assumed I would 'pass the scholarship' and go to the local grammar school. I failed, three times over. I failed the first exam but was given an interview at Coopers' School in Mile End, East London, which I also failed. Then I took a re-sit and failed that too. So that was that and I went with all the other failures (that was about 80% of us then, mostly from the working class) to a secondary modern school for boys, Hylands, which also took in many boys from the local boys' orphanage, the Cottage Homes, who were immediately recognisable because they didn't wear school blazers but charitably discarded tweed sports jackets and baggy loose trousers with deep turn-ups. One made it big in my first year though, becoming the first Hylands boy to pass five O-level examinations when he was sixteen, after doing an extra year, for most boys left at fifteen at the end of their fourth year. I remember his name even now because he became so famous through the school: Derek Chinnery. He was a good actor too and played the lead role in a play about Columbus. Hylands had its heroes and he was certainly one of them.

I was put in the 'A' class and told that preparations would begin straight away to train us for the thirteen-plus examination, the 'Late Developers' — which was the final chance for a few secondary moderners across the borough to make it to grammar school. I wondered how though, when I saw the school library, which was just one bookcase in the corner of the English teacher's room. By the end of my first year I had read most of its contents. But my English teacher at Hylands became my first teacher-hero. He was Mr Clarke, a young Bristolian whose reading lessons with a succession of class readers became the most exciting experiences of my young life. I remember how scared I was, when in J. Meade Faulkner's *Moonfleet* the young protagonist finds the corpse of the pirate Bluebeard and inadvertently pulls off his beard: or the terrifying jeopardy in Robert Louis Stevenson's *Kidnapped* of walking up the dark, decaying staircase in the old house's spectral tower. And then the sudden now-times relevance of a group of urban boys playing on bombsites in C. Day Lewis' novel *The Otterbury Incident*. Books and their words started to come alive for me. And this young teacher cast me as a Greek tribune, in a play about Aesop and his fables, and looking back I often wondered if I felt intimations of trade union struggles to come.

He also opened up the heart of language with me. When he taught us the 'parts of speech', new words which I have remembered all my life came bursting out of his definitions. 'What does an adjective do?' he asked us. He answered: 'an adjective qualifies a noun,' it didn't just describe a noun, it *qualified* a noun! Or 'what does an adverb do?', it doesn't just add to a verb's meaning, 'It *modifies* a verb.' What words were these, and I was learning them. I loved him for it. And when he taught us the 'figures of speech' he went through all of their crazy and astonishing names: he explained simile and metaphor and went on to others with even more beguiling names, alliteration, assonance — even onomatopoeia, giving striking examples of all of them. Then he came to 'hyperbole', what a word! 'It is an exaggeration for the sake of effect!' he declared, and then he quoted Lady Macbeth after the murder of Duncan: 'All the perfumes of Arabia cannot sweeten this little hand.' It was the first time I had met Shakespeare and I was learning to understand and love his words and power of language from this Bristol teacher in his early twenties with a teaching certificate but no degree. I felt that I needed no other teacher but him, that he was teaching me everything, that he was opening up a world to me that I had to dive into.

My other boyhood love was cricket. My father was a fanatical cricketer who had opened the bowling all his life. During the late thirties he had been on the fringe of playing county cricket for Essex, but the war stopped all that. His opening partner for Gidea Park Cricket Club had been the future Essex and England bowler Ken Farnes, who was killed on an RAF training flight in 1941. Later in my life when I read his biography, I was to learn that he had given up work as a city commuter and become a school teacher. When he went to South Africa in 1938–39 as part of the England touring team, he had been disgusted at the status quo in the republic and the conditions of life of the black majority. He became a legendary presence within our house and my father would always talk about him with veneration. It was said that Farnes was faster off the pitch than my father, who was reckoned to be quicker through the air. Strange that they were both East London six-footers, my father was born in Leyton in 1908, Farnes in Leytonstone in 1911.

My father sent me to the Romford Cricket School in the yard in the centre of the old coaching inn, The Golden Lion, in the middle of town, where for ten shillings I was coached for half an hour a week by the ex-Essex opening batsman, Sonny Avery. He taught me the basics of forward and back-foot defence and his insistence on mastering these stayed with me all through my life. At home, in the garden, my father would toss me a leather ball, stand five yards away from me and say 'Right, throw it at my head, as hard as you can!' It always filled me with fear, for I was big and weighty and had a powerful arm for my age. But I did what he said, and he caught the ball every time. He was an astonishing catcher. I must have watched him play hundreds of times (I was his team's official scorer) and I never, ever, saw him drop a catch. He gave me a cloth rabbit when I was very young, when toys were scarce just after the war. 'Where did you get it, Dad?' I once asked him. And he told me. He'd been to a variety concert at an East End theatre during the war and a comedian tossed a couple of these rabbits, holding cloth carrots, into the audience. He stuck out his hand and caught one of them, like the true cricketer that he was. I've still got it, it sits on the floor next to my bookcase, its ears sticking up, the carrot between its paws, telling me again where I came from and the cricket that ran through my father's blood into mine.

Our secondary modern shared a large playing field with the local girls' grammar school, Romford County High, but we only had a miniscule corner of the grounds, with awkward access through a local builder's yard. It was officially anathema to watch the girls at their sports, punishable by the cane: they were grammar school girls and a world apart from us. As for our teachers, many of them were ex-servicemen, emergency-trained in the immediate post-war years and strong, authoritarian disciplinarians who transferred their militarism to school classrooms and corridors, particularly within the ambience of an all-boys secondary modern. The cricket teacher, Mr Kirby, for example, a kind and tolerant man, often whacked me in his technical drawing classes (but not very hard), for talking or not listening, with a wooden pencil holder — his preferred weapon. But he always gave me tremendous encouragement in the under-thirteen cricket team, made me captain and when I got six wickets for no runs against a rival school, sent off my figures to *The Star,* a London-wide evening paper. I didn't get a 'Star' bat, the number one accolade for young London cricketers, but a crisp 'Star' certificate which was lauded by the school. Our form teacher and the school's geography supremo was Mr Siebert, who had been in submarines all through the war. He taught his lessons with real narrative skill with frequent tales of the ocean depths, which gave an added piquancy to the film which was doing the rounds at the time of Jules Verne's fantastical and prophetic novel, *20,000 Leagues Under the Sea,* and Mr Siebert became my very own Captain Nemo. His remarkable aura meant he never had to beat anyone, unlike the PE teacher, a Welshman called Mr Powell who regularly struck my backside hard with a springy plimsoll for my everyday failures to execute a forward roll because of what I was convinced was my grotesque size and weight. He made me feel even more self-conscious and would laugh to the rest of the class while he belted me and then slap me on the back when he'd finished. It didn't seem much like a joke to me, and low self-esteem about my physical appearance haunted me from then right through my adolescence.

But the only teacher I despised was a man called Mr Gamble, who used to tell weird stories to captivate his classes about a mythical polity called 'Gambleland' where rivers ran uphill and the people were quiet, obedient, submissive subjects like he expected his pupils to be. Anyone who spoke out of turn or irritated him would be summoned to the front of the class, compelled to clench their bare knuckles and he would take his sharp-edged metal ruler and strike the flesh of our upper fingers, often causing them to badly bruise and bleed. Looking back, I wondered how he got away with it for years. Parents accepted and agreed with corporal punishment in the main, but that!

And even then I imagined Gambleland as a land of tyranny and pain, an infantile vision of a fascist state led by a sadistic madman. And I learned all this, the very good and the profoundly bad, at a very ordinary secondary modern school in the mid-fifties.

We had an importunate 'scripture' teacher who bundled many of us into the school's 'Scripture Union' where we would assemble and study the Bible during lunch hours and after school, and wear our green badges with the oil lamp emblem. At about the same time I became a regular attender at the local Church of England church, once on Remembrance Day carrying a Union Jack down the aisle, nearly tripping on its long, spearheaded flagpole (which the National Front used to use as weapons two decades after), and feeling that I was doing it all for God and England, whom, we were told, were inseparable. But this was never called brainwashing; we were told that we were behaving like good English boys.

There was a martinet of a music teacher called Miss Arthur, a stern, determined and remarkable woman with an implacable frown who even the most rebellious boy found unchallengeable, who in this boys-only secondary modern amassed a school orchestra of some thirty unlikely young Romford musicians who became more than proficient on their string, woodwind and brass instruments, and who as a music collective won many local awards and prizes. You would see working-class Hylands boys on local streets, among market stalls and sitting over local parks with battered violin cases or carrying trumpets. 'We must have music!' she would emphatically declare in music lessons, and her words have stayed with me for a lifetime.

In 1957 I took yet another examination to gain a tardy place in a grammar school — my last chance. There were many at Hylands who were brilliantly intelligent and who deserved it too, but I was one of the three lucky ones. I got an interview for Hornchurch Grammar, recently built on what were the fields of a local gherkin farm where I would later work in my school holidays. As usual I performed woefully at the interview, but impressed the headmaster in the final minute when I correctly spelt the word 'excerpt'. I was in, and it all hinged on one word and a cluster of consonants. I wondered how life would taste without my Hylands friends whom I suddenly realised I was leaving behind, and with no Mr Clarke and Mr Kirby to boost me. And looking back, I think I felt like Byron's *Prisoner of Chillon,* which I was to study at this new school for my O-level English:

> My very chains and I grew friends,
> So much a long communion tends
> To make us what we are: even I
> Regain'd my freedom with a sigh.

And what new freedoms were suddenly at hand. The resources seemed extraordinary: three separate cricket fields with well-tended grass pitches, not the old single downhill composition pitch at Hylands anymore. Five full-sized football pitches, hockey pitches, tennis courts and an athletics track, and the science laboratories were nothing like I'd ever envisage could be in a mere school. And our classroom to hold our class, '2 Remove' — we were put back a year with students a year younger, supposedly to compensate for what we had missed out at secondary modern — was overlooking the entry onto the playing fields where the girls would stream out in their T-shirts and PE knickers. Such a distraction was like heaven for the boys in our class, but the real measurement of change was our first library lesson. From a single bookcase to a large chamber of thousands of books. During the lesson the teacher in charge of the library taught us about the Dewey Decimal System of organising the tomes. Then he gave us some titles to find. He pointed at me: 'Find me the book called *Mathematics for the Millions* by Lancelot Hobden,' he said, and I set about finding the book like an obedient Labrador finding a shot bird. I found it after a long search and dutifully brought it to him. Later, I wished I'd read it because I was always hopeless at maths. In my first week I thought of my friends I had left behind at Hylands so many times, and how incredibly unfair it all was. I knew nothing about comprehensive schools at the time, but from September 1957 and ever since I would have marched across England to champion them, even at the expense of these enveloping educational riches that I was suddenly a part of which belonged to the privileged suburban youths all around me who were now my contemporaries, although some were my old primary school classmates, now a full year ahead of me and already pitching for sixth form and ultimately university places — their proper sequence of life. And would it be mine too? I wondered.

My fear of P.E. though evaporated during my first year of this new school, and this was entirely due to the P.E. teacher. His name was John Salisbury and he was an England sprinter, a 400 metres rocket who had won a bronze medal in the relay at the 1956 Melbourne Olympics. He became my ideal, and not just because of his extraordinary handsomeness, but because even though I continued to be hopeless at gymnastics, he treated me in a completely contrary way to Mr Powell at Hylands. He was friendly, fair and utterly supportive, never ridiculing or humiliating me because of my size and clumsiness, but talking to me like the big brother I never had. He used to give evening talks at local schools and youth clubs about his Olympic experiences and I would go and help him set up his slide equipment, thinking that just by being there with him I was giving back to him the support and friendship that he was giving to me at school. I remember coming home one February night on my bike from one of his talks. The smog and darkness was so thick, I couldn't see beyond my handlebars. But I didn't care. I felt so proud and pleased to help him, even in the smallest way. When he moved on to another school somewhere in the Midlands after my first year, I felt lost. I suppose. looking back, it was a kind of hero-worship, even love that I felt for him, although at the time I would never have used the word. When I eventually became a teacher, ten years on, I realised that after Mr Clarke, he was my first exemplar.

Looking back, the thirteen-plus approach was not successful. Out of the thirty original members of 2R I was the only one to get to university directly from school, and I was nineteen and a half when I got there. There were other institutional barriers: five streams in a year (six, in our case with the Remove stream) and as I was to find out it was very difficult for us in the Remove stream to gain university entry for an arts subject because we never had the opportunity to study Latin, which was only available for the higher streams and which you needed in order to study subjects like my choice, English, at university. Only three British universities (Hull, Leeds and Wales) would take you without O-level Latin. I was lucky to be eventually accepted for Leeds in 1963. But in 2R we felt a little like a miniature secondary modern within a grammar school. Some students would scoff at us being there and others in our age group definitely classed us as underlings, which was certainly how we felt when we talked about it. 'What are we doing here?' some of my new classmates would say as they dealt with being the school's lowest of the low. My friend Johnny lived on the new council estate of Harold Hill, where his and many other East London families had re-settled from bombed-out neighbourhoods after the war. He seemed lost and completely disorientated at this school. He knew it wasn't made for him and couldn't get home quick enough to play his collection of Elvis albums and tend to his many aquaria of tropical fish, about which he had an enormous knowledge — he was a future marine biologist if ever anyone deserved to be one. But no, even though he was there at this school with all the resources, in his head he wasn't there, for it was a school designed for and for the absolute benefit of the middle class, and unless you moved within that culture and landscape, there was really very little for you at all.

But despite my Hylands years, I was still petit-bourgeois enough to throw myself into the heart of this new learning environment, and my determination to do well at my two loves, cricket and drama, drove me forward. I got a bit-part as Thomas the footman in the school production of Sheridan's *The Rivals* in my first year, and moved on to a much bigger part in the next production, Thornton Wilder's *Our Town*, as Doc Gibbs, in American accent too. In 3R I played my first season, the first of five, for the school cricket first eleven, getting the best batting average and many mentions in school assembly. In 1959 I moved from 3R which was dissolved, into 4B which was the school's third stream after A and Alpha, and before Beta and Gamma, and which was to prepare me for my O-Levels.

But it all was clouded over during our first experiences of the deaths of our heroes. I remember the resentful exchange I had with our art teacher when she dismissed the deaths of the Manchester United footballers after the Munich air crash in February 1958 as inconsequential and over-publicised. The wonderful twenty-two-year-old Duncan Edwards was fighting for his life in a German hospital at the time — he was to die a few days later — and I had seen those young players: Roger Byrne, Tommy Taylor and all the others, a few weeks before at The Valley, when my father took me to see them play Charlton Athletic. Edwards in particular was brilliant: how could she talk about them in that way? And Buddy Holly, who sang all those songs of frustrated teenage love that I felt, and then died in a plane crash in a freezing Iowa in February 1959 and his posthumous hit, *It Doesn't Matter Anymore* being played everywhere. Or the newsreels of my first African hero, Congo's president, Patrice Lumumba, taken in the back of a truck to his death in 1961, his wrists tied, his clothes bedraggled. Or the March 1960 massacre of the peacefully demonstrating sixty-nine black South Africans at Sharpeville and the deformities of apartheid suddenly revealed. And the 1961–62 trial of the Nazi death-camp murderer Adolf Eichmann which told us, in horrific detail, of the murder of millions: Jews, Gypsies, Slavs, communists. It was all around us, and we learned well.

Many school students are lucky enough to meet a teacher who truly changes their lives, and for me it was my new form teacher, also my English teacher. His name was Norman Hidden, then in his late forties, and although I knew none of this then, he had already had a remarkable life. An ex-student of Hereford Cathedral School who had spent some of his childhood in a caravan in the New Forest after his father had returned homeless from the 1914–18 war, a teacher in America, a liaison officer to the US Army in Frankfurt during the latter stages of the 1939–45 war, a left Labour candidate who stood against Churchill's Colonial Secretary Oliver Lyttelton in 1950 in the army town of Aldershot, and he was an ex-Labour councillor in East Yorkshire. He had two broken marriages to German Jewish women behind him: one had been a Holocaust refugee, the other a communist who had returned to East Germany after the war. And here he was, 'The Chief' as we all called him, somehow Head of English in a suburban backwater like Hornchurch in a very conservative grammar school where the Head of History, who was my O-level history teacher, would champion the exploits of British imperialists like Palmerston (who he intimately called 'Pam') and Disraeli ('Dizzy') and say of the hostility between the huge communist nations of China and the Soviet Union: 'Our great hope is that they will, sooner or later, wipe each other out!'

When I began to study seventeenth-century British history and the ferocity of the English Civil War, I was right behind the parliamentary forces, particularly the Round-head rebels like Gerrard Winstanley and the Levellers. Then I learned about Cromwell's campaigns in Ireland, the colonisation of Ulster and the massacre at Drogheda. I was left bewildered, thinking of my grandmother Alice O'Dwyer from Tipperary and her ancestors. Where were they during Cromwell's hideous invasion? How far from Drogheda would they have been? How could Cromwell and those republican soldiers do that? History was beginning to catch up with me and mould its influence around my life.

Something about 'Chiefie' pulled me towards him. He loved poetry and cricket too, which was the best of starts.

In his later years he gave me a short story he had written during his time at Hornchurch called *Six Balls is a Lifetime*, which he told me was about the fearful experience of facing me in the staff/students annual cricket match. 'The glare of the eyeball streaked red and the ball hurtling through at his wicket,' he wrote. He taught me English for four years. During that time he showed us 'method' acting, took us to my first Shakespeare productions, including *Romeo and Juliet* at the Old Vic, where the boys all fell in love with Judi Dench in Zeffirelli's passionate production; and Paul Scofield's epochal performance of *King Lear*, where he declaimed his speeches in a Midlands working-class accent, changing my understanding of Shakespeare in a moment. When I re-read the play after I retired in 2012, I understood the play had new meaning for me about the process of retirement, and I was hearing Chiefie's class-room declamations and Scofield's wonderful voice in every word I read.

Chiefie opened up poetry to me, bringing to his classes now-times poems by Ted Hughes (*Hawk Roosting*), Thom Gunn, D.J. Enright and the American Randall Jarrell in the context of studying Chaucer, Shakespeare, Thackeray and Austen. I began to understand British Imperialism for the first time as he taught us E.M. Forster's *A Passage to India,* and when he showed us the mere five lines of Jarrell's 1945 poem, *The Death of the Ball Turret Gunner,* it hit us like a storm:

> From my mother's sleep I fell into the state,
> And I hunched in its belly till my wet fur froze.
> Six miles from earth, loosed from its dream of life,
> I woke to black flak and the nightmare Fighters.
> When I died they washed me out of the turret with a hose.

We read this in our English class around the time of the Aldermaston marches and the Cuban missile crisis and it carried a meaning we could well understand.

But this was three years after a dramatic encounter with poetry in our O-level English class. We were studying traditional ballads from the *Oxford Book of Narrative Verse*.

One of the set texts was *Hugh of Lincoln and the Jew's Daughter*. Chiefie read it out loud in his feigned Border accent and reached the point in the poem where the Jew's daughter, having tempted the young aristocrat into her house, proceeds to ritually murder him:

> She's wyled him in through ae dark door,
> And sae has she through nine;
> She's laid him on a dressing table,
> And stickit him like a swine.

> And first came out the thick, thick blood,
> And syne came out the thin,
> And syne came out the bonny heart's blood;
> There was no more within.

At this point Anita, the only Jewish pupil in the class, rose from her desk and ran from the room weeping. We were all speechless, including Chiefie; none of us had thought of or predicted such a response, despite the poem's overt and terrifying anti-semitism. Several of Anita's friends went after her, and I remember going too and seeing her crying on the stairs with her friends' arms enveloping her as she bitterly sobbed. When she came back, surrounded by her friends, the Chief apologised and then spoke of how deeply racism had infected the language and its multiple forms of expression. I thought of Anita's father, who I knew well as he owned a bookstall in Romford Market — Bob's Bookstall — where I had bought many cheap second-hand books, and where he would save and show me books he thought I might be interested in. 'What would he think?' I thought. It shocked us all, teacher and the taught. How could a mere poem carry such agony? We began to understand that day messages that Anita, and Bob too, must have known all their lives. For me it was an intimation of the power of language, and in particular the power of poetry.

Much more was to come clear in the Lower Sixth as a result of the school production of Bertolt Brecht's *The Caucasian Chalk Circle* which was directed by a young drama teacher, Miss Robinson, but produced and overseen by the Chief. How he managed to persuade the conservative head teacher to agree to a play by a German communist to be performed at a suburban Essex grammar school in the middle of the Cold War, just sixteen years after the war with Germany, I'll never know, but his powers of persuasion were always formidable. As it was the play had a cast of fifty with many different scenes, settings, costumes and properties, so dozens of pupils were directly involved. I played the part of Simon Shashava, the soldier who falls for the play's protagonist, Grusha Vashnadze, a kitchen maid who cares for the abandoned son of the governor's wife, and eventually adopts him. The play's poetry sent me into raptures, particularly the narrator's revolutionary verses which coursed in my teenage blood:

> O blindness of the great!
> They go their way like gods,
> Great over bent backs,
> Sure of hired fists,
> Trusting in the power
> Which has lasted so long.
> But long is not forever.
> O change from age to age!
> Thou hope of the people!

And the moment that Grusha, responding to the dictum 'Terrible is the temptation to do good', finds the forsaken and starving boy:

> And she rose, and bent down and sighing, took the child
> And carried it away.
> As if it was stolen goods she picked it up
> As if she was a thief she crept away.

As if to seal it, after the final performance the Chief took us to the Aldwych Theatre in the West End to see the Royal Shakespeare Company's production of the play we had acted in on our school stage, with Patsy Byrne as Grusha, the rampaging Hugh Griffith, who had just played the drunken squire in the film of *Tom Jones* as the anarchic judge Azdak, and Michael Flanders, the wheelchaired singer of the double act 'Flanders and Swann' as the narrator. Yes, it was a wonderful and telling production, but we all thought proudly, 'We had done it first!'

Acting in Brecht gave me an intense appetite for the theatre. I spent almost all my pocket money on the cheapest gallery and upper circle seats that I could find in London theatres and on the five-shilling return on the tube between Hornchurch and Charing Cross to reach them. For me, the most extraordinary aspect of watching these plays was seeing the same actors in films in local cinemas one week, and then on the stage the next. So I watched Albert Finney in *Saturday Night and Sunday Morning* or *Tom Jones* in the Hornchurch Odeon, then saw him live on the stage in the name part in John Osborne's *Luther* or as the border rebel Johnnie Armstrong in John Arden's inspiring *Armstrong's Last Goodnight* with Ian McKellen and Derek Jacobi. Or to see Richard Harris in my film of films, Lindsay Anderson's *This Sporting Life,* and a few weeks later to behold him for an hour and a half as the lone actor on the Royal Court stage in Gogol's *Diary of a Madman.* Or to watch, entranced, director David Lean's desert landscapes and Peter O'Toole's acting in *Lawrence of Arabia* and then to see O'Toole a few weeks on in the flesh as the drunken protagonist in Brecht's early play *Baal.* Or to be inside the head of Tom Courtenay's borstal athlete in *The Loneliness of the Long Distance Runner* or share his outrageous fantasies in *Billy Liar,* then examine the truth of racism with him in the National Theatre production of Max Frisch's *Andorra* at the Old Vic.

And the magnificent young women actors who have seemed to be with me all my life, and still are: Vanessa Redgrave in *As You Like It* or Chekhov's *The Seagull;* Helen Mirren as Cressida; Diana Rigg as Cordelia in Scofield's *Lear* and the nurse in Durrenmatt's *The Physicists* and the wonderful Maggie Smith with her comic genius lighting up *Much Ado About Nothing* as Beatrice or in Restoration comedies like *The Beaux Stratagem* or Farquhar's *The Recruiting Officer* with her superb actor-husband Robert Stephens, and Olivier as the absurd

Captain Brazen. It was all a feast of brilliant stagecraft for me, capped by some extraordinary performances like Alec Guinness in Ionesco's *Exit the King,* Brenda Bruce as the immobile half-buried heroine of Beckett's *Happy Days,* Olivier as the petit-bourgeois cipher in David Turner's acerbic satire *Semi-Detached,* or Leonard Rossiter as the soon-to-be Hitler in Brecht's *Arturo Ui.* I felt as close as it was possible to feel to drama and the stage of millions, particularly when I watched the veterans with all their artistry: Peggy Ashcroft playing Queen Margaret in the Henry VI plays, from a sassy teenage princess to an aged and gnarled tyrannical queen all in a day through performances in the morning, afternoon and evening; John Gielgud in Chekhov's *The Cherry Orchard* and Michael Redgrave as the same dramatist's Uncle Vanya. There was Donald Wolfit as Ibsen's *John Gabriel Borkman,* Joan Plowright as St. Joan and Donald Pleasance straight from the film of Pinter's *The Caretaker* now playing Robespierre in Anouilh's play of the French Revolution, *Poor Bitos.* And then, the most moving night in a theatre I have ever known, in the Theatre Royal, Stratford E15 in the midst of the market stalls in Angel Lane — the second ever night of Joan Littlewood's *Oh, What a Lovely War* and the testimony in song and sketch of a million Isaacs and Wilfreds, and the hapless young *poilus* like bleating lambs being herded by their generals to slaughter and oblivion. 'Never, never, never again!' I muttered to myself as I staggered up Angel Lane to Stratford Station and caught the eastward train home.

And what about music? Every school morning for six years I sang hymns in assembly, and their words cast a long sonic shadow. These lyrics were some of the first poetry that I ever knew by heart. In some aspects they seemed beautiful, but when I began to think about their true meanings, I could recognise them as soporifics for all kinds of institutional wrongs and systemic crimes that I read about every evening in my father's *News Chronicle* or *Evening News* which he brought in from work. I learned of

Britain's late imperial exploits in British Guiana, Kenya, Cyprus, Aden and Suez, and as we sang *Hills of the North, Rejoice* in assembly, it seemed to be a hurrah for all these interventions. I never realised that in future years I would be working for revolutionary governments in some of the places referred to in this 'missionary' hymn that was also an imperial tract, as we sang:

> Isles of the southern seas
> Deep in your coral caves...
> He comes to reign with boundless sway
> And makes your wastes his great highway!

Or at 8:30 in the morning we remembered those 'unvisited, unblessed' colonies in the 'utmost west' or those 'far hills, long cold and grey' in the east, where the 'everlasting day' of European civilisation and religion has 'dawned'. It sent messages that we, in Hornchurch, Essex, were truly at the centre of the world and its goodness. And they made us stand up in the hall before classes, hundreds of us who were schooled to be upholders of the dying post-war British Empire, and told to sing such parodies of patriotism:

> Hearts of oak are our ships,
> jolly tars are our men,
> We always are ready,
> Steady boys, steady!
> We'll fight and we'll conquer again and again!

And as if it were true, as if most of us were willing! It became a charade of false chauvinism, sounding stirring but remaining empty.

Or what about the cosy lyricism of *All Things Bright and Beautiful* that were all around us, and the perfect state of the world that God had created for us, with:

> The rich man in his castle
> The poor man at his gate,
> God made them high and lowly,
> He ordered their estate.

while Prime Minister Harold Macmillan reminded us of our bounty, and how we'd 'never had it so good'. We sang it time and time again in our morning hymns, and nobody called it brainwashing.

Except there was one anthemic hymn that we belted out which seemed to be saying so many things at once. It was, of course, *Jerusalem,* and even then Blake raised the temperature of my consciousness. 'Pleasant pastures' and 'dark satanic mills' or 'bow of burning gold' and 'arrows of desire' — what was all this? Was this our country, was this England, was this Hornchurch and Romford? It would take me a lifetime to even begin to answer these questions.

Then there was the other music, the music of our own times and choices. There was Elvis and Buddy Holly, the Everleys and Adam Faith that blared out of the local juke boxes in the coffee bars and youth clubs we went to, but for me it was skiffle, the British home-made versions of black and white American folk and blues classics that came a-strumming from Londoners like Lonnie Donegan, even when he was reproducing the songs of Leadbelly or Big Bill Broonzy. But he did it pretty well when he took Woody Guthrie's *Grand Coulee Dam* to the top of the hit parade, and I learned and sang to myself all its lyrics. Their powerful, beautiful and very American poetry, and their assonance, alliteration and all the figures Mr Clarke had taught me about came to vibrant life as I rode my bike through the suburban roadways of Hornchurch, singing out loud:

In the misty, crystal glitter of its wild and windward
    spray
Men fought the pounding waters and met a watery grave.
Though she turned men's boats to splinters she gave
    them dreams to dream
The day the Coulee Dam would cross that wild and
    wasted stream.

Or there was Lonnie's version of the blues, a signpost to all the blues poetry of Broonzy, Leadbetter and the rest as I whooped from my bike the poetry of *How Long Blues:*

If I could holler
Like a mountain Jack,
I'd go up on the mountain

39

And call my baby back!
How long, how long,
Baby how long?

In 1961 my friend Spud's dad opened a jazz club in Elm Park Hotel, walking distance from where I lived. It was his elder brother whose bike I had once lifted up a tree, so perhaps he remembered that. Anyway, because of my size and height, (my apex in those years was six feet five inches and seventeen and a half stone), he asked me to be doorman and cloakroom attendant. No wages, but free entry and refreshments, and the chance to hear every Friday and Sunday night the best New Orleans bands in the country. There were the bands of Kenny Ball, Cy Laurie, Dick Charlesworth's City Gents, Terry Lightfoot, the veteran Nat Gonella and the 'guv'nor' — Ken Colyer, who'd actually jumped ship in New Orleans (he'd been a merchant seaman) and lived and played his trumpet with some of the Crescent City's greatest musicians. It was the St. Louis Jazz Club, and it was another world just up the road. As I tore entry tickets and hung up the groovers' coats in the cloakroom, I felt like a very lucky man — particularly when surprising guests suddenly came onto the stage, like the San Francisco bluesman and one-man bandsman Jesse Fuller. And when he sang his version of the prison blues, *Midnight Special,* which I had first heard sung through Lonnie's fey accent, I realised where the authentic music had been born, and it only made me want to get there. Here was a black man singing the blues of a black life in a southern Texas city. How vulnerable he was and how careful he had to be.

If you ever go to Houston
You better walk right,
You better not stagger
And you better not fight.
When you walking down the main street
In the middle of town
If you get into trouble
You're jailhouse bound.

40

The clarity, simplicity and narrative of the lyrics told me more about poetry. For I realised the blues was poetry and held all the features of a heightened, intense language, lucid and full of narrative pictures. These were the words that I loved and I was learning more about them every day.

My dear and unlikely friend was Vince, with whom I became very close. He came into the school when I was in 3R, suddenly and explosively. He was born in Bolton and his father was a Flight Lieutenant in the RAF who had been stationed at the now almost defunct Hornchurch Aerodrome. Vince was astonishingly handsome and athletic: tall, muscular with a crop of dark, Beatle-like hair, he was a powerful centre-forward, a dynamic sprinter and a fine cricketer whose skills as an attacking batsman, a deft leg-spinner and a brilliant boundary fieldsman with a throw like a bullet, somehow matched his personality. The girls loved him and the young women teachers blushed when he was around. And yet this boy, it seemed, wanted to be my friend; me — overweight, gangling, clumsy and scared stiff of girls. I couldn't believe it. I used to go to his house next to the aerodrome and we used to play jazz records together, exchange dreams, talk cricket and he would encourage me to find a girlfriend. 'What, me?' I used to say, but he always rallied my spirit and emboldened me. When his northern cousin, a beautiful Lancashire girl, came to stay with his mum and dad, he invited me round, introduced us and left us to get to know each other. It was wonderful. I began to believe in myself more and feel more confident, and it was all down to Vince. We became inseparable, and he became my hero as well as my friend.

When he left the school at the end of the fifth year, I was very depressed. His father had been transferred to Libya, so he had to find a boarding school to do his A-levels. He went to the Palmer's School in Grays, out along the Thames Estuary, an old grammar school, where he became head boy and graduated to go to the RAF Officers' Training College at Cranwell. He won the 'sword' there as the most outstanding cadet, learned to fly and became a Pilot

41

Officer. We stayed in touch, but after I went to University the RAF sent him to fly Hawker Hunters in the colonial war in Malaya. The last time I saw him was in 1966, when he was recuperating from being shot down over a Malayan beach. He had tried to bail out, the mechanism hadn't worked and as he was ejected from the plane he had gone right through the cockpit and his back had been shattered. I couldn't believe it when we met again. He was hunched over, he walked with a serious limp, looked a couple of inches shorter and was about to be invalided out of the RAF. It wasn't the death of the ball turret gunner but it seemed like the end of the athlete and phenomenal crick-eter. What had happened to my dear friend Vince made me hate war, and in particular colonial wars, even more. For what in the hell was Vince doing flying a fighter plane in Malaya, shooting brave people who wanted their own country back from the British? What was going on in the world and how were we involved — in 'the isles of the southern seas' too, what were we doing? Inadvertently, my hero had become my teacher.

And then there was cricket. As I lost weight in my later teenage years, my height and rhythm had made me a prime fast bowler. I was quick with an ability to move the ball both ways off the seam, and when I joined one of the top local clubs, Upminster, I became the first team opening bowler, playing against some of Essex's strongest clubs and best players, getting a stack of wickets. We had a lot of good-humoured moments too. When we played against a team mainly made up of West Ham footballers, including the quietly modest and laughing future captain of England's 1966 World Cup winning team, Bobby Moore, they managed to include, playing as a guest, the England opening batsman Colin Milburn, a rotund, black-grease-slicked-haired Geordie and one of the most powerful hitters in the game. I bowled the first over at him, and he hit my second ball (which was straight and on a good length) so hard and high back over my head — up, up, up and up it went, clearing the row of very high poplars that formed the boundary behind me, that I completely lost the eventual downward slope of its trajectory. I remember bowling about twenty overs to another world cup winner — Geoff Hurst, the Cup Final hat-trick scorer, in a match against Walthamstow Cricket Club. He was an Essex second team regular, a very solid batsman and he scored a very correct 70, but I got him in the end.

But cricket wasn't just cricket, or as C.L.R. James wrote, 'What do they know of cricket, that only cricket know?' Something else was afoot when I played fairly regularly in the summer holidays for a team sponsored by Essex County Cricket Club as a device to bring on young hopefuls, and called 'Essex Young Amateurs'. I was one of the few grammar school boys who were ever picked. Most of the regulars were young cricketers from public schools whose fathers brought them to the matches in their Jaguars and MGs. Some were Essex boys from exclusive schools like Charterhouse or Repton, but most were from minor public schools in Essex like Brentwood, Newport or Felsted. Almost all of them were aloof and unfriendly towards me, from a new grammar school with no cricket tradition which none of them had heard of. I only played because of some of the wonderful grounds and wickets we played on — county grounds like Colchester, Westcliff and Ilford in Essex — and we played Surrey Young Amateurs at the Oval, and also because of the chance of bowling to such talented batsmen — like Alan Knott of Kent and the future England captain Mike Brearley, who opened for Middlesex Young Amateurs. I regularly got wickets in these matches, but strangely, being an obscure grammar school boy in that context was like being a secondary moderner in a grammar school. Excluded from their public school humour, their frame of reference and their exclusive consciousness, I began to understand in my blood about cricket and class, school and class, culture and class in a way that had eluded me before. As James was to tell me in *Beyond a Boundary*: 'Cricket plunged me into politics long before I was aware of it'.

In my last school summer I was picked to play for England Schools against the Welsh Schools at Nantwich in Cheshire. I had been warned that I was going to be observed by the past England captain Freddie Brown, who stood next to the sightscreen at the batsman's end as I began to bowl. I became nervous and self-conscious like I was at interviews, and bowled four grotesque overs with a high number of wides — something I never did in usual circumstances, and was taken off. Mr Brown walked away, back to the pavilion. Although I came back later in the innings and bowled well enough, I was dropped to twelfth man for the next game — at Lord's — and only got onto the hallowed grass as a substitute fielder. It was another dream over, but something real enough was about to begin.

Chapter Two
Miss Cooper's Tears

I began at Leeds University in October 1963 after my usual nemesis of an interview which somehow got me through. After much stuttering and nervous warbling, with attempts to persuade the Head of the English Department, Professor Norman Jeffares (a celebrated W.B. Yeats scholar) that I had watched so many productions by the Old Vic and Royal Shakespeare Companies that I was a precious drama egghead-in-the-making, he told me with a noblesse-oblige type of directness: 'Mr Searle, that was a bloody awful interview but I'll give you a place. I don't care what examination marks you get, just get any two A-levels. But for God's sake go away and read!' I sat there nonplussed. I thought I'd done a lot of reading. I'd got through all the novels of D.H. Lawrence and Hemingway and I'd clandestinely read *War and Peace* and *Crime and Punishment* while sneaking to an unsupervised spot on the building site I'd been working on the previous summer. But I didn't care about his posh accent and superciliousness, I was in, wasn't I, a proud secondary moderner, as I always saw myself, and I'd got there without Latin too. So long live Leeds! I thought.

I was given a room in the male-only Devonshire Hall in Headingley, with its quasi-Oxbridge conventions of daily formal dinners (you had to wear a jacket and tie), weekly debates, and the 'warden' sitting at the High Table in his gown. The meals were served by non-English-speaking and very nervous Sicilian nun-like waitresses who must have been the cheapest of the cheap labour and who disappeared into their backstairs lodgings after every meal. In the room next door to mine was a Guyanese medical student called Sunil who had been a boy at the time of the British 'invasion' in 1953, and in the room opposite a trans-dressing law student called Hilary, who used to dress up regularly as Marlene Dietrich with huge, swelling skirts and sing *Lili Marlene* all down the corridors. The drunkenness of many of the residents, including me, was habitual and raucous, and on the night that the news arrived of John F. Kennedy's assassination the usual noise and bawling of drunken students stopped suddenly in a strange collective sobering-up. In almost an instant there was serious talk, consternation and shock.

For me it was like a discovery of my own country. I was a suburban Londoner making fast and intimate friends with young, mainly working-class men and women, from Wolverhampton, Stoke, Manchester, Blackburn, Durham, Fleetwood and Bradford. I shared a room with a course-mate from Nottingham whose dad worked in the Raleigh bicycle factory in Bilborough. It was almost like going back to Hylands, because almost any of my new friends could have ended up there in this huge lottery of educational futures, yet we had all come through and talked endlessly about it until late at night, every night, with a constantly boiling kettle and everlasting reprises of Dylan's *Don't Think Twice, It's Alright, Masters of War* and *The Strange Death of Hattie Carroll* continually going right through us. On Friday and Saturday nights it was an orgy of music and drink. We became stewards for the Union's weekly hops, sharing the stage with Manfred Mann, The Yardbirds, The Who, Wilson Pickett or The Animals and forming a human fence to prevent infatuated local girls getting onto the stage. My zenith moment was, emboldened by Tetley's Bitter, clambering on stage and hollering a couple of brash choruses of *In the Midnight Hour* with the soulful Pickett. At the time it didn't seem much to do with 'English Literature', but all that and the traumatic relationships we constantly got ourselves involved in with girls on and off our courses, was what we were there for in this city of cold, overwhelming grey where we found unheated flats and bedsitters, where we shivered by electric fires and squeezed endless shillings into the meters.

46

At nights, I would wander through the wasteland of the ridge at the back of our hall of residence with my friend Nick, to talk about our lives and futures. Nick was the son of a Wolverhampton lorry driver from a large Catholic family, a brilliant student who was heading for a First, the only one in our year. We told each other stories of our school experience, me with my eleven-plus failures, and he from a strict Jesuit state-funded grammar school. We both wanted to be teachers, and Nick was clear in his ambition: to become the head-teacher of an urban comprehensive school where all working-class children could find fulfilment and academic promise. We both agreed on that without any demurring, although Nick was to have a four-decade tenure as a lecturer of English Literature at the University of Edinburgh, eventually becoming a professor. As for me, I knew I'd be a teacher and I was sure that it would be at a comprehensive, but I couldn't go any further than that. There seemed to be a lot to do first.

We eventually found rooms in an old house close to the university and spent two freezing winters in our unheated rooms, collecting shuttering and scaffolding planks from local building sites, carrying them home late at night, stamping on them and breaking them up into small enough pieces to put them in our fireplaces and build blazes with them to warm up our rooms while the snow and icy rain fell outside during two cold Yorkshire winters. Nick had a younger brother, Neil, who sometimes came up from Wolverhampton and spent weekends with us. He worked in a butcher's shop and almost every week he would send us joints of pork through the post. Every Saturday morning the front bell would clang, and there'd be a frowning postman with a soggy, bleeding, parcel of meat. Neil always said that pork was most tasty just when it was going off. We had no fridge, so by Sunday lunchtime, when we'd start cooking it, it just started to reek a little. But it became our weekly treat: roast pork, crispy roast spuds and tinned peas. We used to live for

Sunday lunchtimes and this pork sent by post across the heart of England.

Our landlord was Stefan, a middle-aged Pole who had flown fighters for the Polish Air Force in England against the Nazis, and someone had bequeathed him this house as a gift of gratitude after the war. Sometimes he would spend nights in the cellar, wrapped up in newspapers and wake up very early and sing choruses from Polish operas. He became our friend, taking us for meals in the Leeds Polish Club, and when we finally finished our degrees at Leeds, he insisted on taking us both home in his car: first Nick to Wolverhampton, and then me back to Horn-church. It was sheer love and friendship that caused him to do it, and I've never forgotten it. And as I write this in August 2016, in the weeks after the European Union Referendum, when 3,000 hate crimes against Poles in Britain have been registered, and a Polish factory worker called Arkadiusz Jozwik was beaten to death by racist thugs in Harlow, Essex, I think again of our friend and kindest landlord, Stefan Chmielewski.

As for the literature, we read some of it and much passed us by between the starting blocks of *The Anglo-Saxon Chronicle* and the finishing line of T.S. Eliot. But there was nothing that spoke of our own world — it was never taught that way, not like it had been by Chiefie at school, where everything we read seemed to comment directly on how we lived now and what we could learn from it for our now-times lives. Some of our lecturers seemed incapable of speaking in lucid, accessible language. I remember my first year tutor who was, we were told, a poet himself, as well as a distinguished critic. His tutorials were arenas of fear, where you were afraid and reluctant to speak because you were wary that what you said might be considered stupid or inept. Instead, you waited for the tutor to provide the interpretation. Thus the beautiful immediacy of John Donne's love poems like *The Good Morrow* or *The Sunne Rising* was prevented from spreading its radiance and meaning while we were told that the poems' esoteric and metaphysical meanings needed to be unlocked by the quasi-secret critical code which we needed to learn and use as our key. The poems' relationship to our world was aborted in those tutorial rooms, and I wondered what Donne himself, living, loving and testifying like a true human being in early seventeenth century London, would have made of it all. For above all, what does a poet want, I thought. To be understood, on the senses and within the real lives of his or her readers; it must be that, above all. But that wasn't what we were doing. Our teachers were speaking in ciphers, in a language that wasn't ours — wasn't anyone's it seemed, but their own — and we were all learning it, colluding with it, being examined and qualified in it, but it was a betrayal of the poets I loved, from Shakespeare to Blake to Brecht. It wasn't what they wrote for, what they intended their words to mean, what their genius was expressed for. It was Donne who wrote in *The Good Morrow*:

And now good morrow to our waking soules,
Which watch not one another out of feare;
For love, all love of other sights controules,
And makes one little roome, an everywhere.

And it was that very 'feare', of poetry itself — that it must necessarily be difficult, be obscure, even be incomprehensible — that was being driven into us: not the revelation of life, but the secret, hidden alphabet of life. I didn't like it, couldn't accept it, and I was sure that John Donne, who wanted nobody to be an island, wanted no single person to be an entirety in themselves but a human of the world, would never have wanted it either. Poetry was for all men and women; it could not live in the dark, esoteric and obfuscating places. It was forged in the light and the real, to help every person's journey through the world, and the more that I read and studied it, in all its times and forms, the more that I was sure that was true. And with that understanding also came another. That all men

49

and women should be readers, but that the same human beings could and should believe that they had the power and authority to be writers too, that Donne and Blake and Brecht wrote so that we could read their messages, while also being living exemplars as writers: they were showing us how to write poetry while teaching us how to read it. They were showing us how to write our minds on the world, how to re-imagine it, and through the human love and beauty in their words, giving us the cues to change it for the better. More and more, that was how I was seeing poetry, almost as a reaction against how most of our tutors were presenting it to us. It was as if we needed to unread ourselves before we could learn to read again.

In my final year two momentous events happened to me around my quest for the meaning of poetry. The first was that I met Isaac with his words and pictures. A poetry magazine called *Stand* had mounted an exhibition about First World War poets in our union building and a 'War Poetry Seminar' was organised. It may have had something to do with the fiftieth anniversary of the Western Front carnage, but there was a section showing some of the biography, poems and paintings of Isaac, and wandering unknowing into the exhibition room, I became transfixed. I don't know why, but it became one of the key moments of my life, upon which so much of my future was to hinge. Perhaps it was the effect of the simultaneous grim trench realism and simple, beautiful lyricism of *Returning, We Hear the Larks* which captured me, or the hellish lines from *Dead Man's Dump*:

> None saw their spirits' shadow shake the grass,
> Or stood aside for the half used life to pass
> Out of those doomed nostrils and the doomed mouth,
> When the swift iron burning bee
> Drained the wild honey of their youth.

I hadn't read anything like it, with the same impact, since reading *King Lear* with Chiefie at school. I thought about the 'half used life' and my friends in Hylands, of my father's bombed footballing friends and then of the millions who were killed alongside Isaac — like Wilfred, for his portrait was there, near the print of Isaac's sketch of himself in helmet and uniform, on a piece of brown greaseproof paper, the only paper he could find in the trenches. I knew that I wanted to read more and more. I used to pass Whitechapel and Stepney Green on the underground as I travelled the tube between Hornchurch and the West End on the District Line to see all those plays. They were dark, forbidding stations, particularly Stepney Green with its dimly-lit tunnel of a platform with huge iron pillars standing spectrally in the shadows, and I used to wonder what was happening in the streets above. For as I was to learn, these were the streets which Isaac and his friends, artists and poets like Mark Gertler, John Rodker, David Bomberg and his best friend Joseph Leftwich, were to walk along time and time again as young men, discussing art, poetry, and socialist politics, when they weren't reading and quietly conferring at the tables in Whitechapel Library, right outside Aldgate East station, two stops back. Now, standing there, aghast at poetry, in this room in Leeds, it was as if, uncompromisingly, poetry stood somewhere near the centre of my life, and Isaac, a bilingual and very small Jewish poet with parents from Lithuania, was telling me of its power.

Then something else happened which brought me back while moving me on with Isaac. In the last few weeks that we were in Leeds, in the days following our final examinations, four of us found a derelict house like a fully furnished and landlubbing Marie Celeste very close to the university, with its front and back doors unlocked and its every room complete with Edwardian furniture, bookcases, ornaments, magazines, letters and books belonging to one 'Miss Cooper', its old owner. The house had never been cleared or reclaimed, and behind its hedges and overgrown front garden we gained easy entry to its secrets and the private world of Miss Cooper. On its abandoned shelves in the sitting room, next to her desk and

51

worn sitting chair, we found an album of postcards, all with French stamps and photographs of the cities and towns near the battlefields of France and Flanders, with short messages of affection from a French soldier, a *poilu* of the trenches, a young man who opened up his heart to Miss Cooper, telling her of his fear, his anguish, his young soldier's desperate loneliness, to his 'war mother' in another language in a city he didn't know in England, to a young woman he didn't know either, for she must have been young then. Rob, one of my friends, rescued the album from this deserted room, from tramps' mess and an old woman's distant memories, and I never saw it again until 2006, when I visited Rob's home in Ohio, USA and I saw and read these postcards again, another fifty years on from that strange and evocative day in Leeds, Yorkshire, England. The *poilu's* words, still so immaculately kept in Miss Cooper's precious album, from the terrible agony of the trenches, made me think not only of fifty years before in Leeds, but of Isaac and his last torments too.

There was yet one more echo of Leeds and Isaac for me to contemplate. In 2014 I was looking through a bookshop and came across a thick book published by Oxford University Press: *Collected Critical Writings* by Geoffrey Hill, my first year tutor at Leeds in 1963, whose tutorial had filled me with that 'feare' of participating, the nervousness about talking about poetry. By that time Hill was eighty-two, was an eminent poet and critic, had been a Professor at Boston University and an Honorary Fellow at Oxford and Cambridge colleges, and in 2012 had been knighted for his services to literature. I had known none of this before, but as I flicked through the eight-hundred-plus pages of his book I found one particular essay which leapt out at me: *Isaac Rosenberg: 1890–1918*. I found it to be full of insight, passion and indignation. Hill asked his readers to consider the key question affecting Isaac, and there was nothing esoteric or speciously 'literary' about it. Asked to find the most succinct description of Rosenberg's 'desire' he wrote, '"I would say "the desire to free his voice". To free his voice from what? From the condition of being regarded, or disregarded, as an expendable "young Hebrew", a slave in the vast pool of London labour; subsequently, by single extension, as an unidentifiable waste item in Field Marshal Haig's ever-increasing expenditure of blood and treasure.' His words hit me like a hammer — why didn't he talk like this, say such things fifty years earlier when we were studying Jonson, Marvell or Donne? I read his words with excitement and regret in equal parts: excitement because his writing and its content was so fine and precise, regret because half a century ago I lost such a ripe opportunity to grow inside. 'If only Isaac had been there then,' I thought; 'even as his words are now,' maybe Geoffrey Hill and I could have met with them, could have grown with them, both of us, and be better equipped for further words and further life. An opportunity missed, I thought.

During our last term at Leeds a professor from McMaster University in Hamilton, the steel city of Canada, came to our department seeking recruits to teach an English Literature course which all first year students in all arts subjects had to pass — a compulsory subsidiary course. You taught for about eight hours a week, and as payment you were granted an 'Ontario Scholarship' to study for a master's degree in English, and given a small stipend to pay for lodgings and other basics. It seemed like a very fair offer, so three or four of us signed up for it. So I spent the summer (after receiving my degree from a very limp-handed Duchess of Kent) working on a Romford building site to get the money for my ticket, and I was off. I remember the last weeks that I spent in Leeds, the endless pints of Tetley's mild, hearing and dancing to The Who at the last hop and seeing Pete Townsend smashing his guitar into the amplifiers as the band finished with a storm of sparks and a billowing cloud of smoke at the end of a chorus of *My Generation*. Then having to endure the union coffee bar lobbying of one Jack Straw, to vote for him as the next year's union president. 'Will you vote for me?' he implored timidly. And even as I write this I see him on our television, the obsequious and Bush-serving ex-Foreign Secretary and leading Blairite now turning seventy like me, caught out in a sting asking for £5,000 a day to help willing payers gain influence in Parliament. His manner seems just as servile and demeaning as it was fifty years ago in Leeds University Union.

Anyway, I knew I was getting away from all that as I climbed on to the VC10 for New York, taking the long way to Hamilton. I didn't know anyone in the Apple, but I had the telephone number of a Jewish girl I'd known in Leeds from Columbia University who had been on an overseas student course. I rang her, but she was out of the city. Her father, who answered the phone, was very friendly and invited me to meet him for lunch on Broadway. I walked from the very cheap hotel where I was staying and saw a young slick-haired policeman leaning against a shop doorway, his holster bulging, chewing hard and twirling his truncheon. 'Excuse me,' I asked him, 'could you tell me how to get to Broadway?' He looked at me quite quizzically, surprised by my accent. There was a pause. 'Broadway?' he repeated after a few seconds, 'I never heard of it.' And he carried on twirling. Welcome to New York, I thought.

When I eventually found Broadway and met my host, he was very different; warm, hospitable and full of humour. He led me to, of all places, the Playboy Club. 'What?' I said, 'are we going in there?' 'Of course!' he said, and he bought me an expensive meal, joked with the scantily-clad waitresses as I stared agog, and plied me with drink, telling me all about his business and his daughter. As he shook my hand and left me on the sidewalk outside, I could see through a half-drunken haze the Museum of Modern Art, very close by. 'What?' I said to myself, 'Isn't Guernica in there?' So I staggered in and stared at Picasso's anti-fascist masterpiece for the best part of an hour, looking up and apologising to him for my state of being. 'Everything you can imagine is real,' he once said, and I believed him. But I never forgot its images, its power and its message, and the extremes of culture I had experienced within those three New York hours.

I took the Greyhound to Hamilton via Niagara Falls, cast my eyes at the city's huge steelworks, reminding me of the views of Sheffield's Don Valley I used to have when I hitched my way from London to Leeds — and set about finding somewhere to live. I moved into a small attic flat in a large house in Dundurn Street. In the ground floor apartment lived Evie, a Mohawk woman, her white boyfriend Donnie, a steelworker, and their infant son, Donnie Junior. Evie and Donnie were kind and friendly, and insisted that I came down in the evenings to watch their television with them. Evie offered to do my washing and Donnie, always with a can of Labatt's beer in his hand, loved to talk to me about his work. Once or twice they went out while I looked after little Donnie. But could they drink! And when they drank, could they fight! I remember one night hearing a huge hubbub downstairs: shouts, cries, thuds, things being thrown, crashes and howls. Then it all became quiet. I was worried and went downstairs, tentatively. Evie and Donnie were stretched out, drunk and comatose, on the Chesterfield still covered in Perspex as they had bought it, and little Donnie was tottering and whimpering, his feet treading on broken bourbon whiskey and vodka bottles. I picked him up and tried to bring his parents round. They eventually woke up, sobered up and sent out for pizza. But it was quite an introduction to Canada.

In Hamilton, I met Bill, a draft resister and hater of war. He was my age and from Brooklyn, where his father owned a small ice cream factory in the heart of Bedford-Stuyvesant, a venue of fierce riots the year before, where local disenfranchised blacks were fighting back. Bill knew all about this on his pulses, for he had worked on the floor of his father's factory during Bedford-

Stuyvesant's most incendiary months. Now he was in Canada to avoid the draft, as well as studying for a master's in Psychology. I got to know him while I earned a few extra dollars as one of the subjects of his experiments, reacting to flashing lights in a darkened room. We became friends as he explained to me his disgust at what US servicemen were doing in Vietnam. I thought of Vince and told Bill all about him. He nodded, he held in his breath and assured me that he was never going out there. He had to be very careful about crossing the US border — his local draft board were onto him, he told me. I thought about being free in Canada, and Bill reminded me of the thousands of slaves who escaped through the networks of the underground railway to find freedom this side of the frontier. It wasn't so different for young Americans — most of them white this time around — like Bill and his compatriots, who had come to Canadian universities to escape the horror of war. I thought of Isaac and his millions too, for whom there seemed no escape, yet compared him to Bill, who was resisting war and the hell of the Mekong. Isaac had enlisted in the Suffolk Bantams, who specialised in physically small soldiers, and he had done it to ensure an income, however meagre, for his impoverished mother, and thus provoked a dreaded and implacable journey to the trenches.

Bill, my Geordie friend Bert and I would wander the streets of Hamilton, drink with the expatriate Irish, many of them steel workers, in the local Cork Town Tavern, and we'd talk about our lives in other countries. Bill introduced us to writers like Marshall McLuhan and Herbert Marcuse, both of whom seemed a bit too much for me, and he took us to New York in his pick-up van and we got a taste of the mangled ruins of Bedford-Stuyvesant and Jones Beach on Long Island, where Walt Whitman would sit on the dunes near where the tide met the sand, creating his long lines of *Leaves of Grass* to the sound of the crashing surf. And what were we doing now, a century or so later: chucking a frisbee around and sharing in hippy heaven? It didn't seem comparable somehow, yet Bill and his own internal and external struggle against soldiery changed my life and way of thinking. "Hey, Chris baby!" he would greet me every time we met, clasping my hand and shoulders. All my life since I've thought of him as the best of America, and wondered how he spent his life; always, I knew, on the side of peace.

At the University, I took the opportunity to use the thesis requirements of the MA course to write a dissertation on Isaac's poetry. Nobody in the English Department there had read him or knew anything about Isaac's poems, but the Shakespeare specialist agreed to read them and become my supervisor. What I did find though, was an immense interest among Canadians in the ordeal and suffering of the First World War trenches, and some powerful accounts had been written, like Phillip Child's *God's Sparrows* and Charles Yale Harrison's agonising realism in his *Generals Die in Bed.* Everywhere I went in Ontario, every small town, I found war memorials remembering the slaughtered Canadians at places on the Western Front like Vimy Ridge, Passchendaele and Amiens, and when, the year after, I travelled west to teach in Alberta, I found the same. It seemed uncanny that the young Jewish working-class East London poet had so much in common with thousands of Canadians of his time and his age who suffered from the same madness. As I was in the middle of my work for my dissertation there arrived the fiftieth anniversary of the Battle of Vimy Ridge, a part of the larger Battle of Arras, where 3,598 Canadian soldiers were killed and 7,004 wounded between 9–12 April 1917. Newspapers like the *Toronto Globe and Mail* and the *Hamilton Spectator* carried large-scale headlines, maps and accounts of the battle, the first to involve all four divisions of the Canadian Expeditionary Force.

So *Break of Day in the Trenches*, *Returning*, *We Hear the Larks* and *Dead Man's Dump* were as much a part of the Canadian experience as they were the British, and the more I showed them to Canadian colleagues and students, the more they became interested in Isaac. Hamilton was quite a Jewish city too. Many of my students were young Jews whose family and cultural background was not so different from that of Isaac. One of my first moves in tackling the dissertation was to visit and confer with the local rabbi of the synagogue near the university, and he was very encouraging. I told him that I wasn't a Jew, I knew no Hebrew or Yiddish, and asked him whether he thought I could do justice to Isaac's poems. He was friendly and positive and said that he thought it was an excellent idea for me to continue, so I came away full of enthusiastic intent.

My main purpose in my thesis was my argument that Isaac was not primarily a war poet, or a lyrical poet only concerned with a disgust at war and huge empathy with its victims, but, as I wrote in its introduction: 'Rosenberg's work evinces a central idea, a certain cyclical design and adherence to a conscious theme that evolves from the confusion of the early poems, through the apocalypse of trench verse to the final preoccupation with mythopoeic form. It is an idea which involves tyranny and the rebellion against tyranny, revelation and final reward.' This 'plan terrific', as Isaac called it, had its precedent in the poetry of Blake, another visionary London poet, and for Isaac 'the reign of Blake is yet to begin.' In his final months in the midst of the barbarism of trench warfare, Isaac was writing fragments of mythical verse drama, such as *Moses* and *The Unicorn*, drawing on his Judaism, so to categorise him as a 'soldier poet' is to misunderstand and misinterpret the wholeness of his vision. He wrote of his intentions in writing *The Unicorn* to 'symbolise the war and all the devastating forces let loose by an ambitious and unscrupulous will'; but right up until his death in the last days of the war, he was seeing beyond its horror: 'I am determined that this war, with all its powers for devastation, shall not master my poeting; that is, if I am lucky to come through all right. I will not leave a corner of my consciousness covered up, but saturate myself with the strange and extraordinary conditions of this new life, and it will all refine itself into poetry later on.' These words from the torment of the battlefield became as a clarion call for me and my own awakening consciousness on this new, compelling continent.

I was anything but satisfied with what I wrote, but I thought, 'Well, it's a start. Isaac is going to be with me a long way after this, and I shall always be returning to him.' I finished my course, handed in my dissertation and jumped on the Canadian National Railway at Toronto to go out West. I had very little money and got as far as Edmonton, Alberta, where I had a friend to stay with. I was about to start work as a trackman on the railway, but I thought I'd have one last try at getting a teaching job — I couldn't find anything in Edmonton — and travelled a couple of hundred miles south to Calgary to see what that city held for me. I walked into the English Department on the University of Calgary campus and asked to speak to the Head of Department, like a navvy walking onto a building site in London to ask the gaffer for a job. Professor Guy, the man in charge, who I later learned came from a mining family in Nova Scotia, explained that on that morning a colleague teaching the same course that I'd been teaching in McMaster had left and they needed an immediate replacement as the academic year began in two days. 'Then I'm your man!' I said. He made a quick telephone call to McMaster to get an instant reference, and I was in! I couldn't believe my luck, and sent thanks and blew a kiss to the memory of a friendly nun sitting near me on the Canadian National, who had given me a 'lucky dollar' before she had got off the train at Winnipeg.

Looking for a place to live, I bought and scanned the *Calgary Herald* and there was a bedsitter advertised on 14th Street NW. Not being accustomed to a grid street system, I turned up at the equivalent number on 14th Street NE. When I opened the door, a young man, his wife and their baby faced me. They were perplexed when I referred to the advertisement in the paper. It was soon apparent that I had come to the wrong street, wrong house. I explained I was looking for a room so after a brief conversation, they gave me one in the old wooden, crumbling house they were renting. They were both radicals, Mary was an organiser in the anti-Vietnam War movement (and that wasn't common in very conservative Calgary) and Pat, her husband was a mature student at the university, later to become President of the Students' Union. There are lucky days and lucky days, but this was just about their apex: a job, a place to live and two new friends, all in one day!

I spent a year in Calgary. In many ways it was a deeply backward place. I remember anti-Vietnam war marches through the centre of the city and the hostility of many Calgarians: 'Yer fuckin' yeller-bellied sonsofabitches, yer commie bastards,' was what we heard, and the city's fathers were mortified when hippyism suddenly struck their sons and daughters. They saw it as a plague coming up from San Francisco via Seattle and Vancouver, and when Calgary's first love-in was promised in the city's largest park, Riley Park, the esteemed benefactor who had donated the park's land to the city, the now retired Judge Riley, heard of the event and demanded his land back. And yet my students were full of life, progress and friendliness. As I write this, I'm looking at a large fossilised dinosaur vertebrae given to me by one of them, whose father was a warden in the Dinosaur National Park in the Badlands to the south. Another took me on a trip in her rattling Oldsmobile to Vancouver, Seattle and then back to Calgary, via the Grand Coulee Dam. Looking down at its hugeness and sublimity with Woody's words and brilliant poetry filling my head, I marvelled at how boyhood dreams could become real.

As for my job in the University, I was enjoying the teaching and friendships I was making with colleagues and students. I was just about the youngest and certainly the most junior member of staff, so I was often given what were seen as mundane tasks, although I never saw them that way. When the most eminent and influential Canadian literary critic, Northrop Frye, came for a day as a guest lecturer in the Department, I was asked to look after him. I spent the day with him, taking him from meeting to meeting, and finally to his lecture. I had read his book on Blake, *Fearful Symmetry,* and admired the way that he sought to show structure and clarity in Blake's visionary genius, for until his book was read and absorbed, many scholars still saw Blake as a maniacal radical with little form or coherence to his poetry. But for Frye, Blake's language was 'a literary language with its own idioms and its own syntactical arrangement of ideas,' and he went on to assert that 'the sources of art are enthusiasm and inspiration: if society mocks and derides these, it is society that is mad, not the artist.'

I had read Frye's book shortly after finishing my dissertation on Rosenberg, so my mind was still full of Isaac as I perused his words. What he wrote about one London poet began to impact upon my love for and study of another. In *Fearful Symmetry* he wrote that 'the imaginative mind, therefore, is the one which has realised its own freedom and understood that perception is self-development.' Wasn't that Isaac too, I thought, and his determination and pragmatism to take everything in his life, including the most brutal and horrific conditions around him such as those in *Dead Man's Dump,* and turn them into poetry? I took the opportunity, as we sat drinking a coffee while he waited to give his lecture, to ask him what I'd always wanted to ask him since reading his book. 'Why did you write it?' I said. 'Why did you, a Canadian, spend so much time thinking and writing about a London poet who lived his life so far away from you?' He looked at me and said, very quietly, just a handful of words. 'Ahh, but I grew up in the mind of Blake,' he said, smiling, and he walked off towards the lecture room.

I thought about this, and have never forgotten it. In Leeds, I had listened to celebrated guest lecturers like F.R. Leavis and William Empson and tried hard to read their books, but I had never heard or read anything like what Frye had said to me with such lucidity, honesty and nakedness. For since I first read him, hadn't I grown up with Isaac? Hadn't I lived with his words as if I were talking with him, asking him about his use of language, even here, between the Rocky Mountains and the prairies on another continent? Didn't I see him as a friend rather than a poet to be studied? In my university years it had been driven into me that what I needed to achieve more than anything, as a student and critic of literature, was something continually referred to as 'critical detachment'. But wasn't that the antithesis of what Frye had just told me about his pursuit of meaning of the words and images of one of the great revolutionary poets of any tradition? 'Grow up in his mind,' he had said, and what could be more empathetic and less critically detached than that? No, to understand a poet with any kind of fullness you needed to reach out and seek to share his life, whether he or she were alive or dead, for the poetry they made is certainly alive: it never dies.

Between November and March, Calgary is a cold, cold city, and when I wasn't wandering its icy streets or preparing my classes, I was trying to write a novel. I called it *Poilu,* and it brought together two protagonists from the past and the present around a woman called Miss Cooper, the 'war mother' of the French soldier, whose portion of life we had found in that derelict house in Leeds. When I read Isaac's many letters from the trenches in his *Collected Works,* I was deeply moved by his raw emotions, the ambitions he nourished for his poetry and his sense of desperation and entrapment. Like many trench soldiers he signed up not for patriotism, but for the meagre wages that he gave to his mother. Even he, with the power of such an imagination, could not have envisaged the untrammelled horror that he was to experience. In *Dead Man's Dump* when the limber full of ammunition crushes the bodies of his dead and dying comrades, scraping the face of a soldier in his last moments of life, he finds an apotheosis of war poetry, poetry that his letters illustrate with even more repugnance. As I read them, I thought this is what this *poilu* sees every day around him, and his letters to Miss Cooper are the way he tries to find some hope and sense in the future, for the present is a hell-hole with neither. The novel is a succession of the *poilu's* letters to his war mother, and they are interspersed by episodes in the life of a student at Leeds and his friends; their dissipation, their emotional entanglements, their relationships, their drinking, their examinations, the entirely metaphorical trenches of their lives from a generation that has not known and will not know either war or a soldier's life. Although the soldier is French, I knew that he was also Isaac, and I was trying to ease my way into his mind and his reality. I thought too about the physical differences between myself and Isaac. He was very small and the only regiment that would accept him was the Suffolk Bantams, who had no barrier against size and height. I wondered about my own six feet five inches and how long I would ever survive in a trench for people ten inches shorter than me. Through the winter I wrote this novel in the freezing evenings and early mornings in that old wooden house.

Forty years later I returned to Canada to teach at York University in Toronto, and I was determined to search out my old friends Pat and Mary in whose house I had stayed during my year in Calgary. I eventually found them in Victoria, on Vancouver Island. I also met their daughter Laura, who, as an infant, had slept directly below me in a very warm downstairs room. She didn't remember me, how could she, she was only three when I left. But she remembered something else which shivered my consciousness. She told me that she remembered as a baby during the nights when I was writing upstairs, dreaming about a soldier, who came every night to her bedside, held her hand and spoke to her, helping her sleep. She remembered him as kind, smiling and fatherly.

I told her what I had been writing in the room over her head those four decades before and we both gasped. Mary added that after I left they had searched the attic which hadn't been touched for many years, and they found a World War One soldier's uniforms, medals and diaries. I wondered whose house I had been living in all those years before, and I thought again of Miss Cooper, Isaac and my *poilu*, and how very close the past is to us.

As for my novel, I kept its handwritten pages with me while I travelled all through the summer of 1968, up the Alaska Highway to Yukon, Dawson City and Whitehorse, Skagway, Alaska; down to the British Columbia coast to Seattle, then on to San Francisco and Berkeley where I stayed with my old American Literature professor at Leeds, Doc. Tracey. He took me to the 'Vietnam Commencement' in the main university concourse which honoured those resisting the draft, and the wildest dance I'd ever been to, organised at the Carousel Ballroom by the local Hells Angels chapter and featuring Janis Joplin and Big Brother and the Holding Company. Janis was singing *Summertime* with huge power and beauty as we walked in the dancehall. At Berkeley I passed the insurgent singer Phil Ochs singing *I Ain't Marching Anymore* in the street, and groups of Black Panthers strutting their pride at every turn. The impact of the war in Vietnam was everywhere. I met returned soldiers on the Greyhounds, on the trains, in diners, bus stations and on the streets. They were often angry, outraged and shattered. On the boat down the British Columbian coast I spent a lot of time talking with a late middle-aged couple about just about everything, and as we neared Seattle, where they lived, they invited me to stay in their home for a week or so. They had a son, Ted, about my age, who had just come back from Vietnam — he had been drafted, and they hoped that I could befriend him and help him out of a terrified isolation. I spent a week with him, talking, drinking and driving around Seattle. We became good friends and he confided all kinds of hellish experiences with me, but he believed that what he had done was a real benefit to Vietnam and its people. I took the opposite side and we argued and discussed it for a week and neither of us changed, although hearing his opinions that the US way of life was the model for the world and its peoples and all he was trying to do was to bring it to the Vietnamese people, although I could never accept them, with the love and generosity within his family I could see where they had been born. He never wanted to accept the truth of the damage that U.S. systems of exploitation and domination were bringing to the world. After a week we said our good-byes at Seattle Bus Station much more friends than enemies.

Summer of 1968 in the USA: to say that it was the summer which changed my life would be an understatement. Everywhere I went I found ferment, protest, and anger at America inside America. The assassination of Bobby Kennedy in L.A., which I heard news of in the very same city just as I was jumping off the Greyhound at its bus station; the shooting of Martin Luther King in Memphis, the demonstrations against the Democratic Party's congress in Chicago and that of the Republicans in Miami, the Poor People's Campaign finale in Washington D.C. and the making of Resurrection City, the city of shanties in the grounds below the Lincoln Memorial as a living tribute to King. Everywhere I went – on Greyhounds, in diners, in bars, from a world of jukeboxes and loudspeakers, Aretha was crying out her song, *Think.* with its chorus a huge repeated shout 'talking about freedom!' It was a love song about a young woman's release from a constricting relationship sung so powerfully, but hearing that word 'freedom' in so many contexts, it seemed to be a living commentary on so many aspects of U.S.A. 1968, its sound echoing in every corner of such a vast country.

I crossed the frontier at Nogales, went on to Mexico City. As I was sitting on some steps at the university, struggling with a guide in Spanish, a young man, clearly a student, approached me and started a conversation in very good

English. He wanted to know all about me, and then he asked me, 'What do you want to see?' I said: 'Well, the murals mostly,' and he took me proudly around his campus showing me the revolutionary explosion of public art of the great socialist muralists, Diego Rivera, Siqueiros and Orozco. My eyes and mind were staggered by them. 'What next?' he said. 'What about Teotihuacan?' I asked. We found a bus that took us out of the endless city, and we were right there. He told me the history of the titanic pyramids and took me to their summits. And as we were saying our goodbyes and I was giving him my thanks, I met two German young men of exactly my age: Gunther and Klaus, both Bavarians. We seemed to become friends immediately and their English was brilliant. So we decided to travel on together, first to Veracruz and then to Tabasco and Villahermosa. We talked earnestly about our countries as if this were an opportunity all three of us had been waiting for. We went deeply into the wars between our nations, the second one in particular, which had given birth to all three of us, about Nazism and the hope of lasting peace. Travelling, laughing, eating, swimming on the beach at Veracruz, sleeping in the same cockroach-crawling cheap hotel rooms together, endlessly talking about our lives and what they could be, we pledged our friendship and swore that there would never, could never be another war between us or our peoples. Our generation would stop all that ever happening again, we declared, we would never let it happen again! And as the waves of the Gulf of Mexico pounded on the Veracruz sand, we believed it of ourselves. As I write this now, we would all, the three of us, be in our seventies, and I have often wondered if Klaus and Gunther still remember our pledges, made before that rolling surf. And I thought too of Isaac and millions like him. The only Germans they had ever faced, their overlings had told them they must kill or be killed. Now here were two young Germans, exactly my age, who I was not facing with guns, but befriending, sharing the closeness of life — sharing rooms, sharing thought and laughter, sharing the future.

As we talked, I told them a story my father had told to me, which had in turn been told to him by a German client of his, with whom he had established a close post-war friendship. He had been one of Rommel's troops in the Egyptian desert, and he said how for weeks his platoon faced a squad of British soldiers, with a stretch of no-man's land between them, where there were some small, deserted farm buildings with one surviving cow in one of them. Both sides wanted milk, so between them, during a clandestinely-arranged meeting across the barricades under a white flag, they made an arrangement. On alternate days, soldiers from each side would be allowed by their enemies to venture from their trenches and milk and feed the cow in an official and secret truce which continued for several weeks. How absurd is war, we decided, and we swore that we would be those soldiers for the rest of our lives.

And then on to Resurrection City, which was an instant shanty town erected right in front of the Lincoln Memorial, built by thousands of protesters who had arrived in Washington from all over America — made of corrugated iron, duckboards, shuttering planks, wooden boxes and casks, all kinds of materials lifted from construction sites, making shanties erected in front of one of the world's great monuments. And then it rained, how it rained. One of the City's organisers, William Rutherford, described it in this way in the book *Voices of Freedom:* 'We had terrible weather at the time. The city was bogged down in mud and rain. Resurrection City was as bad as any battlefield there could have been in any of the wars with the foot soldiers slogging through the mud.' And the warzone image was extended by Rutherford as he described the police tearing down the City on June 24: 'The police in this long blue line moved forward and they actually fired tear gas and we got a good whiff of tear gas, those of us who were supervising or serving as observers for the evacuation of the camp. And there was smoke from the tear gas rising from the ground, again, like an abandoned battlefield. As you moved forward across the

The Poor People's
Campaign, Resurrection
City, Washington DC,
June 1968

site, it was literally at the end of a major battle, a battle of the poor, and they had lost.' For Rutherford, Resurrection City's destruction was 'the Little Bighorn of the Civil Rights Movement, the end of hopes and dreams of many.' For Jesse Jackson, it was both a culmination and a presage: 'The first time I had ever really experienced tear gas was in Resurrection City. They drove us out with the tear gas. They gassed us. They shot Dr King. Now they were gassing us. I was determined to keep the struggle moving — if you will, to keep hope alive. I left there with an awful sense of betrayal and abandonment.'

The contradictions were ripe in Resurrection City. I was sitting eating a sandwich on a bank above the pool below the Lincoln Memorial, when a middle-aged white man — he had all the accoutrements of a university academic, with notes, briefcase and sports jacket — walked over to near where I, and a large group of black men and women, were sitting. They had leather jackets, afros, combs in their hair and they waited until the white man started speaking, or as it turned out, lecturing. He began to talk about Gandhi, his life and ideas. The black group listened awhile until one interrupted, 'What you talkin' about man?' he asked the speaker, as his friends began to heckle. The white man began to explain that Gandhi was one of King's inspirations, and he wanted to tell people about him, so they'd know about the man who set King on his civil rights path. His listeners became irritated and annoyed. 'What you saying man, the King got his own people, not you!' said one, among a chorus of dissent. 'Yeh man, and there ain't going to be no Gandhi when we come!' 'Go home, man,' they shouted. Impossible to make himself heard, he shook his shoulders, picked up his notes, jacket and briefcase and walked away, disconsolately.

Shortly after this I was standing by the pool staring and marvelling at the huge multi-racial crowds, when the young black man next to me who was about my own age, began talking to me and asking me questions. He told me he was a primary school teacher, a Washingtonian who lived just a few hundred yards from the White House. He noted my accent and asked me what I was doing there. I explained that I had been teaching in Western Canada, and had come to support the campaign, saying how important it was to people all over the world. 'Come with me!' he said with a big smile and we walked for about a mile or so until we reached a big tenement block behind the White House. He took me up a staircase to one of the upper floors, unlocked a door and invited me in. There, about to sit down to a meal, were his family — his parents, his sister and brothers and some grandchildren. He introduced me, we shook hands, another place was laid, and I sat down and ate with them. I told them about my mother, father and sister in England and my impressions of Resurrection City and the campaign, and something too about my life and work in Canada. I didn't stay long, but the sense of family warmth and friendship was immense and I carried it with me all over America. When I went back to Resurrection City, Coretta King was speaking on Lincoln's steps where Martin had declaimed his dream five years before. Then she sang *Come by Here, O Lord* with great beauty, using other words in the verses to set out the dimensions of poverty: 'Someone's jobless Lord, Come by here'; 'Someone's homeless Lord', 'Someone's crying Lord'. And she was followed by songs from Eartha Kitt; Aretha Franklin; Pete Seeger; Peter, Paul and Mary and Mahalia Jackson as thousands and thousands listened and promised. It was the America I had dreamed of: the country of Walt Whitman, of Woody, of Broonzy and the leaves of grass were growing all around me.

No more so a few days later in New Orleans, a city of myths for me, set on fire by my years on the door, tearing tickets at the St. Louis Jazz Club. But it's a long way from Elm Park to Bourbon Street, and in a dimly-lit, dingy, sweating room I heard the music of masters. The rococo, curlicuing clarinet played by Louis Cottrell, the dancing notes of the tiny Creole trumpeter Ernie Cagnolatti, the

hoarse tailgate slides of Waldron 'Frog' Joseph, the sometimes tickling, sometime rampaging snares of Louis
Barbarin, younger brother of a famous Crescent City
drum family, the blues-baked, rattling piano of Fatman
Williams, all in an ensemble of sheer life and beautiful
energy. But before I got too enraptured about my dream
city, sitting on the levee above Jackson Square I got
another message. I was talking to a man sitting close to
me, smoking and looking far out across the Mississippi.
He was friendly enough and telling me how, despite continually trying, he couldn't find a job. 'So what do you
think the problem is?' I asked, with a stranger's naivety.
'It's fucking whitey,' he said, 'won't fucking give me one.'
The real world of the blues, outside of the music, guitars
and horns, hit me, darkly and nakedly.

Yet strange and wonderful were the people you met on
the buses and trains across the Americas in 1968. On the
bus between Mexico City and Acapulco I found myself
sitting next to a young Chicago lawyer called Joan. We
were the same age, with twin spirits: it was sheer
serendipity for me and we never stopped talking. Her devotion was to the struggle for true civil rights for all
Americans, and how she could apply the law to its realisa-
tion. We got off the coach at the beautiful silver town of
Taxco and wandered its streets while our driver had his
break. We stared upwards at the rose-coloured colonial
double towers of the church, and began three days sharing
and exchanging our lives, our commitment to a better
world spanning the Atlantic and our dreams for the
futures of our countries. In Acapulco, we walked along its
beaches, ate its food and struggled with its people's
Spanish and watched in wonder at its blissful sunsets and
at the divers who plunged off high rocks, spearing into the
Pacific from more than fifty metres above.

Then we were away to different destinations, she to
King's funeral in Atlanta, me to Washington and Resurrection City. We met again a few weeks later in Chicago and
the warmth was still as strong as she showed me her city,

71

meandering through its South Side, with me sensing the blues everywhere. She saw me onto the Illinois Central at the Windy City's main railway station and I was going south again to Alabama, Mississippi, Florida and the Caribbean. We never met again and lost touch, but the power of her love for justice never left me and sprang up in my blood many times during the next fifty years.

A couple of years ago, and struggling with my computer, I tried to find her on Google. As I knew it would, I found her life had been dedicated to civil rights and she had become a US District Judge in her home city. Then I read on, profoundly shocked at what I read. One evening in February 2005 she had returned home from work. As soon as she entered her house, she knew that an intruder had been there. In the basement she found the bodies of her husband, a fellow lawyer, and her elderly mother, both shot in the head. The murders pointed back to a white supremacist, one Matthew Hale, who was in prison awaiting sentence for attempting to solicit Joan's murder. Hale was a leading member, the 'Pontifex Maximus' of the so-called 'World Church of the Creator', who had used the online bulletin board the 'Arayan Update' to publicise Joan's home address and photographs of her family, branding her a 'probable Jew' and a 'Kike and nigger-loving traitor' and asking members of his 'church' to end her life. It was an unsuccessful litigant whose case for millions of dollars of medical compensation which Joan had dismissed, who was eventually convicted for the murders following Hale's heinous invitation.

Reading of this in 2015 and remembering well the passion of Joan's social love and thirst for justice in 1968, I could only curse the racism of America and its demonic persistence. But I knew too in my brain and my senses, the determination of those who spend their life resisting it. Joan is ever one of them, and four and a half decades later, I recognised its true cost, for her, for America and for the world.

Chapter Three
Caribbean Jump

It was cricket which took me to the Caribbean, and my love for Caribbean cricketers. I grew through my boyhood with the exploits of 'the Three Ws' of Barbados — supremos Frank Worrell, Everton Weekes and Clyde Walcott batting in my heart and the sounds of the 1951 calypso by Lord Beginner, *Victory Test Match*, celebrating the West Indies victory over England at Lords, ringing in my ears. I always supported the West Indies — particularly against England, and when I met some of their players and got their autographs in 1957 when they played against Essex at Ilford, I was overjoyed. I'd never seen anyone bowl quicker and with more fire than Roy Gilchrist, and with more grace and physical beauty than the great Barbadian pace bowler, Wes Hall. Working in Canada, I'd been away from cricket for two years. Now I was determined to go back to where I believed its true soul was, not at Lord's but in those islands.

I had a Grenadian student at Calgary called George Brizan, who was later to be Grenada's prime historian, and when I told him I wanted to teach in the Caribbean, he helped me find some local schools. I settled on Bishop's High School in Tobago, wrote there and the head teacher immediately replied with an offer of a post. So I was fixed up for September 1968: all I had to do was get there. I took the long route, eventually flying from Miami to Jamaica, where I planned to catch the Federal boat through the eastern Caribbean islands to Port of Spain. On the flight to Kingston I sat next to a very friendly Jamaican government civil engineer, and he invited me to stay with him at his home in Kingston while I organised my ticket on the Federal boat the *Maple* which, with its sister ship the *Palm*, travelled up and down the islands of the short-lived

Federation of the West Indies, as a vestige but also a potent reminder of Caribbean unity, along with the cricket team and the regional University of the West Indies, with its campuses in Jamaica, Barbados and Trinidad. My new Jamaican mentor took me around Kingston and Spanish Town, and the projects that he was most concerned with, the major one being what to do about The Dungle, the giant slum that had been built by its homeless residents on a garbage dump on the shoreline just outside the capital. I had never seen anything like it before, a gigantic shanty town that looked impossible to penetrate, the setting of H. Orlando Patterson's vibrant novel *The Children of Sisyphus*. It was an eye-opener, for a young Englishman, of what those 'isles of the southern seas' could be like in reality.

As I had a full week before the *Maple* left harbour, and I had very little money, he took me to the University of the West Indies campus at Mona, towards the hills behind the city, built on the grounds of an old sugar estate. He introduced me to some students who were spending the vacation there, and one was an ex-Bishop's High School student from Tobago who, when he heard that I was on my way to Tobago to teach at his alma mater, insisted that I stayed on the campus. He told me that there were lots of spare rooms during vacation time, nobody used locks and keys, and why didn't I just take one, put my stuff in it, and sleep there. It wouldn't cost me a cent, he said. So I'd been in the Caribbean a week, had another week to go in Jamaica, and it had been free all the way so far. I couldn't believe my luck, or my Caribbean hosts' generosity.

As I sat with them at nights around an open-air bar many cross-Caribbean issues arose, but particularly their concern about one of their tutors, the Guyanese historian Walter Rodney, whom they admired and dared to emulate. Rodney, born to working-class parents in Georgetown in 1944, had done brilliantly in his undergraduate studies at Mona in 1963 when the University of the West Indies was still the University College of the West Indies dependent on its London University godfathers. He had received his doctorate from the School of African and Oriental Studies in London, had gone to teach at the University of Dar es Salaam and then returned to take up a position in Mona, where his socialist ideas and open critiques of the Jamaican power structure had soon made him an enemy of the government of Hugh Shearer. The tawdry sex scandals affecting the prime minister, and his corruption, certainly gave all kinds of satirical scope for the Mona students. There was strong support amongst them for Rodney, which grew into determined action three months later in October, when Shearer declared Rodney to be *persona non grata* in Jamaica. This provoked the 'Rodney Riots', when students and many Jamaicans came out on the streets to protest. Rodney lost his position at Mona, eventually returning to Dar es Salaam, where he was to write his hugely influential book, *How Europe Underdeveloped Africa.* When he finally returned to Georgetown in 1974 to teach at the University of Guyana and to write his epochal *History of the Guyanese Working People,* with others he founded the Working People's Alliance, which powerfully argued for socialism and effectively opposed the government of Forbes Burnham. In 1980 he was to be assassinated by supporters of Burnham. But that was to come. Certainly in July 1968 he was the main man for these students at Mona, and the radical ideas of many of them found agreement with Rodney, and looked forward to events in Grenada more than a decade later.

The Federal *Maple* was a Caribbean working ship plying between the islands during the nights, with passengers getting on and off during the days, when it unloaded and loaded up freight at each stop and gave those on board a full day to visit Antigua, St. Kitts, Montserrat, Dominica, St. Lucia, Barbados, St. Vincent and Grenada before it docked at its southern limit at Port of Spain. Very much a West Indies vessel, I befriended its

75

Barbadian Third Officer who, when we reached his island, took me to his home to meet his family. We had a delicious meal and then he insisted on taking me all around Barbados in his small car. This was the island of Weekes, Worrell and Walcott, as well as Wesley Hall, to me a true island of heroes and I savoured every square yard of its coralline and gently undulating landscape. But it was also the anglocentric setting of the terrible imposition of British slavery and plantocratic fortune-making, where Bussa and many other brave men and women had made their great rebellion in 1816, which was so savagely put down by the colonialists and their soldiers.

I learned a lot on the *Maple* as it wove between these islands. I got to know a young Peace Corps worker called Sally, who had finished after two years of trying to set up basket-making cooperatives in Jamaica. She was racked with doubts about what she had been doing. Why had she been treated with so much suspicion, even hostility at times? Why was being an American, representing the US government, so often a burden? Why were the Jamaican people so unenthusiastic about making baskets? What had she been doing there for two years? We talked about all these things and many more, and they impacted strongly upon me. How would I be perceived, as a teacher from the old colonial power? How could I avoid becoming a prisoner of history?

As I left all the remarkable people that I had met and learned so much from during the bursting months of 1968, I knew I would never see them again, but the discussions, arguments and friendships, however transitory, we had forged had turned pages in my life, and as I travelled on the overnight ferry between Port of Spain and Scarborough, Tobago with a violent storm crashing against the surging boat with scores of Tobagonians below decks crying, howling and praying as we went through the Dragon's Mouths straits that separate Trinidad and Tobago, with the hull creaking and moaning all around me I thought, well even if this is it, it hasn't been too bad, has it? And after a tumultuous night, as the ferry, ironically called *Bird of Paradise*, floated smoothly into Scarborough dock, my sweat subsided as I said to myself, 'Well, maybe that's normal.' I felt ready for anything and wondered to myself, 'What would Isaac have made of all this?' He'd been on a long sea voyage when he stayed for a sojourn in South Africa in 1914 as a part of a treatment for his weak lungs — maybe he'd had a similar quasi-cyclonic experience when his ship neared Cape Town. Who knows? I felt he was with me.

As for Tobago in 1968, it was just about the apex of natural beauty — I'd never been to anywhere like it. I managed to buy a bargain Lambretta motor scooter with the last of my Calgary earnings and it opened up the island for me, from the lowland south to the volcanic ridges stretching across the island's backbone to the north and the fishing villages all around the coast. Everywhere I went children and teenagers would scream out 'Ay, Django man!' evoking the name of a notorious long-haired and stubble-chinned spaghetti Western white man hero whose films were showing regularly at Scarborough's beachfront cinema. Adults were more curious and very friendly, particularly when they learned that I was a teacher at 'Bishop's', which was reckoned to be Tobago's prime school. I remember parking up my scooter on the cliffs above St. Peter's Bay, a small settlement to the south of the island. An elderly man was clearing his plot, his cutlass in his hand. He called me over, and with a big smile asked me who I was and where I was from. I told him I was a teacher, from England. 'Ahh, England,' he said, 'and do you know John Arlott?' So for me, here was true fame. A man tending his garden in one of those 'isles in the southern seas' we used to sing about in school assembly, was asking me if I knew the great cricket commentator with the Hampshire accent whose succulent voice took cricket all over the world, here too. 'Man, I love his voice!' my sporting friend said, and we spoke of our favourite cricketers, in particular his

Caribbean compatriots and the legend of Worrell, Weekes and Walcott. And I felt at one with him and all the world because of a game we both loved.

At the back of the school, along the road to Plymouth village, was the house where Learie Constantine, the great Trinidadian cricketer and activist, now retired, lived. I had first heard about him from my father, who had played against him in the Thirties in a charity match at Romford. My father had been much impressed by him, not only by his all-round cricketing skills as an attacking batsman, fast bowler and brilliant outfielder, but by his friendly and dignified demeanor. He had come with my father and a group of his teammates to the local pub, The Unicorn, after the game. I had read about his many tussles with English racism as set down in his book *Colour Bar,* especially his successful 1943 legal case against the Imperial Hotel in London's West End. The hotel had barred Mr and Mrs Constantine and their daughter from staying there when Learie was in London to play an international match at Lord's, even though he had already paid his deposit. An American client had declared: 'The Imperial is coming to something if you are going to take niggers in!' and the hotel management had succumbed. Learie's legal riposte was swift and the hotel was publicly shamed. So to know that this national and local hero and icon of my father and friend and house-mate of C.L.R. James, whose *Beyond a Boundary* I was reading and nourishing, was living so close to where I was teaching, somehow gave me a powerful feeling of familiarity and pride.

As I settled into the school the students were full of vibrancy, creative energy and humour, and every class became a pleasure, despite some of the alienating irrelevance of the texts that the London-based GCEs compelled us to study. Getting through Jane Austen's *Emma* became something of an ordeal for the A-level students and I. Perhaps it was after one of these classes that the headmaster, a Barbadian and something of an anglophile as far as education was concerned, called me into his office and told me that the tradition was that for December's annual prizegiving, there was the annual performance of a dramatic production by the students, customarily an extract from a Shakespearian play. Now as much as I loved Shakespeare, I could see the cultural absurdity of this, particularly in the context of the Caribbean playwrights who were coming to the fore. So I made this point and I could see his discomfort, particularly when I proposed that we perform *Moon on a Rainbow Shawl* by the Trinidadian actor and writer Errol John, which had been very warmly received when produced in London. Set in East Dry River, a working-class neighbourhood of Port of Spain and written in Trinidad's 'nation language', it exposes the poverty, landlordism and other hardships of those struggling for survival in the sister island. John's father was West Indies fast bowler of earlier times, George John, and his son's play has a sub-plot about racism within West Indies cricket. This was something ripe in the minds of many Caribbean people after a long struggle, led by the Trinidadian writer and activist C.L.R. James and described in *Beyond a Boundary*, to appoint a black captain for the West Indies team. This finally became a reality with the appointment of Frank Worrell in 1960. As for Errol John, I had seen him play Othello at the Old Vic in 1963, the first black man ever to play the part in the famous theatre, with the brilliant Australian Leo McKern as Iago. I was much impressed by his performance, watching from the gallery over many empty seats, for his performance had received poor reviews from the British establishment theatre critics who didn't like the manner in which he spoke his lines. Now, at last in Trinidad and Tobago, I realised the inflections of his speech and I could hear his Othello in the people's voices around me, and yet there was still a residual complex amongst them that the Queen's English was bound to be superior, and anything Caribbean, anything local, especially speech, must be inferior. It was an

Lyle Alexander in
*I Thought You Loved
the Fishermen*:
Tobago 1968

attitude that I was certainly not going to reinforce or tolerate, and a few days later I met with the headteacher again and explained my position, saying that I and the students would write our own play about the devastating Hurricane Flora, which battered Tobago in 1963. He reluctantly agreed, and looked at me strangely. Why would I, an Englishman, want to put on a play about Tobago using Tobagonian speech? I could tell that he didn't, or was unwilling to, understand, but I think he wanted a quiet life and a play for prizegiving.

I found a flat overlooking the surf of Rockly Bay and its plummeting pelicans, just outside of Scarborough and owned by a canny local businessman of Madeiran roots, Mr Gomes, whose general store was on the ground floor. As I marked my students' essays in the late evenings, I could hear the relentless lapping of the waves to the front, and from the back of the flat came the beautiful melodism and stomping joy of 'Our Boys' Steel Band, whose pan tent was just behind the flat. As they played into the night the tunes of Sparrow and Kitchener's racy calypsos and ballads like the theme from Zeffirelli's film of 'Romeo and Juliet', it prompted me to hire the beachfront cinema for the school and take all its students and teachers to a special matinee screening of the film showing them that it wasn't just spaghetti westerns that came from Italy. They loved it as it touched their Caribbean teenage hearts.. Many weekends I took the Friday night steamer to Port of Spain, staying in the wooden shed that my colleague Cyril, the Geography teacher, had installed in the corner of a bleak barrack yard in East Dry River. The yard was marshalled and stewarded by a burley, no-nonsense policeman resident called Clifford, who like his neighbours, seemed more than a little surprised to meet me, a gangling, long-haired white man from London, as I turned the key in the lock of Cyril's shed, opened the door and beheld the old and bare mattress that covered the entirety of its floor. But once I had explained who I was and that I was a teacher-friend of Cyril, they welcomed me with jokes and friendly needle, inviting me to join their nightly relaxed 'liming' sessions around the yard's single communal shower and faucet. It struck me then, and I think about it now, would any of them have found the same warmth and hospitality that they showed to me in that East Dry River barrack yard, in the streets and blocks of London, had they made the passage?

When I went into Ishmael Khan's Port of Spain store, I bought Earl Lovelace's novel *The Schoolmaster* – I was to interview him in Grenada fourteen years later – I was served by a bright-eyed and vibrant East Indian young woman called Patsy. We began to talk and very soon were seeing each other, taking walks on the Queen's Park Savannah or around the lush tropical trees and shrubbery of the Botanical Gardens. I began to love Port of Spain; its vibrant cosmopolitanism made a huge impression on me and made me wish that London could be that way. I went to a concert featuring the calypso power of the Mighty Sparrow singing his moving tribute to the late Martin Luther King, and much less serious songs like his ribald calypso *The Lizard*, telling the story of a teacher called Mildred who carries on teaching her lesson even though a curious lizard has climbed up inside her skirt. The Trinidadian audience went mad with laughter. I also went to a reading by the great local novelist and humorist Samuel Selvon, whose dialect-emphatic novels and short stories like *The Lonely Londoners* or *Ways of Sunlight* were to entrance and influence me so powerfully in my upcoming London years.

As Patsy and I walked around downtown Port of Spain, along Frederick Street or across Independence Square, we found ourselves the targets of direct racist invective by some liming bystanders. I remember well the hostility because I had never personally experienced it before. 'Wh'appen white boy, you have a nice coolie girl there!' I hated it, and suddenly I began to feel, in a much slighter and less enveloping way, what thousands of people in my own country must have felt – in Smethwick, in Notting Hill and Brixton, in Moss Side, Handsworth, Liverpool 8,

82

Southall or Chapeltown. For Patsy it was much, much worse. How did she feel, being abused and belittled by men of her very own city?

Every opportunity I got in my classwork, I encouraged my students to talk and write about Caribbean matters and the issues that truly concerned them. In January 1969 some four hundred students, many of them from the Eastern Caribbean, occupied the computer suite at Sir George Williams University in Montreal as a protest against racism in the University's grading systems. On February 11th the occupation was broken by aggressive police action, resulting in ninety-seven arrests, including several students from Trinidad and Tobago. This was seen as an outrage by the Bishop's students — some had relatives who were students there, and others had dreams of going there or to other Canadian universities. They wrote passionately about Sir George Williams' injustices and with even greater anger and eloquence about the farcical 'Operation Sheepskin' colonial shenanigans of the following March.

The Second Battalion of the Parachute Regiment of the British Army made an 'amphibious assault' on the small Caribbean island of Anguilla, and were followed by 120 members of the London Metropolitan Police. This was in response to 'unrest' in the island at its proposed and compulsory unification with the islands of St. Kitts and Nevis as a single unitary state. Britain's Victorian and Palmerston-like 'invasion' of this tiny Caribbean island may have made it the laughing-stock of the world's press, but for the children of Tobago, itself a smaller sister island, following events day by day, it invoked profound vexation and resentment. It was another step towards the eventual black power protests which broke out in the streets and army barracks of Trinidad and Tobago in April 1970, just over a year later. And as more news came through of the racist degradation of apartheid in South Africa and the British attempts to conciliate the white Rhodesian pretender Ian Smith during and after British Prime Minister Harold Wilson's discussions with him in 1968 on *HMS*

Fearless, students brought the issues to drama with an elaborate mock-United Nations General Assembly session on the future of South Africa and Rhodesia, with the faces of South African and Rhodesian representatives blanked out by flour, which, I thought, made a change from whites impersonating blacks by the use of boot polish, something my own skin still remembered from my days as Balthazar. But these international manifestations of racism were met in these young people's own island every time they or their parents walked inside a Scarborough bank. Whether it was the island branch of Barclays, the Toronto-Dominion or the Canadian Imperial Bank of Commerce, the same sight would greet them: light-skinned bank tellers and never a black face behind a counter. It was the outrages of Sir George Williams University and Anguilla come to their own island, and once they were set free to write, their indignation came boiling out: Canada, Britain, South Africa, Rhodesia, Anguilla and the streets of their own island capital; the truths were beginning to connect up, and a strong awareness of them, and what I didn't know then, but found out two years later, when I read his book written from a Californian prison, *Soledad Brother*, was that a young black American called George Jackson was writing from his cell: 'There is no turning back from awareness'.

Jackson also wrote: 'I know that the most damaging thing a people in a colonial situation can do is allow their children to attend any educational facility organised by the dominant enemy culture.' Bishop's was a government-funded Church of England school in a newly-independent nation that was an ex-colony. Yet it retained most of the trappings of an elite colonial school. It followed a predominantly London syllabus, with some Caribbean emphasis in subjects like Agricultural Science, History and Geography. The students read *Jane Eyre* for their O-level English just as I had done, along with *The Long and the Short and the Tall*, a play about a group of British soldiers with diverse regional British accents, set in the Burmese campaign of the Second World War — and yet there was

84

nervousness and reluctance about producing *Moon on a Rainbow Shawl,* partly because it employed characters speaking in a national Caribbean dialect.

At Bishop's almost all the literature texts were straight from the English canon or following the London University General Certificate of Education rubric. It was as if I was bringing lilywhite Hornchurch into the throbbing heart of the Caribbean, supplanting the brilliance and beauty of Caribbean speech and language with a code that was foreign, dominant, white and unreal. I began to understand how the imposition of colonial culture through the school system had been so monstrously effective for decades and how its efficacy was still working in a post-colonial context, still blotting out the achievement of Caribbean writers. We had but one class reader of Caribbean texts — *West Indian Narrative* it was called, edited by the Trinidadian scholar Kenneth Ramchand. How the students loved and responded to its stories and extracts from the novels of their own writers, how the words exploded in their minds! When we read from Barbadian George Lamming's *In the Castle of My Skin*, Jamaican Andrew Salkey's *Hurricane*, Guyanese Jan Carew's *Black Midas* or Trinidadian C.L.R. James' short story *La Divina Pastora*, or when they shared the riotous humour of Trinidadian Samuel Selvon's London story *Brackley and the Bed* from his *Ways of Sunlight* collection, literature suddenly became true, about their world, about their lives. Their eyes, their enthusiasms, their minds lit up with meaning.

For me too, I sensed their freedom. It was truly liberating, and a long, long way from teaching novels like *Emma* to my sixth form A-level class, with its characters and their prosperous nineteenth-century southern English life with all kinds of unmentioned connections to the slave trade. What was I doing, teaching this? I thought. I remember one lesson with *Emma*. It had been a long, long day, it's true, and I'd been out in a rum shop the night before and it was the final lesson of a humidly hot afternoon. I must have been talking like a senseless drone about Emma and Mr Knightley as I felt my head gradually dropping down towards my desk. Then suddenly, Zelma and Annette, two of my students, were jogging me: 'Sir! Sir! You head falling on the desk! You all right, Sir? Wha' happen? You sick Sir?' I'd actually fallen asleep while teaching, the only time in a classroom lifetime. I apologised and we all laughed about it at the time, but when I thought about it, I knew that despite Jane Austen's artistry it was *Emma* that had unwittingly caused it. Its irrelevance, its alienation, its neocolonial subjugation of all things local in the human life and mind of the Caribbean, its history and its future. All her characters, her themes, her settings were estranged, white, faraway and imperial; there, as Fanon was telling me in his classic text, to put white masks over black skins. For there was nothing that was Caribbean, local, black or life-true about *Emma*. It represented a distant and repressive perspective of literature, and I was teaching and promoting it! I too had studied *Emma* for my A-level English, but now, not in Hornchurch, England but in Tobago in the Caribbean, Jane Austen had never taught me so much.

All this made me feel that the play we were about to write and perform had a special significance. I suggested to the classes that I taught that they write about the experiences of Hurricane Flora, and to talk to their families about it before they did. They wrote some powerful accounts (some of them are set down in my book *The Forsaken Lover,* which details its process) and from these writings I began to mould together the skeleton of a play, about the impact of Flora on the lives of a group of people living in a small Tobagonian fishing community. Then it was up to the actors to elaborate and create the dialogue between themselves, and they did this brilliantly, with tremendous verve and humour, loving their language. We introduced song and stylised dance around 'pulling seine', when villagers come to the beach

86

to pull in the nets laid by the fishermen, and the hurricane effects, using African drums, flying palm branches, coconuts, sheets of galvanised iron and piping, wood and buckets which were hurled on to the stage from the wings. Within this melee the chief character, Hawkins, a fisherman played by a vibrant young fifteen-year-old called Lyle Alexander (who eventually became a senior officer in charge of the Army Reserve in the Trinidad and Tobago Defence Force), shouted his indignation towards the heavens:

> Jesus, Jesus I thought you was a friend of the fishermen,
> I thought you loved the fishermen.

It wasn't Lear on the storm-blasted heath, but the power of Lyle's outraged delivery on a Tobago stage where the hurricane had brought real wrath and destruction had a deep effect upon the prizegiving audience who were astonished by their children's performances and the way in which they had re-lived history and the real, terrifying hours which they had been through just a few years before. As for the headmaster, he seemed astonished by the short play, but any doubtful feelings he might still have had disappeared when the play and its actors won the national schools drama competition, in the face of the elite schools of the sister island like Queen's Royal College, which still carried through all the colonial and imperial mores.

As for me, a few days after the prizegiving performance I was off to Guyana, a country I had always wanted to visit, not only because of its great cricketers like Rohan Kanhai and Lance Gibbs, but because I remembered strongly October 1953, when, still a primary schoolboy overjoyed by England's Ashes victory at the Oval, I had read the *News Chronicle's* headlines about British troops being flown from Jamaica to British Guiana, and the cruiser *Superb* and the aircraft carrier *Implacable* steaming there to re-occupy the South American colony. Why? Because of the threat of a properly elected Prime

Minister, dentist Cheddi Jagan, who was bringing something called 'communism' to British Guiana through his Progressive People's Party government. Churchill's Tory government had issued a statement through the Colonial Secretary (one Oliver Lyttelton, Chiefie's erstwhile opponent at Aldershot in the 1951 parliamentary elections) which declared:

> Her Majesty's Government has decided that the constitution of British Guiana must be suspended to prevent Communist subversion of the Government and a dangerous crisis both in public order and in economic affairs... the faction in power have shown by their acts and their speeches that they are prepared to go to any lengths, including violence, to turn British Guiana into a communist state. The Governor has therefore been given emergency powers and has removed the portfolios of the Party Ministers. Armed forces have landed to support the police and to prevent any public disorder which might be fomented by Communist supporters.

I didn't know what all this meant at the time, but it etched 'British Guiana' in my boyish consciousness, and it compelled me to go to there if I ever got the chance. Well, now I had the chance, and I could also see the reality of all those jungle scenes in my old stamp albums. What I didn't know was that I was to interview Cheddi Jagan two decades on in Grenada. He would tell me much about those 1953 events, and their relevance to the dangers facing the Grenada Revolution. Our paths were to cross again, by letters this time, in September 1993, after our school in Sheffield had raised quite a large sum of money for medicines for those suffering during the 1992 cholera epidemic in Guyana. By that date Cheddi Jagan had been elected as President of his nation and I had sent the donation directly to him. He wrote us a very warm letter of thanks, saying how our students' fundraising work 'reflects positively for future generations' and that the Guyanese people 'will ever be grateful to them.'

But that was far in the future and in December 1968 I met some young Canadians in Georgetown who asked me what my plans were in Guyana. I said that I didn't have any. They were 'CUSO' (Canadian Universities Service Overseas) a sort-of Canadian equivalent of the Peace Corps, and they suggested that if I wanted a sense of the Guyanese interior, I should go to Bartica, on the banks of the huge Essequibo River, and on the edge of some very thick bush. Having seen the huge, tree-trunk-thick anacondas at Georgetown Zoo, I felt more than a little trepidation, but armed with the address of one of their CUSO colleagues, a teacher known as 'Bartica Bill', I caught a bus, then a boat where the Essequibo, the colour of dark rust, pours out into the Atlantic. There seemed to be no real settlements on either side of the river, only bush and thick green, until Bartica, where I disembarked and looked for Bill. In this last staging post before the bush, the refuge of gold prospectors called 'pork-knockers' (I knew something about them, having read Jan Carew's classic novel of their lives, *Black Midas*), I asked some children playing at the dockside if they knew a 'Teacher Bill'. They all knew him, everybody knew him, and a whole platoon of his students took me to his wooden house, on the edge of town and right next to the river. It was a real pleasure to meet him, and he immediately asked me to stay with him while I was in Bartica. He was from Toronto, so we had a link there, and as we were both teachers, we exchanged many experiences about classroom approaches. Then he got up from his table overlooking the massive river, and asked me, 'Would you like a swim?' 'A swim?' I thought, 'in that?' I had been spoiled in Tobago with some of the most beautifully serene beaches in the Caribbean, and as I stared at the liquid khaki of the Essequibo where you couldn't see an inch under the surface, I was more than a little worried. 'Hang on,' I said, 'what's in the water? What about alligators, piranhas — do anacondas swim?' He laughed and assured me, 'Listen. I've swum in here every day for the last two years — I've never seen any of them.' And he stripped to his shorts and plunged in, going out a good fifty yards. I managed about ten, trying to see under the surface at every stroke. The only obstacles that I found were the stone-hard trunks of fallen and submerged greenheart trees.

Bill's hospitality was warm and generous, and as we drank in the town's last-ditch saloon rum shops, everybody seemed to know him and quite a few of our drinking partners knew London too, and spun off names of streets and underground stations as if they were just outside, rather than a mighty river with thick wild bush coming down to its banks. But I was soon on the boat and back to Georgetown again, and the long drive to the airport at Atkinson Field, a converted US air base. At Port of Spain I still had a few days left, so I decided to go to Grenada. I paid very little money to travel there via St. Vincent, in an old and decrepit-looking motorised boat which buffeted between the islands. After St. Vincent we made our way through the Grenadines, stopping at Bequia and Carriacou, then, with the next stop Union Island, we came across a cluster of craft, with their crews appearing to be searching the waters and picking up objects floating in the sea. A crewman told me what had happened. A boat carrying local Vincentian workers who had been building an American hotel on one of the small palm-fringed islands, had been overloaded, capsized and sank with a number of lives lost. 'They was too many men in the boat,' he declared, 'they was trying to save on money.' I looked at the debris in the water and felt my blood boiling. I had already seen in Tobago the impact on Tobagonians of a US-tourist industry, of the models of often servile service work which it entailed and its mimicry of things and ways American. Huge new tourist complexes were being planned and constructed to expropriate large-scale profits out of the island. Here was more of the same, with tragic consequences for Caribbean working people. Our boat too searched the wreckage in the sea for bodies or survivors and their property. 'They was trying to save on money,' and many men had drowned. It was America provoking and causing death in what they supposed was their backyard. I was to see it and know it again. And this had happened in the seas where the Union Island-born seaman, Hugh Mulzac, had learned his craft and his skill. Mulzac was the first black man in America, where he emigrated, to win a Master's licence. For twenty-five years he tackled bigotry and racism for his right to become a ship's captain. It was not until World War Two that he was given a ship, and he served with courage and distinction in the heat of the maritime conflict. These were Mulzac's waters — what would he have thought if he could have seen this betrayal? In the closing words of his life story, *A Star to Steer By,* he wrote:

> And if, therefore, there is any sense I can impart to the younger generation it would be this: commit yourself! Fight for the liberation of oppressed people everywhere, fight for an honest, moral political system, fight for the fullest appreciation of every human need, for fighting for the good life for all people is the only way to live and win it for yourself. Thus does life become worth living.

Every human's life contains crucial events and moments which break consciousness and provoke future action. There, on this old, almost unseaworthy boat making circles around these few square metres of the Caribbean Sea looking for the dead, those killed by American profiteers, I began to understand the true power relations of the world, those compelled to serve them and those who take enormous benefit from them. These were the last days of the year 1968, and I also knew that through this year, young people like myself were realising the same things in Paris, London, Toronto and across the USA. George Jackson's words, set down in the same year in his Californian cell, would always come back to me when I remembered those moments, and they stick to me still: 'There is no turning back from awareness.'

When I finally stepped off this boat in St. George's Harbour in Grenada, it was the day before Christmas Eve and I felt knackered. I found a cheap bed and breakfast on the other side of the tunnel under Fort George, where other tragic events were to take place a decade and a half later and my close friends were to be killed by their own erstwhile comrades. As she gave me a key for my room, the landlady told me not to worry about the sounds coming from the room next door, and as I lay down on the bed, I could hear a man's oratory coming through the wooden grille at the top of the dividing wall. 'He's a local politician, and he practices his speeches every night before he goes to sleep,' she had told me. Even this man's extraordinary rhetorical and elaborate Queen's English didn't stop me sleeping, and up with the pelicans diving around the fort next morning, I shared a taxi to Pearl's Airport across the green crest of the island's main range with another politician, who the taxi driver collected from a large gated house in L'anse Epines, a prosperous seafront location on the south-western corner of the island. As we drove across Grenada, he seemed to be pleased to have the company of a white Englishman, and as we rolled down the steep road on the other side of the topmost sublime peak, the Grand Etang, he commanded the taxi driver to stop, invited me out of the car and took me into a plantation beside the road, which he knew so well that I assumed he owned it. He went up to a nutmeg tree, plucked a fruit and showed it to me, proudly and proprietorily. 'This is our fortune!' he proclaimed, and stood tall in his light tan skin and a smartly-fitting trop-ical suit. There were a few much more darkly-skinned and less expensively-dressed labourers observing and tending the trees and the soil around them with their hoes and cutlasses who didn't much look like the joint recipients of that fortune. Further down the road near what, more than a decade further on, I was to know well as the village of Birch Grove, some women had a small stall and were selling bananas. It was a brief but engag-ing lesson which was to stay with me and help my understanding of this same island a dozen or so years later. As he dusted down his suit and sat back in the taxi, giving his eye to the taximan to drive on, I felt I had learned a little more about the realities of class in the Caribbean.

Back in Tobago I got my head down to my teaching, and my scooter rides around the island confronted me with all kinds of evidence of its colonial history, its centuries of slavery and its people's resistance. On the headland above Scarborough was the fort which had housed the colonial soldiers, my forebears, who had kept the cruel status quo for all those years over the descendants of a people, some of whom I could now call my friends. In the soldiers' cemetery next to the fort was one stone-covered grave which was at right angles to the others. When I asked my friend the Trinidadian archaeologist John Llanos about this, he told me that the soldier who had been buried in the non-sequential grave was a private who had committed suicide during his service. Nobody seemed to know any more about him or his life, so I set my imagination to work. I imagined that he had been a young soldier, maybe a London recruit, who had been so disgusted and angry at the system he had been sent to protect and risk his life for, when he had seen its reality and its cruelty and oppression it was too much for him to bear. A strange and maybe fanciful optimism perhaps, but one I took to my heart and my consciousness — for why wouldn't he, I thought, forced to act out such a commission, trapped in a role from which he could find no escape. And wouldn't there have been similar young men in all the colonies all over the world who might have harboured similar thoughts — from Africa, to China, to India, to the Pacific, in all those places we used to sing about in *Hills of the North, Rejoice!* — all those men of my age and younger, and this man whose bones lay close to me now, I could have been him, couldn't I?

John was a dedicated searcher of history. In his small house on the road to Bacolet he had a whole cabinet of Arawak and Carib artefacts — he insisted on giving me

93

one, the ceramic head of an animal whose nose had been snapped off or rubbed away between giant eyes. It sits on my windowsill here in Sheffield even now. He told me he had found it with other similar pieces near the beach in King Peter's Bay — named after an Amerindian chief who had held sway around there during the arrival of the first colonialists. He also told me in a very excited way, about a rebel called Chubb, whose life and death story he had found in some previously undisclosed documents. He had found details, he said, of a slave rebellion on the north-western coast of the island, on an estate called the Bloody Bay Estate, where on June 7 1771, the slaves rose up and killed their manager and overseer, before scattering inland, up to the thick forest of the island's central ridge. Soldiers were called from Scarborough, and the rebels finally surrendered on 22 June. But that was only one part of his story. He also said he had found papers relating to an 'Enquiry into the Slave Trade' which had been held in London in 1790. Certain evidence had been given about the execution of rebellious slaves in Tobago, and the names of two of these slaves were Chubb and Sampson. There was an account of Chubb's sentence of death by sword and fire, and a witness had said that before Chubb's arm had been severed he had kicked up sand saying, 'Buckra, today you see me but by tomorrow I shall be dust like this,' and those present, including his gaolers, had been much impressed by his courage.

By sheer coincidence a group of us, teachers and sixth-formers, from Bishop's had been part of a school field trip the week before to find the source of the Bloody Bay River, which runs out into the sea through the bay named after the battle that was fought between the competing colonial powers of England and France, many years before Chubb's rebellion. It was part of the island that was completely unpopulated and behind the bay the river fell through the volcanic ridges on its way to the sea. During our ascent to the top of the ridge and following the course of the river, we counted seventeen waterfalls with beautifully translucent

94

pools at their bottoms. The geography teacher who led the field trip had miscalculated both the distance and the difficulties of scaling the falls. We became lost, and with no camping equipment we had to spend a very cold and shivering night near the crest of the island, hunched up against each other as the water poured past us. So much so, that when we finally set off to return to Bloody Bay, a search party had been sent up the river to find us. For me, I had never seen countryside so intense and beautiful as that we passed through to find the bubbling source of that river and to look ahead and back to see the distant sea miles down the deep and seething green escarpments both in front of us, and behind us. I thought of Chubb and his comrades who had rebelled, fled and scattered up this very ascent, through its thick forest with only this diaphanous and plunging river as their guide, of their days of suppurating heat and their icy, almost polar, nights as the ceaseless, freeborn water splashed relentlessly one side of them. What would they have been thinking, what way back was there for them, what future as the armed and revengeful men behind them were in full and merciless pursuit — my countrymen too.

Strange and compelling how the imagination drives you. For me, it told me to write another play for my students to consider, develop, change and transform by the midwife of their astonishing power and poetry of language. I brought together John's revelation of the story of Chubb — of his courage, defiance and vulnerability and his impact upon one of his captors, his gaoler, who I imagined having something of the consciousness of the man whose body was buried in the right-angled grave at the fort in Scarborough, a young soldier fraught with doubt about what he had been told by his 'superiors' he must do to his nation's enemies. I thought of Isaac and Wilfred and their trench poems — 'I was the enemy that you killed, my friend.' And I decided to set the play at the 1790 London enquiry into the slave trade that had considered Chubb's insurgency and his trial and execution,

Cora Tucker as Chubb:
Half Moon Theatre,
Stepney, 1985

that John had told me about. In bringing these strands of history together I was, consciously or unconsciously, testing my growing faith and belief in human empathy upon myself and my own writing.

I left the play *Chubb* with my students and colleagues before I came back to England. They performed it for the next prizegiving in December 1969, just five weeks before the Black Power upsurge in both Trinidad and Tobago, where many of them came out on the streets in support of their sister islanders and to make their point against the predominantly foreign and white power structure which controlled and sought to exploit and despoil their lives. Reading about the rebellion back in England, I thought Chubb and his comrades would have approved. It was a long step too for Bishop's to put on such a play, and I wondered how much persuasion the headteacher needed to agree to it. Of course, I never saw it, but with Lyle and his friend Erol playing the parts of Chubb and Sampson, I thought, how could it have been less than inspiring? Ironically enough, I didn't see it either when it was performed by the Half Moon Young People's Theatre in Stepney, East London, in 1985. I had left it with an ex-colleague when I moved up north to work in Sheffield and he had no forwarding address for me in those pre-internet days. After its stage production at the Half Moon it was taken by their young actors and performed at fifteen schools in East London and Lambeth, and provoking discussions after each performance and some stimulating teaching material in a teaching pack for the schools, it was used as a curriculum vehicle for education about the slave trade and its consequences. The Half Moon version of the play made Chubb into a woman character, giving the narrative even deeper dimensions. It wasn't until two years after the performances that I learned about the Half Moon production, and I was sent some powerful photographs of the staging and its actors, as well as the poster of the play, and the young woman Chubb stares down at me now from my wall as I write these words. He/she has travelled a long way. I eventually changed Chubb into a story, and it was published as one of my short stories in the collection *The Black Man of Shadwell* in 1976.

I had been accepted for a Master's course in Education at Exeter University, so by June 1969 I was homeward bound. I left Tobago on the night voyage back to Port of Spain on the sister ferry of the *Bird of Paradise,* the *Scarlet Ibis.* Scores of my students had come to my flat overlooking the dockside during the afternoon and evening, and we had a final party with the calypsos of the Mighty Sparrow and *Hey Jude!* of the Beatles at full volume. They wouldn't go home, and when the *Scarlet Ibis* steamed off at 10.00pm, I could hear them shouting and repeating 'Django! Django!' until we were round the headland. I was staggered. All I could do was scream back 'Tobago! Tobago!' until we were well out to sea and set towards Trinidad.

I'd booked a ticket back across the Atlantic on the *SS Montserrat*, better known as by its predominantly Caribbean passengers as the 'Monster Rat'. It was a regular emigration vessel, mainly for Trinidadians but it also stopped to take on more travellers at Cartagena (Colombia) and Willemstadt, the port capital of Curaçao. There was a real stew of people on board, good food, plenty of wine with the meals, and a wonderful group of young Trinidadian women going to be nurses in Britain and give so much to the National Health Service. When I think of them now, I think of all the Caribbean nurses that have helped me and my family for all those years between, and how they all must have deservedly retired by now, and I say to myself 'long live the NHS and the part you played in it!', but then they were young women full of energy, verve, song and dance, but they were going to an uncertain future in a land still racked by racism and the dictums of Enoch Powell. And I thought too, what are they leaving, perhaps for always? And the poem of a young Tobagonian girl in one of my classes came back to me, about the last hours on their homeland of a migrating family:

> It was their last visit
> We were all standing, close together
> With our minds based on each other,
> Saying farewell.
>
> Down the close, darkened road
> They made their way,
> With faces grimly gay
> Saying farewell.
> They boarded the ship
> Without looking back...

Had it been like that for these young women? For the risks taken, the huge gamble of life in emigration, the chance it might be good, the danger it might be bad or even disastrous, the jeopardy in the choice once made: these Trinidad young women knew all this, but on their voyage out, most of the time they hid it under merriment and a huge optimism of the will.

Yet five years later, when one of my Stepney students whose parents had made the same voyage from St. Vincent and St. Lucia, wrote this in her English class, the lives of these young nurses and what their first half decade of life in England had been like, worried and nagged at me:

> I can just imagine when my mum got off the boat, all sorts of things going through her mind, thinking what life would be like in England, leaving all her friends and family behind, thinking if she would ever go back there and see them. My mum has never gone back on a holiday, but she is hoping to go sometime this year. She does not like it very much over here.
>
> For other people who emigrate to other countries they run into a lot of good luck and for other people, well, it's just working day in day out in a country they don't really like. Once you get on the plane or boat there's no second chances. You can't change your mind, it's just too late and you think to yourself, what have I done? You lose all your friends and they think, 'I hope she's doing the right thing, emigrating like that'.

As for me, I was going back to the land and the city of Isaac and I, and on this ship of migrants, of dramatic departures and arrivals, I read again the two books, both by Caribbean revolutionaries, which alongside Jackson's *Soledad Brother*, have had the most influence over my life. The first was James' *Beyond a Boundary,* into which I poured my own cricket experiences of sport and class, and began to fathom them with a new understanding. The second was Frantz Fanon's *Black Skin, White Masks.* As I read the Martiniquan's translated words over this most brutal ocean where the bodies of dying and resisting slaves had been hurled to their deaths two and three centuries before, I suddenly made political and cultural sense of his truths of language, how it alienates when it is an oppressive, imposed force, but how also, when forged within the endless seascape of the imagination, it can begin to set us free. Isaac too, en route to Cape Town to stay with his sister and rest his panting lungs, had a long, long Atlantic journey. Did he think about and create in his huge mind, similar insights? Only the waves knew, and with all the history they held, they weren't going to tell me anything. I needed to find Isaac's streets to know that — for as his great ancestor Blake had reminded us: 'Our streets are the ideas of our imagination.'

Chapter Four
Devon Interlude

But first of all there was another year's study to do, in Exeter in Devonshire, a city and a county I'd never been to before. I was lucky to get a grant from the Social Science Research Council, I had some stimulation and friendly tutors and a cohort of English teachers my own age who were earnest to discuss and formulate ideas of teaching and education, so all that was very positive. But I missed the verve, the humour, the creative joy and critical outlook of my Tobago students so much, that I think that almost any other setting would have paled. I had been more than spoiled on that extraordinary island.

One of my new colleagues was a white South African who had come on this course direct from a jail in his home country, where he had been imprisoned for anti-apartheid activities. He had us acting out scenes from his incarceration in classes that explored empathy in the classroom, in which we all sought to share each others' experiences through our imaginations. I tried to act his desperate emotional loneliness of solitary confinement. It worked too, and I thought that I began to understand the agony of apartheid and the punishment of resistance to it in new ways. It became a new lever for me to use in poetry as a means of such imaginative empathy in my own classrooms of the future: Chile, Belfast, Oman, Spain, Wounded Knee and South Africa itself all beckoned. And then another student called John, a seemingly quiet and serious man who had come to the course after a decade teaching in his home industrial town of Runcorn, between Manchester and Liverpool, began to tell a story from his own childhood. As he remembered the polluted factory air in his town, and how as a ten-year-old boy he had come downstairs from his bedroom to do what he usually did and feed his pet rabbit, he began to weep convulsively as he told us of the morning that he had found his rabbit dead, poisoned by the industrial fumes. It made me remember that I was certainly back in England again, and this was a teacher in his mid-thirties. Another event that sharply reinforced where I had returned to was when another course-mate called Granville Williams, who was later to become a founder and organiser of the Campaign for Press and Broadcasting Freedom, organised a busful of students to go to the plush Devon resort town of Torquay, to protest against a meeting organised by local Tories featuring Enoch Powell, then riding a tide of popularity after his racist and provocative 'Rivers of Blood' speech. As we chanted and waved placards outside the meeting, the stupefied conservative looks on the faces of those who attended, again told me very clearly that this was certainly England.

There too was a first year student, Yana Mintoff, daughter of the anti-colonialist and socialist prime minister of Malta, Dom Mintoff. Nine years onwards, in July 1978, she was to achieve national renown when she hurled three bags of horse dung from the public gallery onto sitting MPs in the House of Commons, as a protest against British troops in Northern Ireland. With her was another protester, the blonde-haired Chris Gibson, a future founder of the Haringey Cricket College in North London, a pioneering venture which very successfully developed cricket skills with local black working class teenagers. I had been back for just two months and it was as if the worst and the best of Britain were at odds with each other that day at the so-called English Riviera.

But my year in Exeter was most marked for me by meeting two remarkable women, both well into their seventies. The first was one of my tutors, a woman called Marjorie Hourd. Her interests penetrated the heart of childhood, child psychology and children's imaginative writing, particularly poetry. In 1949 her book, *The Education of the Poetic Spirit*, had been published, a pioneering work about the close relationship of the child's development, the teaching of English and imaginative writing. In it she argued and demonstrated that similar critical standards can be applied to children's poetry and the child's mind, as to the psychology and creative expression of adults. She had us studying children's writing using critical standards and methods that we might use to study Wordsworth, Blake or T.S. Eliot. In the preface to her second book, *Coming into Their Own,* co-written with Gertrude Cooper, she writes about 'the child's world of ideas' and how when children 'are thinking poetically their mastery of it is direct and sure.' It is 'felt in the blood and felt along the heart.' She also describes a process which I was to understand time and time again in my future teaching life in Stepney and Poplar in East London, in Mozambique, Grenada, Bethnal Green and Pitsmoor in Sheffield; Toronto and Manchester, something Marjorie wrote she 'would define as the *creative-critical principle*, an activity which turns art into a great educational force and finally shapes one's taste and discrimination.' She applied that same respect to children's poetry as she did to studying *The Rime of the Ancient Mariner* or the works of Keats, whom, she reminded us, wrote that 'if poetry comes not naturally like the leaves to a tree, it had better not come at all,' or Shelley, whom she quotes as saying that 'the source of poetry is native and involuntary, but requires severe labour in its development.' How many times in the coming five decades I was to remember Marjorie and the words that she gave to us in that classroom in Exeter, with her warmth and humour, so many ideas and insights which I was to use, apply and recreate in many places in the world.

The other woman who had such a deep effect on me that year was the novelist Jean Rhys, born in 1890 in Dominica, one of the islands that I had briefly encountered for a day on the voyage southwards to Trinidad on the Federal *Maple*. She was living in a Devonshire village, in the isolated hamlet of Cheriton Fitzpaine. A white woman, the daughter of a Welsh doctor, she had arrived in England in 1910 with aspirations to study at the Royal Academy of Dramatic Art. These hopes were soon deflated by the death of her father, and she was left to cope as best she could with little or no money and few friends, drifting from chorus line to mannequin parade to artist's studio as a model — and from one seedy hotel room to another, feeling the ire and prurient suspicions of many an English landlady. Her journey to Britain and subsequent experiences, like thousands of men and women from the Caribbean who were to arrive half a century later, was 'a journey to an illusion', although for her it was devoid of dimensions of racism. But exploited economically and sexually by the 'lost generation' of artistic men in London and Paris who promised her much but left her with little, her early life was close to the loneliness and alienation of the protagonists of her early works like *Quartet, Voyage in the Dark* and *After Leaving Mr McKenzie.* Even after the publication of these novels, now recognised as minor masterpieces, she remained in obscurity until the appearance of *Wide Sargasso Sea* in 1966. By this time she was living alone in this Devonshire village. From her *Letters 1931–66* comes this passage in a letter to a friend:

> This place, which I imagined would be a refuge, is a fore-taste of hell at present — it has hardly stopped raining since we arrived, and I wish the bloody River Exe would make up its mind and wash this whole village and the damp fields and the cows right away and finish (Me with cows). Instead of that it oozes and drips away... No cash but who cares?

When I heard that she was living alone in a village relatively near Silverton, where I was living, I wrote to her and asked whether I could come and talk to her about her novels, which had impressed me greatly, particularly *Wide Sargasso Sea,* with its recreation of the life and agony of Antoinette Bertha Cosway, Mr Rochester's mentally sick wife in Charlotte Bronte's *Jane Eyre,* locked away and secreted in the attic of Thornfield Hall. She too had been a white Caribbean woman.

She agreed to see me, so on a damp Sunday in February, when there were no buses, I walked the ten miles or so to

Cheriton Fitzpaine. Before I found her bungalow, I had a drink in the village pub. I remember well the icy and hostile glares from the pub's all-male clients, as I sat at the bar with my beard and long hair. Her home was one of a row of cottages called 'Land Boat Bungalows'. I remember the name well, for it seemed to suggest her own characters, washed aground in their lives, and, as she put it when we sat down and talked in her cold, damp front room: 'they are all wrecks, trapped in the Sargasso around them. They cannot get free.' She told me that she felt like a stranger in this village: 'Some of them think I'm a witch,' she said, 'and that's what they call me.' We discussed the Caribbean, and she told me how much she had loved the people of her island with its sheer mountains, deep green foliage and legendary 365 rivers. 'It is sublime!' she declared. She told me that thirty years before she had returned there, and even in the Thirties she had been appalled by the growing Americanisation and the deformities of tourism. Later she wrote to me: 'I'd never go back for it must be changed out of all knowledge now, and that would sadden me. I tell myself that they can't cut down the mountains or coop up the sea, but I am not convinced.'

My lasting impression of her was of a woman of great kindness and warmth, despite the blows of her life. Sitting with her, drinking tea in that small lounge, at the age of 80 she still wore bright red lipstick and thick, scented powder and she seemed to move around her bungalow like a woman in her twenties. I remember looking out of the window at the damp Devonshire hills, and thinking of her characters so far from the Caribbean, drinking towards cracking point, dependent upon the patronage of male dilettantes, yet capable of reviling and resisting them with both rage and insight: 'Her heart began to beat heavily. The buzzing noise deafened and benumbed her. She felt as though an iron band was encircling her head tightly, as though she was sinking down into deep water...' It was then finally, and through the musings and brilliance of this white Caribbean woman, that I realised quite starkly, that I was back home.

Chapter Five
Stepney Swing

I started teaching in Stepney in September, 1970. I had little idea of the school I was getting into, and should have done some research. If I had, I would have discovered that its Church of England governance was certainly not slumbering, and that it was founded by one Sir John Cass, a wealthy City merchant and alderman with definite Caribbean and slave-owning connections, who signed away a portion of his wealth as he died in 1718 to found a school for East London children. Every year, on 'Founder's Day', the school's pupils were marched to St. Botolph's Church in the City of London, to hear a service of remembrance and be given red feathers for their buttonholes. The legend was that as the founder died making his bequest, he coughed up blood which soaked the quill he was using. The ecclesiastical inheritance was still strong: the Chair of Governors was rector of Stepney Church; the Vice-chairman was the rector of St. Botolph's. As for the teachers, several were Church of England priests, one of whom would, on a daily basis, patrol the corridors complete with dog collar, academic gown and brandished cane. Organised to emulate a public school 'house' system, the four 'houses' were in fact called 'guilds' to reflect city business confederations.

What I also didn't know at the time was that the school stood on a road where Isaac had lived. In his day it had been called Oxford Road, now, redeveloped with post-war blocks of flats and this school, it was called Stepney Way, and ran down to the churchyard of the Chair of Governors' church. Isaac would have known intimately the terraced houses and narrow streets of the area, and regularly walked back under the trees half-hiding the tenement blocks of Stepney Green, right up to the Mile

End Road. Earlier, when he was a boy, he lived in a house on Jamaica Street, a little closer towards Whitechapel, and before that, when his family had arrived in Stepney from Bristol, they lived in number 47 Cable Street close to Shadwell, south of the other arterial road through Stepney, the Commercial Road. I found a flat very close to all these addresses, in Albert Gardens, a Georgian square off Commercial Road, with a beautiful glade of plane trees and a statue of a barefoot, idealised agricultural labouring boy looking out over the main road, sickle upright in one hand, rake in another, standing in front of a wheatsheaf since 1904. Erect, Grecian-featured and pre-Raphaelite, he didn't look much like a local boy. Many of the square's residents were Jewish families, and bustling mothers would take their children across Commercial Road with its heavy eastward traffic, to Marion Richardson Primary School, just opposite the square. On the next street along were the remnants of the first Dr Barnardo's home, and in the other direction towards the city, was the derelict East London Maternity Hospital where many of the parents of my students were born, and next to it was 400 Commercial Road, the handsome Georgian house of the Bishop of Stepney, which was to become an important place for me. As I came home from school, or in the mornings, I would see and hear the birds in the plane trees. It was not returning and hearing the larks as in Isaac's most famous trench poem, but certainly the sparrows, the pigeons and the starlings.

I discovered that I had a co-tenant in the flat, a rat which lived in the Ascot heater in the bathroom, which was just about the warmest place in the abode. One night, my friend Bernie stayed with me and I put out a mattress in the hallway for him. He woke up to find the rat staring at him. He jumped up, spluttering, and the rat scampered back to the Ascot. Bernie turned it on and opened the flat's front door. It jumped out of the heater and ran out the door and that was the last I saw of it. I thought of another rat, one with 'cosmopolitan sympathies' in Isaac's poem *Break of Day in the Trenches,* crossing backwards and forwards across lines of trenches and creating a strange unity between German and British soldiers. But where this Stepney rat went after his runaway exit from 22a Albert Gardens, I never knew.

I used to dream some nights about meeting Isaac, sitting on one of the benches in Albert Gardens, or in the churchyard of St George in the East, under Hawksmoor's huge stone tower and the glades of plane trees. One night I dreamed that he was sitting in Albert Gardens on the bench next to the statue of the reaper boy, and that he had come back from the trenches for his last ever leave.

'What's it like there, Isaac?' I asked him. He replied, 'I can't describe it, it is hell. I can only say what it's truly like in my poems. I wonder why I am there. I'm a hopeless soldier, and it's not that I hate the Germans that face us, they are just like me — why would I want to kill them? But it's all too late now, I'm entrenched, I can't get out. And my mother needs my separation allowance — how would she live without it? But just wait, when this war is finished I shall write such poetry! I will tell my readers everything — I shall hide nothing, for there can never be another war and such a terrible waste of young lives of those who have never been allowed to live! Your children and those you teach must never have to face this! They will write poems, they must never shoot guns and be slaughtered by bombs and bullets. They must grow like these beautiful trees.' And he waved at the plane trees.

And I would wake up, sweating, shaking.

As for the school, if I thought I had met vicious streaming in my own education, it hardly compared to what I found at Sir John Cass. There were five streams before you reached the 'Remedial' stream, which wasn't a class with small groups and more teachers to give close attention to students' learning problems. It was simply another class of more than thirty students with a single teacher: the rock bottom stream. As this class gradually rose up the school, the students became more and more disaffected and gained less and less self-worth and more and more self-contempt and consciousness of their own exclusion. As an English teacher I taught two fourth year classes, one a non-examination ROSLA ('Raising the School Leaving Age') class which, since the recent law change, meant that they were compelled to stay on at school until they were sixteen, despite almost all of them hating every moment of it. As a drama teacher I also taught all the second and third year forms for one lesson a week.

Three incidents very early on in my time at Sir John Cass gave me a keen insight to what I was dealing with. The first was when I was present at a Business Studies class with a combined cohort of fifteen-year-old girls, most of whom were being prepared through this class to join typing pools in City offices. The teacher, in her singular authoritarian way, was reprimanding the girls for their lack of interest and motivation, but then went on to call them all 'cheap'. I knew well how much of a contemptuous insult this word was to young East London women, and after the class I asked her why she had used that word. 'Well they are, aren't they?' she said, and I was shocked. I taught some of these girls and found them to be full of wit, humour and warmth, and I couldn't understand how any teacher could use that word. Then one dinnertime, I found one of my first year students, a boy called Timmy, about to be on the end of the unsheathed cane of the patrolling priest. This Timmy was in my first year English class, and his writing, particularly his poems, bristled with life and beauty. I asked the priest what he thought he was doing, and told Timmy to leave the room. The conversation I had with this man of God was anything but cordial, and I thought, that's another enemy made. I remember one of the many supportive letters I was to receive in the wake of the *Stepney Words* furore shortly to explode at the school. This one was from a veteran ex-pupil who went to the school in the Thirties. 'Our family was very poor in those days,' he wrote. 'The teachers at the school seemed only interested in canning (sic) us.' The berobed priest's image came back to me, and although he was a grotesque caricature of the worst of the school, I wondered how much had changed.

The third event was about poetry. I asked one of my low-stream classes to write about how they saw themselves at school, how they saw their futures. Among many poems of optimism, despair, egoism and complexes was this untitled and anonymous piece left on a desk, which I picked up after the pupils had left the classroom. I looked at it, studied it and tried imaginatively to fill in its spaces as I have done for four and a half decades since. It became the preface of the anthology which was published in May, 1971; *Stepney Words*:

> I am just a boy
> > with a lot of dreams
> But what's the point
> > I won't get nowhere
> I'm just ordinary
> > nothing special just
> > > ordinary
> Got no chance in this
> > world unless you're
> > > clever
> Which I'm not

Many years later I befriended a poet, born in Barbados in 1909, called Peter Blackman. From a working class family (his father was a stonemason, his mother a laundress); he gained a Church of England scholarship to an elite colonial school and went on to study for the priesthood at Durham University, before becoming a missionary in the Gambia. When he experienced the racism within the church and discovered that white priests were earning more than their black colleagues, he returned to England and became a mechanic for British Railways and a militant within the British Communist Party, as well as friend and confidante of Paul Robeson and a celebrated socialist poet. It was at the Half Moon Theatre in Stepney in 1980 that he gave a speech about poetry, saying this after reading an extract of Whitman's *Leaves of Grass*: 'We do not pay enough attention to our exploration of the ordinary. You are ordinary, I am ordinary, so what do we fuss about? Yet it is such stuff as we that human society is made. What we must try and do is get at the ordinary, and so work that without any suspicion of deterioration we see in the ordinary and out of the ordinary that we bring excellence, without elitism. That is what we want; in the ordinary is the excellent. The ordinary people, the ordinary, the men and women who go to work every day. It doesn't matter what they do, out of them comes excellence, not can come, but comes excellence. If you're interested in poetry remember that you're occupied with words; you must drench yourself in words, and you must take ordinary words and out of ordinary words you make beauty, you make glory', and quoting the *Book of Job* he concluded: 'You make the song of the sons of God when the morning stars first broke out!'

It was some ten years after I read this anonymous Stepney child's poem that Blackman spoke these words, yet I immediately thought of that poem when I heard them, and all the poems that came after it in the classroom and all the others that I have taught since. Words of the ordinary: ordinary words, whether those of these children, or of Donne, Blake, Rosenberg, Owen or Whitman. I suddenly realised he had found the true source of the poetry that I had loved, and I had found it there, in Stepney.

Inspired by Marjorie and Isaac, I started taking my classes out into the streets around the school with their pens and their notebooks, asking them to write down what they saw: the houses, the few trees, the birds, the people who passed them by. We went by the river towards Wapping and to Shadwell Park. Right opposite the school was the churchyard where there were still the discernable mounds which signified the mass graves of the Great Plague of 1666. We acted out imaginary scenes from that catastrophe, and then sat on the benches to write poems. On one October morning, two eleven-year-old girls,

Lesley and Karen, sat down together on an iron bench. Lesley wrote this:

Autumn Morning in Stepney Churchyard

The church was standing in a spot where the light of
    a thousand candles was glowing in the mist of the
    morning,
And the faint beams of sunlight came through, and
    the cold air was gently overflowing and in a second
    it was gone.
The churchyard was dead and the birds only were there,
And the leaves were falling,
               falling,
                falling
And the dew that lay by the ever-lay leaves is fainting
    into the background to die.

And Karen wrote:

The grass is covered by brown leaves,
The sun is peering through the trees,
The dew on the grass is delicate
Like a baby's tear.
The grass mingles with the graves,
Behind the graves there dwells fear.
The church is ancient with its dull-coloured walls,
Surrounded by black railings
Surrounded by trees
All ancient.
So I'm sitting on a bench as the sun goes down,
Night draws in, all goes calm.

As I read these poems for the first time I thought of Blake and the *Garden of Love:*

So I turn'd to the Garden of Love
That so many sweet flowers bore;

And I saw that it is filled with graves
And tombstones where flowers should be.

And Karen's simile, comparing the autumn dew to the delicacy of a baby's tear, where did she conceive that? Had she seen it as she kissed goodbye to her baby brother or sister before she walked to school that morning? I could only imagine, only try to enter her world. And wasn't this beautiful London oasis near the very place that Donne had worked as a minister, and at the end of the road where Isaac had lived and grown to poetry? And I wasn't imagining it, it was real: here was the true place of London poetry, forged as ordinary people passed by, to and fro, morning and evening, to walk through the rare trees of East London to Stepney Green underground station, and here were two eleven-year-old poets forging their craft from their ordinary words and vitally original figurative language. And wasn't this the same young poet Lesley who would write so powerfully about her own imaginative process a few weeks later in another *Stepney Words* poem that she called *Loneliness*: 'my mind a mad menace on the loose.'

We went further afield in our walks, all around the local streets and few open spaces, taking notes as we walked. When I took the same class to Shadwell Park, overlooking the Thames, Sharon studied the boats, the riverside, the derelict docks and cranes and the people all around her, and later at home she wrote this poem from the notes she took.

A Trip to Shadwell Park

The cool gentle breeze that moves the ripples of water
    and causes it to crash against the concrete wall,
The barges never going anywhere just continue to sway from
    side to side like they are nailed to the bottom,
Distant shouts from passengers aboard a pleasure cruiser,
The droppings of sweets and crisps, luring pigeons,
Old people with nothing to do, watching the action,
Small children too young to go to school amuse themselves
    by running round, exploring, investigating things.
The friendly atmosphere that joins everything, everyone
    with everyone.
Friendly people, amongst them an old woman ridden to a
    wheelchair,
A man with his camera giving us hints on our camera,
An old frame of a pram stuck in the mud with water flowing
    over it.
The smells

Refreshing smells
The river, with a mixture of smells,
Oil and sewerage
Small patches of flowers giving a mild scent to the air.
Two Pakistani women and a baby, neglected, unattended
    talking their way, keeping themselves to themselves,
Would the park and its people let them in on the act?
And the old woman,
The old Jewish woman wishing for her childhood back -
To think we were giving her so much pleasure.
Birds hovering above the picture,
The lifelike picture,
Everyone taking part.
A man unaware of everything, in a deep sleep
Stretched out on a bench.
People everywhere, on their own or with friends, enjoying
    the beautiful weather.

Back in the English classroom the poems came teeming
out about the lives of the poets and the lives of others,
particularly the old. It was as if these children had a particular empathy with the old people they saw all around
them;

I'm old and frightened
In this darkened world
I'm shut behind bars...

Or:

I live on my own
In a cold damp room,
No one to talk to
No one to see

My children are married
They live far away,
My husband died
On a cold winter's day...

Or the blind man who passed them:

As I walk along the street
As blind as a bat I think
I will never see the world
'till I die

114

As a blind man
I can't see one thing
In this lovely world
Dark is a terrible thing
To live with.

Or there was Timmy's poem, and I thought again of Blake and *Infant Sorrow*. Timmy called his *The Chance:*

The Chance

Here I am lonely in my mother's womb
As I am lying here, I am wondering
Just whether to come out and see the bright world.
But maybe it's not a bright world.
It's maybe dull, but I can't tell if it is a dull world.
I will not be able to get back into the womb if it is dull.
It is just a chance I will have to take.

Or there were the poems about school, some of them not so far distant from Blake's *The Schoolboy* and these two verses:

Ah! Then at times I drooping sit,
And spend many an anxious hour,
Nor in my book can I take delight,
Nor sit in learning's bower
Worn thro' with the dreary shower.

How can the bird that is born for joy
Sit in a cage and sing?
How can a child, when fears annoy,
But droop his tender wing
And forget his youthful spring?

For Blake's questions were being partly reflected, partly answered in these other London poems written nearly two centuries later. One began by asserting:

My classroom is dim and dull
My teacher sits there thinking,

While Susan, a fifteen-year-old, wrote in her *Going to School*

Going to school is hard,
It takes me all day to get up out of the warmness,
And go out to the coldness.

115

> I think of the lessons ahead of me and then I think of the
>   teachers.
> You get freedom out of school
> And you get locked up in school just like a prison.
> The bell goes at ten to nine
> Five more minutes of freedom!
> The bell has gone and I am bored.

Sandra considered the school day:

> We're to sit and work.
> All day long we sit.
> The pips go. We rise.
> We leave. All regulated.
>
> Step out of place
> We get told off.
> 'Wear school uniform!
> Wear flesh-coloured tights!',
>
> It's sickening how these things go,
> They never know what we think.

And Gillian told a short story of one of the school's allies
in *The Tall Man with the Grey Hair*:

> A knock comes at the door
> A tall man
> With grey hair
> Steps in.
> 'I understand'
> Says he
> 'You have not been at school'.
>
> Mum's face
> Grew long and yellow,
> 'Haven't you?'
> Says she.
> Her long boney hand
> Came swiftly round my face
> And the tears run
> down my face.

These were nearly all girls writing these poems about
school, and their criticism stung. Sharon walked the
streets of her imagination along her own *Lonely Road to
Education*:

Out into the open air into the fresh atmosphere.
Everybody neatly dressed,
Working men, school kids.
None talking to each other.
Just the clip clop of the heels
Clashing against the ground
And their alternate dips into the puddles left by the night rain.
Everyone trying to occupy themselves but no one speaks.
Out into the open air into the fresh atmosphere,
For a quiet walk to school.

And how these children responded to the challenge of imaginative empathy. I remembered Chiefie teaching us to put ourselves into the minds of the ball-turret gunner, or the colonised and alienated subjects of the Raj in Forster's *A Passage to India*, or how he urged me not just to act the soldier Simon Shashava in *The Caucasian Chalk Circle* or Doc. Gibbs in Thornton Wilder's *Our Town* but to become them: what would they think, what would they do? I would cycle around Hornchurch imagining what daily decisions a small-town doctor in Grover's Corners, New Hampshire would take in his daily work, or how a soldier would think and act faced by the enemy. Now I was teaching mainly white Stepney teenagers to become Bangladeshis, their new nation facing the effects of natural disasters and invasion, and in East London facing the racist violence of Powell-influenced white youth. Peter wrote this, one of many 'feeling the pain' and agony of others once far away, but now living in the next street:

They kick us
They boot us to the ground
For no reason,
They call us names
They make jokes about us.
We live in a house that's derelict
But we are grateful,
For it is better than nothing.
They cannot feel the pain,
But what has happened in Pakistan
And to my parents,

117

For I know not what has happened
To them.
The tidal wave
It came so quick
They were terrified in their tracks.
Helpless,
My wife and children
Dead,
Thousands dead and drowned.
Why?

These poems were in the forefront of my mind one Saturday when I went into Whitechapel Library. This had been the meeting place of Isaac and his friends in the first decade of the century, the one precious space open to them where they could find seclusion, warmth and a venue for reading and study. It was from here that Isaac, Leftwich, Rodker and their friends would begin their night walks around Whitechapel and Stepney, and discuss the news and ideas of art and politics. I saw that the library had become a photography gallery for a week or two, showing the work of a young photographer whose name was Ron McCormick, a graduate of the Liverpool College of Art and the Royal Academy. The exhibition was called *Neighbours* and, a leaflet told me, they were all photographs of Spitalfields, where the photographer also lived. I was captivated by his images of children, of the aged, of families in their homes or on their doorsteps, of the streets and blocks where many of my students lived, in the same way that I had been surprised by joy at their poems. I asked Alec Ayres, the librarian, about the photographer. 'Why don't you leave a message for him in the comments book?' he said to me. So I did, telling him of my students' poems and how his images had moved me in the same way. I also left my address.

The very next day he called on me at Albert Gardens. We talked, then walked the Stepney and Spitalfields streets like Isaac and his friends, and ended up at his flat on the first floor of an old, dilapidated Georgian house in Princelet Street off Brick Lane, its ground floor being used as a paper bag, box and rolls of string store by its

Jewish owner. On the way he used his camera like a third eye, stopping and snapping at everything that fired his interest: he never went out without it. His flat was basic, with homemade furniture and a bathroom which also served as a darkroom. I met his wife Linda and their beautiful baby daughter Nancy. I had some copies of my students' poems, and Ron and Linda were deeply moved by them. He exclaimed in his Liverpudlian accent, and when I pointed to some of the similarities between his photographs' visual images and the words and figurative power of the poetry, he nodded and marvelled. He offered to come to some of my classes, bringing blown-up prints of some of his photographs to see how the young poets would react. I thought this was a tremendous idea, and we discussed the photographs we should use and how we should use them. Very quickly we became friends, through the agency of poetry and photographs.

Ron became a regular presence in my classes, particularly my first year class, and his photographs became powerful and provocative stimuli. His pictures of an old man in the market with a Sainsbury's shopping bag and stick was the source of Jimmy's poem:

I'm old I need rest
Maybe it's the gardening I do
Maybe it's the long walks I take
Maybe it's in my mind
At night in bed I rejoice the rest I'm having
My muscles are getting stiff
Sometimes I get rheumatism in my legs
I'm getting very old I need rest

When Carol saw Ron's picture of an Asian girl standing alone in front of a half-demolished wall, she wrote:

I am just a lonely mermaid
I only have myself to look at
I have no friends like the people on the beach
When I see the children playing on the beach
I wonder why no one will play with me
And why I'm so lonely

Ron transcribed her words across the wall, as if they were graffiti. And spurred on by a photograph of a pigeon rising up to fly, Marion wrote like an eleven-year-old urban John Clare:

As it lifted up off the ground
Its wings spread like leaves
Its tail opened like a fan
Its feet curled up tight.
It sees a spot of white on the grass
It swoops round and dives at the bread
It comes to the grassy ground
It comes to the piece of bread
It swoops it to its beak and eats it
Then it walks around for more bread.
Its feet go up and down
Its wings are like cobwebs
Its feathers are scruffy
Its colours are like a butterfly's
Its patterns are like an artist's.

Ron was helping them to observe, to notice detail, to think in figurative language, to empathise, to make whole stories from single images. When Ramona looked at his photograph of a doll on a Petticoat Lane market stall, with an elderly woman with a cigarette between her lips looking on and the stall holder next to her, she created this story-in-poetry:

The Stall and Me

'Earrings for sale, knuckle dusters, watch straps'
The man who owns the stall cries, 'Second-hand beads!'
He stops talking as a lorry rushes past and drowns his voice,
The exhaust choked his words into a cough,
Lorry after lorry
Car after car
I sit here waiting patiently
Waiting for someone to buy me
For someone to take me home and love me.
Once again the man resumes his voice and yells,
'Cowboy suits, buttons, buckles'.
An old age pensioner wanders to the stall
Clutching a one pound note.

The owner got up off an old orange box that his backside
  lazily rested upon,
The old lady's small grey eyes wandered over my body...
The owner grabbed me and said
'This 'ere doll's a real bargain,
Only two pound ten.'
The woman said, 'I've only got a pound, and it's my
grand-daughter's birthday tomorrow.'
She explained how this was all she had left.
The owner said, 'I'm sorry luv; I don't give fings away,
What about these beads?'
But the lady still insisted that she wanted me.
The owner, being a kindly man, said,
'Go 'ome and bring me another ten bob.'
A small tear fell from my eyes
As the old lady slumped off.
The owner knew he would never see the old lady again...
Dolls have feelings too, you know!
The owner of the stall
Ran after her, thrusting me into her hand.
The next day her grandchild pushed me past the stall,
The owner was still crying out.
He waved and smiled —
Perhaps he'll be there forever
But he'll always be just a stall owner.
I'll never know his name
And I'll never forget his dirty little stall in Petticoat Lane.

As we walked the streets, there, naked and explicit, were
the settings and subjects of both Ron's photographs and the
children's poetry. We considered another way of bringing
the two forms together. Why not an anthology combining
both? But to do it with beauty and respect, we needed some
money, which neither of us had. Ron scraped together a
frugal living designing book covers, posters and his photography occasionally made the papers, and I was a probationary teacher. So we decided to ask the school, to see if it
would provide funding. The Sir John Cass Foundation was
wealthy enough, owning land and many houses north of
Victoria Park, and we thought that this might be the kind
of project that they could support. We put together a
'dummy' compilation of poems and photographs and called
it *Stepney Words,* showed it to the head teacher, and

awaited his response. He seemed to be quite enthusiastic at the outset of our meetings, but said it was an idea that needed approval of the school governors. He also said that a previous English teacher had come up with a similar idea without photographs, which she wanted to call *The Star in the Mud,* but that had not been approved and she had left the school soon after. So we went away and waited.

I had an intimation of what might be coming one morning when the Chair of Governors, the Reverend Gibbs, approached me in the corridor outside the school staff room and told me that he'd been reading some of the poems. He didn't say much about them, but said of the children-authors; 'You have to remember that they're all fallen children, that they're all in a state of sin.' And that was it, he walked off. I stood there, deeply affected. What did he mean, what was he saying? When I told Ron, he was perplexed too. We thought about the poems: there was only one, written by a fourteen-year-old girl in my class — the very lively and confident Kim, that was explicitly about religion. With her conviction, passion, complexity of thought and sense of justice, she had written this untitled and unexpected poem, entirely of her own motivation.

> I once saw a man in Nazareth.
> He was born in a stable.
> Now, two thousand years later,
> That man has caused poverty
> Not able,
> Not able to see what he has caused
> Or who has suffered for him —
> But when palaces rot and children cry,
> Who then will carry that cross?
> Not him.
> Money and government shelter this man,
> For churches must rot without it —
> And remember who caused that man's
> terrible death,
> Now it's us that carry the cost.
> Though, when I complain,
> I still feel the pain

For others that are paying the cost,
One day I will be able to say,
'You're not the only one
on that cross.'

Was this poem the reason for Rev. Gibbs' response? Ron and I couldn't work it out and felt we were in the middle of some ecclesiastical argument. So we decided to get another church view, and arranged to meet Trevor Huddleston, the Bishop of Stepney, to show him the poems. So we knocked on the door of 400 Commercial Road. He was friendly and warm, and for me, having read his searing critique of the apartheid regime in South Africa, *Naught for Your Comfort,* he was something of a hero, despite me leaving organised religion behind, many years before. As the priest of Sophiatown on the outskirts of Johannesburg, where he had befriended many of the key figures of the South African resistance movement like Nelson Mandela and Oliver Tambo, he had fought against racism, and set down his experiences as an early exposure of apartheid. We left copies of the poems with him.

As we left his house, I thought about what I had learned about his life of Christian socialism. Before he came to Stepney he had been Bishop of Masasi in newly-independent Tanzania and become a close ally and friend of its socialist president, Julius Nyerere, whose government was giving aid and succour to the soldiers of FRELIMO, the Mozambican liberation movement, who were operating over Tanzania's southern frontier and creating liberated zones in the Portuguese colony's northern provinces of Cabo Delgado and Niassa. Huddleston's Masasi diocese was in the south of Tanzania and close to FRELIMO's bases. I wondered how such a man could share the same Church as the Chair of the Sir John Cass governors, and was even more nonplussed when I learned of the career of the Vice-chairman, the Rev. Derek Harbord, Rector of St. Botolph's Church in Aldgate on the eastern edge of the city, who proudly announced himself on the church's notice board as 'One of Her Majesty's

Judges (rtd.).' He had been a High Court judge in colonial Tanganyika, in its pre-Tanzania era and a pillar of British imperialism. As for Huddleston, Nyerere described him as 'a fighter in the struggle for the triumph of human equality and dignity in Africa. He is also a human being who exudes warmth and friendship towards the men, women and children whom he meets; he enriches the lives of those with whom he works.' I marvelled how these two men, now both working for the same religious institution in East London, but with such different human perspectives, were now reading and forming opinions of the poetry that my young students had written in a school under the control of the Church.

When we called in to see Huddleston a few days later (he lived just around the corner from me), as I walked in to his office he looked at me directly and pronounced: 'Christopher, I love these poems. These children are the children of God!' To say I was taken aback would be taking it mildly, for Rev. Gibbs's opinions were still reverberating in my brain. He said that he would certainly support the proposed book being published, and would help us in whatever way he could. Ron and I were both heartened, and we decided to show the poems around the community to get further support. We went up to the top floor of Latham House, a tower block almost next to the school, to meet the recently retired dockers' trade union leader, Jack Dash, who did his keep-fit exercises and weight training on his tiny fifteenth-floor balcony overlooking the now-defunct London Docks and their derelict cranes. To the establishment and its press, Jack — with his communist politics and record of leading many official and unofficial strikes — was the devil incarnate. While we were at his flat Ron took the photograph which we used for the eventual cover of *Stepney Words,* which was also Jack's view from his balcony. He loved poetry, and said he wrote some himself, and he was deeply impressed by the poems, especially because he recognised the names of some of the poets, from families who were tenants of the council estate next to the

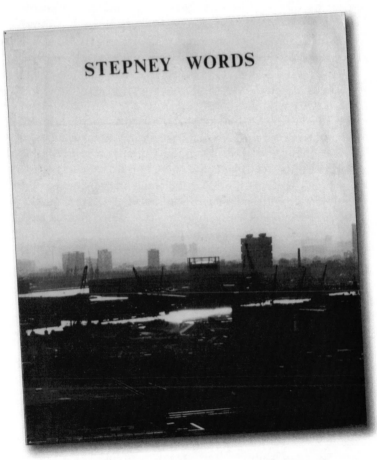

Photograph,
Ron McCormick©

126

school of which his block was a part: Mountmorres Estate. 'Anything I can do mate,' he said, 'just let me know. I've got some good contacts in the press.' And he gave me a paperback copy of his autobiography, *Good Morning, Brothers!* with a preface which he said would be his epitaph:

> Here lies Jack Dash
> All he wanted was
> To separate them from their cash.

So by the time we got the words of the Governors, we already had some strong support for the anthology, and promises of donations towards its publication from many people, including my friend Rob Morrison, a young Australian science teacher at the school, Chiefie and my old school friend Pete, a local plumber and Alec Ayres from Whitechapel Library, Isaac's intellectual home. It had been a friendly librarian at Whitechapel Library who had encouraged the teenage Isaac to move ahead with his first published poem, *Ode to David's Harp*, in 1905. When I told my students of the idea to publish their poems with Ron's photographs, they too were full of enthusiasm.

The only negative opinions, unfortunately came, as we feared, from the school governors. I was invited to one of their meetings where they said, they thought the anthology was 'unbalanced', too 'gloomy' and couldn't I find some more 'cheerful' poems to make it more positive? The poems should be about 'the lighter side of life', they insisted. To me, still deeply affected by Marjorie's affirmations of the 'creative-critical principle', this was very hard to take. I remembered the song that Woody Guthrie used to sing, how those in power always wanted to silence and wipe away 'the pictures from life's other side.' These governors did not want the children to write about the real world. As I said later, they wanted the cockney sparrow to sing cheerfully from his cage. The collection held within it deeply contradictory impressions of the poets' home neighbourhoods, exemplified by the two views of Stepney which we had set side-by-side:

I think Stepney is a very smokey place
But I like it
People in Stepney do things wrong
But I like them
Everything in Stepney has its disadvantages
But I like it.
It does not have clean air like the country
But I like it
The buildings are old and cold
But I like them
The summer is not very hot
But I like it

WE LOVE YOU, SEARLIE!

TEACHER Chris Searle at the school gates yesterday trying to coax the pupils back to classes

And:

I come from Stepney, lived there all me life
Loads of cheap markets
Bargains at half price,
Jumpers and skirts, trousers cheap
All muddled up in any old heap

Dirty old women, shouting out their wares
Everybody stinks, nobody cares
All greasy dirty things bunged into bins,
Stinkin' rotten hole is Stepney.

EVEN a threat of no football next term couldn't break the Great School Poetry Book strike yesterday

Six-hundred pupils at the Stepney school spent all day in pouring rain defying teachers and singing outside the school " We Shall Overcome."

Mr Chris Searle, the teacher whose sacking caused the strike, pleaded with them to return to their classrooms.

And we aren't going back to school until they say you can stay

From
The Sun
28 May 1971

Banners

" You'll get soaked or run over," he shouted. " You should fight through the proper channels in the proper way."

But the pupils shouted back: "We love you Searle. We're not going back until they say you can stay. The rain's our problem, sir."

At one point, PT master John Roberts vaulted the school's 5ft wire fence and threatened:

"Come back or I will go on strike. There'll be no football next year if you don't."

Still the pupils stood

Pictures by
ROBERT KEMP

firm and, waving giant protest banners, explained why they wanted 24-year-old Mr Searle to stay.

Said 16-year-old Zelmada de la Cruz: "He's the best teacher we've ever had.

"Thanks to him, we have a club for seeing films at half-price and lots of other things.

" He gives up four nights a week to help us. Now we are showing we want to help him."

Slums

And Mrs Phyllis Samuel, mother of a 15-year-old pupil, said: "He is the only teacher who lives here in the slums and tries to understand the children."

Mr Searle sacked for publishing a £300 book of poems by the children without letting the

school governors see it —was not talking about the uproar.

The National Union of Teachers is investigating his case and he said: " I am in a difficult position. I cannot say anything."

But fifth-former Peter Neve, aged 16, of Formosa House, Ocean Estate, Stepney, said: " My sister Michelle wrote one of the poems. She was in the papers and on TV.

Pickets

" Some of the teachers don't like kids being able to do that. They can't hit at us, so they hit at the man who helped everyone."

The school would only say Mr Searle was fired for " flagrantly " ignoring instructions.

It was not because of the content of the book, said a statement.

Meanwhile, the storm threatens to go on. Some of the pupils said they would even picket the school next week when they are officially on holiday.

SITTING it out . . . four pupils putting their point with a huge poster

The affectionate and sentimental were adjoined to the stark, the dismissive and the ruthlessly realistic. Both were true, both were original, both, in different ways and from different standpoints, were critical. I felt as if they were manifesting Marjorie's principles: this was a part of her 'education of the poetic spirit'.

Ron, Linda and I thought that we shouldn't be deflected. Linda had spent a lot of time typing, pasting and checking, and keeping records of everything we did. Ron had found a printer along Brick Lane, a Mr Weinberg, who had an astonishing personal history. He'd shown him the poems and he was very keen to do the printing for a very reasonable price. We found out much later that he was Issy Weinberg, the son of Baruch Weinberg, a Jewish socialist militant who had escaped from Tsarist Russia and become a writer, printer and instigator-founder of the Yiddish 'Workers Circle' in East London. 'He was a worker and a dreamer who longed for a different life to the one people had, not only for himself but for others,' Issy said of his father. 'The Workers' Circle Friendly Society helped Jewish workers and craftsmen survive when they were on strike for better pay and conditions'. He had passed his printing skills onto his son, who had inherited his tiny Brick Lane printshop. The beauty and skill of his printing was a source of immense pride to him. So it seemed that we were all set, and we couldn't have found a more fitting and masterly printer. Ron had done the design and production and had come to school especially to photograph the eyes of a second former called Angela, so he could put the image directly above her poem called *Mirror*. It looked beautiful, as did his landscape over the river, docks and cranes taken from Jack's balcony, to which he gave a sepia gloss, making it even more evocative.

So with our own money and donations, we published *Stepney Words,* calling ourselves by the name of Reality Press, and paying for 2,000 copies. It all came to just over £300, which, considering the sheer quality of the printing, we considered very reasonable. As soon as we had copies,

I tried to find the home addresses of all the poets by searching for them in the school registers, and I began visiting their homes and taking around their complimentary copies, from Limehouse in the east, all around Stepney, Shadwell and Whitechapel, to Spitalfields and as far as Clerkenwell to the north. I was received with both surprise and warmth by parents, who were not only taken aback to get a visit from a teacher, but delighted to see their son's or daughter's creative writing in print, and in such a fine publication too. I'd met some of them before, particularly the families who lived close by, and some knew me through the film club I'd set up at school, which had become quite popular. We showed some good films too, both English Sixties' classics like *A Taste of Honey* and *The Loneliness of the Long Distance Runner*, as well as quality American fare like Marlon Brando in *One Eyed Jacks* and Paul Newman in *Cool Hand Luke*. It was an innovation which sometimes got packed houses, and it introduced the students to some fine films. I welcomed students from neighbouring schools like the nearby Stepney Green Boys. School. Some teachers warned me that this would only breed trouble, but it never did. But as far as the home visits with *Stepney Words,* it gave me a face-to-face opportunity to explain to parents why we'd done the book as well as compliment the skills of their children's work in their own front rooms. We also sent copies of *Stepney Words* to people we admired and who we thought might be interested.

We had some more than encouraging replies. From Suffolk A.S. Neill, the libertarian educational pioneer of Summerhill, ordered several more copies. From Yorkshire, the champion of comprehensive schooling in the West Riding and author of the campaigning *Children in Distress*, Sir Alec Clegg, wrote a letter of support to the *Times Educational Supplement*, saying that *Stepney Words* had 'so moved me by its depth of feeling and by the statement that it made as a whole, that I took what was for me, after 26 years in Yorkshire, the wholly unprecedented step of sending a modest contribution to the next issue.' James Britton, education author and Professor of Goldsmiths College, University of London, called the poetical language 'unliterary... but full of honesty and conviction,' and the playwright Arnold Wesker, himself a Spitalfields boy, sent us an unpublished poem from his own boyhood, *Sitting Waiting for Auntie Ave,* as a contribution to the next issue which was already in our heads.

A group of the poets took part in a 'Festival of Racial Harmony' at the People's Palace in Mile End Road, which later became a part of Queen Mary College, University of London. On a stage famous as the venue of trade union rallies, political meetings and the East London concerts of Paul Robeson, the *Stepney Words* poets read their poems in front of slides of Ron's photographs. They did the same a week later in a morning school assembly, except accompanying them was not *Hills of the North Rejoice* and *All Things Bright and Beautiful* but the Hollies singing *He ain't Heavy, He's My Brother* and Nicky Thomas' rampaging early reggae version of *If I Had a Hammer.* The students were almost dancing in the aisles when he came to the final chorus:

It's the hammer of justice
It's the bell of freedom
It's the song about love
Between my brothers and my sisters
All over this land

And this was a message ringing out over a post-Powell East London, multiracial and internationalist to the core.

Jack Dash had been true to his promise. So true, it got me in all kinds of trouble! He'd shown the poems to his contacts in *The Sun* and the *Daily Mirror,* and the next thing I knew was that both tabloids were running big features on the *Stepney Words* poets, quoting several of the poems in full with photographs and pen portraits of their writers. I doubt if either paper ever published more poetry, before or since. There was also another profile of

Ramona and Pauline with
Stepney Words, in *The Times,*
on the day of the strike.

the book and its authors in the last ever issue of the *Daily Sketch,* which ceased publication after its *Stepney Words* edition. This meant, of course, that hundreds of the Sir John Cass parents and their friends read these poems, and the local paper, the *East London Advertiser,* not to be outdone by the nationals, also did a double-page spread. Suddenly, the contents of *Stepney Words* were everywhere. We'd made sure that we sent a copy to the headteacher, and I waited for the reaction, not really knowing what would happen next.

It didn't take long. A few days later I was sent a letter telling me that I would dismissed at the end of the school year. As this was late May, with the school year ending in

July, I had less than two months left. To the school governors I was simply a 'probationary teacher', nothing else, and it would be simple and straightforward to get rid of me. The headteacher, Geoffrey Barrell, was the author of what was considered the standard textual authority of the employment laws regarding teachers, called *Teachers and the Law,* so the governors must have felt that they were on safe enough ground. I was offered no opportunity for a hearing or a chance to put my case for continuing my employment. I had been summarily dismissed, clearly in a way that, as my union lawyers later pointed out to me, was totally contrary to common employment law — and by a man who had written the accepted book on the subject! Some irony indeed! I thought at the time that it must have been the biggest headmasterly own goal in educational history.

But more of this later. It was the week before the final half term of the year. Sitting in my classroom during the lunch hour, several of my third year class came in and sat down with me, which was quite usual. They must have noticed that I was looking a little glum, so they asked me what was bothering me. I told them: I'd got the sack and I wouldn't be around from September onwards. They asked me why, so I told them. They found it hard to believe. 'What, you're getting the sack because of the book you did of our poems?' They were astonished. Then shortly after the bell rang for afternoon school, and we went our different ways.

After that, at the time I had no idea what was happening. As I understood it much later, Michelle, a girl in my class whose poem was in the book, told her brother in the fifth year, and soon it was all around the senior pupils. I didn't teach them, but several of them were film club regulars. The fifth year had games all afternoon at Fairlop playing fields out in Essex, and on the coach home they discussed what they should do with one of the women PE teachers. The next day was very strange. I could tell that something unusual was up, but

I didn't know what. At the end of the afternoon a first year girl, giggling as she passed me in the corridor, gave me a big smile and said something like, 'You wait until tomorrow Sir, you'll see!' I decided to get right out of the way, so that night I went back to my parents' house in Hornchurch and stayed there, wondering what tomorrow would bring.

When I came in the next morning, I got the tube, walked up Stepney Green and came through the school's side entrance and into the staff room. Already there were some huge sounds coming from the green at the front of the school, sounds only comparable to Upton Park on a Saturday afternoon. It was pouring with rain too, but none of the strikers seemed deterred as they sang with a huge sound *We Hate the Governors* and *Roll out the Barrell!*, punning on the headteacher's surname and evoking memories of communal sing-songs at Saturday Morning Pictures. They also took John Lennon's peace anthem, *Give Peace a Chance*, changing the words slightly and singing out: 'All we are saying, is give Chris a chance.' Most of the teachers were amazed and uncomfortable, although as I learned much later, some of them had some idea of the proceedings. The Head of Art had been approached the previous day by students in his class as to whether they could use his room, paper and paint to make banners and placards. He had left his door unlocked to give them access. Rob Morrison, the Australian science teacher had acted similarly. Even though there were only a handful of children in the school and pickets stood at the students' entrance, the Deputy Head entered the staffroom just before the morning bell with her customary declaration and armful of registers: 'The children are waiting! The children are waiting!' I went upstairs to my class on the first floor. There wasn't a student present; they were all outside on the green with the reporters and photographers of the local and national press milling around in the rain beside them. 'What would Baruch and Issy Weinberg have made of all this?'

I wondered, all inspired by a children's poetry book set and printed in their tiny Brick Lane printshop.

It seemed that the evening before, after school, there had been a mass meeting on the green, and a strike vote of raised hands, just like the dockers, had been called and approved. The strike leader was a fifth-form girl from a local Gibraltarian family called Zeinaida, and she and Jackie, from my fourth year ROSLA class, had alerted the *East London Advertiser* who in turn had contacted the national press. The *Advertiser* sent a young reporter, Steve Nice, who a few years later achieved pop fame as Steve Harley, the lead singer and songwriter of the pop group Cockney Rebel, whose song *Come Up and See Me* became a big, big hit. That morning he was one of the soaked reporters with their even wetter notebooks, scouring the green and Stepney churchyard for the word from the young strikers. When a group of them tried to find shelter in the church's large porchway, *The Times* reported that they were shooed away by a very angry Rev. Gibbs, but undeterred they carried on singing and waving their banners.

One by one the teachers ventured outside to order or implore them to come into school, but to no avail. Eventually, I went out too, thanked them profusely and told them I was going to fight the sacking through my union, and asked them to come back to school, out of the rain. 'No!' scores of them declared from behind their banners, 'Not until they give you your job back!' and they waved with their determined smiles. There were parents there too, I noticed. One of them, I knew, was an active trade unionist, a postal worker who had recently been on strike. He seemed to be teaching them how to picket at the main school gate. I thanked them again and went back into the staffroom where teachers were already taking sides. The priests in the school, the 'guild wardens' and the hierarchy were very much on the side of the head and governors, but the younger teachers were much more divided. Some simply couldn't believe that the students

PUPILS THREATEN LESSONS BOYCOTT

Strike teacher fights for job

ENGLISH TEACHER Chris Searle will return to the Sir John Cass-Redcoat School, Stepney, when the spring holiday ends on Monday to give his class more poetry lessons—and to fight for his job.

Mr. Searle, 27, refuses to comment on his sacking by the board of governors after poems written by pupils were published in a booklet called "Stepney Words".

"It is now in the hands of my solicitor," he said. "I cannot say anything on the specific subject of my job at the moment."

Mr. Searle, who lives in Albert Gardens, Stepney, has the support of the 900 pupils, many of his fellow teachers and most parents.

Hundreds of the children staged strikes last Thursday and Friday and some are threatening to boycott lessons again on Monday, but they are expected to return to school until there are new developments in the dispute.

Mr. Searle, who gained an English degree at the University of Leeds and an M.A. at McMaster University in Ontario, Canada, said the children enjoy writing poetry because it is the best way in which they can show "their own uniqueness."

He added: "It helps them to believe that they are people, not just kids. It helps them believe in themselves."

FATHER'S FIGHT

The 37-year-old father of one of Mr. Searle's pupils is making a lone fight for the teacher's reinstatement.

Postman John Sadler, a sorting officer, isn't used to the door-knocking he is doing for petition signatures — but his foot-sore efforts have already earned him 100 supporters.

John — a militant during the recent postal strike — has been delivering his critical views on the "heartless" governors of Sir John Cass-Redcoat School to his Stepney neighbours.

After a week's holiday with his family in Somerset he will canvass for support on the Ocean and Stifford Estates, Stepney, before handing the petition to the governors.

His daughter Pamela, 14, is a member of Mr. Searle's after school cinema club and she was one of the first to strike.

'GOOD TEACHER'

John said: "The fact that all these children came out on strike is proof enough that he is a good teacher. He puts a lot of his own time into running clubs after school. He is devoted to his job.

"At the most the governors should have given him a rap across the knuckles."

Mr. Searle, who is single, spent three years teaching at the University of Calgary, Canada, and at schools in the West Indies before joining the staff at the Stepney school last year.

MEETING BISHOP

A group of pupils met the Bishop of Stepney, the Rt. Rev. Trevor Huddleston, yesterday morning (Thurs.) in the hope of arranging a meeting between themselves and the board of governors.

Said fifth-former Zeiniada De La Cruz: "We just want to talk it over with the governors. We want to put our side.

"Mr. Searle is a great teacher. He's more like a friend to whom we can tell our problems. We're really going to fight to keep him at the school."

Spokesmen for the striking pupils outside the Sir John Cass-Redcoat school, Stepney Way. They are (from left). Jackie Tolley 15, Zeiniada De la Cruz 16, and Sylvia Bullman, 16.

Photo — Kenneth Newman

were capable of organising a protest and strike that had been so effective, and suspected that I was the instigator. But these children lived within the ethos of strikes and labour protests — some of their parents were very much a part of that culture. Also there had been recent large-scale strikes of dustmen and postmen, and the docks had been in a long industrial turmoil with the onset of containerisation. So there was nothing unusual about strikes in the midst of their lives. It was the same for the generations of school cleaners, who were all local women. They had refused the school hierarchy's orders to wash away the slogans written in chalk and paint by the young protesters. When I thought about it, I wasn't surprised. I had got to know some of them quite well, including the veteran, Lil, who lived in a terraced house in Bromley Street, very near the school. I would walk past her house every morning at about eight o'clock, and many times I passed her husband Bill on the doorstep. He was an ex-sailor in both the Royal and Merchant Navies, and he would invite me in for a cup of tea, always putting a dose of rum or whisky in my cup as he gave it to me. 'You need that boy, what with those kids!' he used to tell me with a big wink. It certainly used to perk me up for the day ahead. Lil, just back from her early morning shift, would look on ruefully with sometimes a few choice words.

Very swiftly, two petitions started circulating in the staffroom; one in support of the governors which attracted a majority of signatories, and one in support of me. I hadn't been at the school long enough to know many of the teachers very well, but I was still astonished that so many of them should support the governors. Then I began to understand something of the dynamic that was at work. I sat in the staffroom, as I usually did, next to the special needs 'remedial' teacher called Burt. He was from St. Lucia, the only black colleague in the school. We quickly developed what I thought was a friendship, and spent many lunchtimes talking about the Caribbean. He lived in Harlesden, North London, and one Saturday invited me over there, where I spent the morning with his family, before he took me to visit the Credit Union, which he helped to organise. It had been a warm and fascinating day. Now when I sat down next to him the day of the strike and the passage of the two petitions, he seemed uncomfortable, nervous. 'What's up, Burt?' I asked him, for I had never seen him like this before. He leaned towards me slightly and said, almost whispering: 'I'm sorry Chris man, but I can't be seen talking to you or sitting with you. I've got to think of my family and kids. If the head thinks I'm your friend, who knows what could happen. I'm sorry man.' And that was it; he walked away and we never really spoke again. It hurt me more than anything, and showed me clearly how much fear was around these teachers. But my Head of Department spoke up for me. He was something of a loner around the school, but a deeply intelligent man, born and bred in Stepney, and a teacher whom the students loved and respected. Although his very formal teaching style and mine were just about polar opposites, we got on well and I trusted him and admired him very much. He had little or no time for the school hierarchy or time-pleasing teachers who never opposed it. He didn't like petitions either, and sent in a personal letter to the governors giving me his strong support. He, and the teachers who signed the minority petition for me were brave. They knew that the headteacher and the governors were powerful men (and they were all men, all white) who held positions of power and leverage, and they all defied the ambience of fear that was like an indoor cloud across the staff room. Four of the teachers who signed the governors' petition were persuaded to give evidence on behalf of the governors at a later hearing, recalling that I had spoken in support of the children of Holland Park in a private staffroom conversation, when the West London children had organised a strike in support of one of their teachers, Mrs Rousseau, when her contract had been prematurely ended in December 1970. *Ipso facto*, because I supported that schoolchildren's strike, I must have organised the strike at Sir John Cass. I was astonished to hear a private conversation between colleagues quoted in quasi-legal proceedings. But I could only put it down to the level of fear and intimidation which was created around a group of school children's assertion of their right to organise and protest around their own poetry. When I thought of their action and courage on the green at the end of the very street where Isaac had lived and walked with his friends, I could only marvel and wonder what he would have thought of it all.

The strike carried on until the half-term holiday. The headteacher called in Zeinaida and other fifth-formers for a futile meeting, but they refused to change their demands. Zeinaida told the *East London Advertiser*: 'We have most of the school out here today — we'll have twice as many tomorrow. We'll have every school in East London out on strike.' On the second day a large group of the strikers marched through the City and along The Embankment to Trafalgar Square, carrying banners. The secondary boys of the school on Ben Jonson Road (another poet!) nearly opposite Sir John Cass, Stepney Green School, had climbed the tall iron gates of the school to join the strike on its first day after their headteacher had tried to lock them in, and as the news was carried around the borough, the girls of Tower Hamlets School along Commercial Road came out, as did the students of Robert Montefiore School in Whitechapel. Such 'secondary action' gave the students' protest more and more the character of a mature industrial strike, and it was only the interruption of the half-term holiday that seemed to quieten things down.

Half-term was something of a respite for me too, but not for long. Suddenly messages of support were reaching me from many quarters. Local members of the National Union of Teachers turned up at my door, promising support; the Deputy Head of Robert Montefiore (who was subsequently to become London's first black head teacher) M.S. Mitra, sat down with me for two hours, helping me with a letter for the Inner London Education Authority; Ron set up a meeting for me in his flat with the historian and Queen Mary College lecturer, Bill Fishman — author of classic East London working class histories like *Streets of East London, The Insurrectionists* and *East End Jewish Radicals* — and he advised me about fighting back and kept me laughing all afternoon with his wit and narrative. Tony Smythe, who led the National Council for Civil Liberties (now 'Liberty') gave me his time and advice, and Trevor Huddleston had gone public with his support on the first day of the strike, and was quoted on the front page of *The Sun* under the head-line 'Please Don't Sack Sir; Bishop hits out at "stupid" decision', saying of the governors of this church school: 'I just don't know how they reached this stupid decision. I'm certainly going to take this up. The poems were excep-tionally good and deserved the widest audience.'

Marjorie Hourd had seen the children's march to Trafalgar Square on the television news, and wrote to me: 'I nearly wept when I saw your kids crossing Trafalgar Square on Friday — I felt that all I have fought for in nearly forty years was indeed coming to pass.' And as for Chiefie, he was now a teacher educator in Tottenham All Saints College and Chairman of the Poetry Society, and had led the campaign for the remains of the revolution-ary poet Byron to be re-interred in 'Poets' Corner' of Westminster Abbey. He had also founded a poetry journal called *Workshop.* He wrote a piece called *Protest Poem* which was published in *Tribune:*

They've sacked Chris Searle today
Anonymous men in clerical grey
Who govern with absolute rule
This voluntary aided
Church of England
Ever so Christian school

It may be joy, it may be misery;
But suffer the children to write what they see
Quickly the answer came back:
They gave him the sack, the sack, the sack
From this voluntary aided
Ever so Christian school

We'll publish some poems, the governors said,
The ones that are pretty — and pretty nigh dead!
The rest of course will never do
They're far too fresh and much too true
For this voluntary aided
Victorianly faded
Ever so Christian school

We cannot say the writing's pornographic
It merely shows the people, the streets, the traffic
But we'd prefer the bright-eyed vision narrow
Into the dead old cliche, 'cheerful cockney sparrow'
In this happy, oh so happy
Church of England school.

The Children's March to
Trafalgar Square

And so they've sacked Chris Searle today
Who broke their first commandment: to obey.
Governors who preach the truth, the life, the way —
Get down on your knees and pray, pray, pray
For your ever so Christian
Tarnished and faded
Your ever so Christian soul.

Here were the two teachers that I admired and loved the most; the two people that had given me so much and helped me grow as a person, as a teacher, at entirely different times and phases of my life, and the two writers who had taught me most about poetry and 'the poetical spirit'. And then Chiefie told me that he had a copy of Marjorie's *Education of the Poetic Spirit* which had been published in 1949 and which he had read when it first came out. He gave it to me, and I have it in front of me on my desk now, and to me it is an amalgam of both of them, a huge shout for poetry, and an endless hurrah for children and the insight of their writing.

My life began to change irrevocably after that first extraordinary day at Stepney Green. Every newspaper prominently carried the story of the strike and its ramifications, and during the night after the first day of the strike, Bert, an old friend from Canada, took me down to the Fleet Street all-night café, Mick's, to wait for the first papers to come off the presses. As we sat there, nervous and self-conscious in an ambience of constant activity and movement as the printworkers and junior journalists milled around the counter in the packed-out room of the gulping of teas, loud conversations and exclamations and the clashing and scraping of knives and forks against plates filled with sausages, bacon, eggs and chips, I remembered that this same street was where Isaac, the young school-leaver, had found his first job in an engraver's firm. It was a job he had hated, in the centre of what he called in his poem *Fleet Street,* a 'shrieking vortex'. Now, even in the middle of the night, this street never lay down, never slept while there were newspapers

143

to produce. I couldn't believe it; the children's faces as well as mine were everywhere in their pages and even the most notorious right-wing papers — the *Daily Mail, Daily Express, Daily Telegraph* and *The Times* were sympathetic. *The Guardian* had contacted me to write an article, Nicola Tyrer, the *Evening News* reporter, did a long interview at my flat, and the *Sunday Times* columnist Peter Lennon asked me for an interview with some of the poets and we all met in my bedsitter with plenty of cups of tea. It was an engaging encounter. One of the girls in my class, Cheryl, produced a piece of writing which she read out loud to an engrossed Lennon, who ended his article, titled 'Poetic Injustice?' with it: 'What have we learned at the end of the day at school? Precisely nothing, although facts have been pushed through our minds. We're like machines being programmed with orders. We carry them out and then we are fed with more. It is like a long string which cannot be digested enough to please them. I would like to chop the string to leave a loose end to join up again to a new, worthwhile life at school.'

I was contacted by Fred Flower, the Principal of Kingsway Further Education College and eminent language scholar, whose books I had read, with a very tempting job offer, and the educational publisher Routledge and Kegan Paul wrote to me asking whether I had written anything for publication. I sent them my M.Ed thesis that I had written on racism in language, based on my teachings in Tobago. Published under the title *The Forsaken Lover* (the title of a poem which one of my students had written), it was, a few months down the line, republished as a paperback by Penguin, and in 1972 won the Martin Luther King Award. I was all right financially by that time as the National Union of Teachers had secured my salary from the Inner London Education Authority, so I donated the award to the liberation forces fighting to free Zimbabwe from Ian Smith's rule — something my Tobago students had been passionate about. I was interviewed by the Jamaican novelist Andrew Salkey for the B.B.C.

144

Caribbean Service, so wondrously, some of my Tobago students, thousands of miles away across the Atlantic, heard me talking about their poems. Andrew became my very good friend too. I had shown Chiefie my novel *Poilu,* and he wanted to publish it through his own Workshop Press. Suddenly a lot seemed to be going on. I thanked Fred Flower for his generous offer, but when I thought of what the students had done for me, I felt that I had no other option but to fight hard to get my job back and prove them right. Mightily surprised, I also said the same thing to Paul Beasley, the left-leaning Labour leader of Tower Hamlets Council and Chair of Governors at Bow Boys Secondary School, when he visited me one night, advising me to apply for the vacant headship at the school. There was also a precedent to win, the NUT lawyers told me. It was important to win the right for probationary teachers to have a hearing if they were threatened with dismissal. That was the priority. My case hinged on the need to secure that precedent and I was determined to win it for me, and for other teachers like myself. And I thought of the young woman teacher who had worked so hard to compile *The Star in the Mud*; what had happened to her? Until this day I have never met her or even known her name. But I have always felt she was my colleague and my friend, still teaching somewhere in a classroom that I would never know, still teaching poetry, still encouraging her students to write.

Ron, Linda and I talked about our next step. With all the publicity we had sold out the first edition, reprinted and nearly sold that out too. Linda was processing all the sales and sending out the books, and it was soon clear that we had enough money to publish a second collection. I certainly had enough good poems, and others were being sent in, so we compiled *Stepney Words, Number 2.* By this time the summer holidays had started and a group of us had taken over the old, disused Bethnal Green Fire Station and had converted it into a combination of summer school and adventure playground. It was proving to be very popular with local children, and some Sir John Cass students came over from Stepney. When one of them, Maxine, saw a bare white wall, she took up a paint brush and with absolute spontaneity she painted:

> This fire was put out by water
> Our fire is in our hearts

Just as she had printed it, a small boy stretched up with a paintbrush and painted a black line through her words.

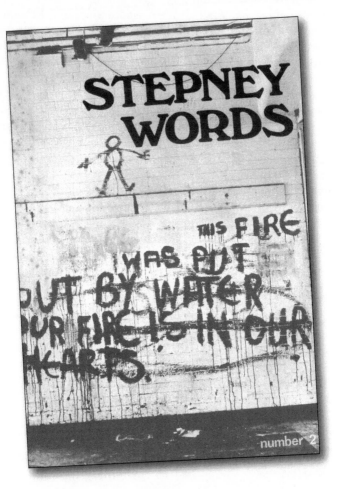

Ron and I both looked at it, Ron photographed it and the image became the cover of *Stepney Words, Number 2* — made in Bethnal Green. It sold just as quickly as the first edition and included both Ron's photographs next to the poems and the drawings of a fourth-former, a docker's son called Jimmy May. Jimmy was in the school's lowest stream, dumped into a non-examination ROSLA class for two years until he was sixteen, eager to start work yet being given little preparation or encouragement for it. The school called his class 4R, which provoked memories of my own very different 'R' Class experiences. Jimmy and his classmates called his class '4 Rejects' and they felt angry and resentful about how the school had categorised them. But how they would talk and write about their lives, and joke and laugh too. I used to love being with them.

Jimmy never wanted to write much, but he was a very good artist and the students in his class would write poems and pass them across to him to illustrate. Then he would sit with complete concentration and focus. His picture of an elderly couple beside Gary's few lines weeps empathy, as his image reflects the words, so stark and simple:

There are lots of old women
Men as well
All sitting in rooms and
Looking at hell

They wonder if they shall
See the world or even
See the sky as well...

And when his classmate Kathleen wrote her short poem about a young boy being taken from his grandmother into care and adoption, inspired by a moving photograph, Jimmy was there, sitting next to her to add his own visual heart to her words:

She holds him tightly
Tears rolling down her cheeks
She thinks this may be the last time she will see him,
Gone, gone for ever

147

Into a different world,
New people, new home.
Then she kisses him
And slowly he walks away
Into the dark and lonely street.

In 1972 Jimmy's drawings in *Stepney Words 2* also inspired the BBC documentary makers of the *Man Alive* series to make a film about him, and the prospects of millions of young people like him all over Britain. *Born to Fail?* it was called, and it shows Jimmy, having left school, carving up meat and making sausages in a Stepney butcher's shop, still trying to persevere with his drawing. In one moving sequence he organises all his family members, in turn, to contribute to a collective portrait while sitting around their dinner table in their Shadwell council flat. Jimmy, from his school's bottom rung, from the 'Rejects' class, becomes a teacher of art — the pursuit he loves best — and a very effective one too. And one tailpiece. Last week, as I was going through some photographs of the events around the strike, I found one from the Press Association of the students marching down Victoria Embankment, laughing, singing and waving banners. I had it blown up to see if I

Drawing by Jimmy May

148

could identify some of the demonstrators at the back of the march. Suddenly there was Jimmy, smiling and holding up a drawing of a twenty-seven-year-old man with a beard and leather jacket. 'Blimey!' I thought, 'that's me!' and I thanked his loyalty, his courage, his humanity and his art and that of all those with him, even in my seventies, sitting here at my writing table in Sheffield in 2015.

As for our Bethnal Green Fire Station project, it became very popular with local parents and their children, though not so much with the local police chiefs. To them, the idea of a group of local radicals taking such initiatives on their manor was simply not acceptable, particularly when a young policeman, Colin, joined in with us, gave his all, and became the partner of one of the organisers, staying nights with her in one of the disused rooms above the main chamber. 'Watch him! He's a police plant!' was a constant warning, but I never believed it, and after a few weeks he was told to leave the force for such fraternising with the enemy, and was deeply shocked and disillusioned when his superiors framed him on the charge of leaving his warrant card unattended during the nights he stayed at the fire station.

Then one morning I was sent a message by the poet Adrian Mitchell. He had read about our project in the *Evening Standard,* and sent us fifty matinée tickets for a performance of his play *Tyger,* about the life of Blake, being performed in the West End by the National Theatre Company. It was a joyous afternoon at the New Theatre of St. Martin's Lane, with boisterous dialogue and the marvellous music of Mike Westbrook, and the children, fascinated and engrossed, had a compelling and utterly surprising time. At the end of the play, the actor playing Blake, Gerald James, invited them all up on the stage for the finale, with the actors dancing, singing and jumping around with them. Yes, they were Blake's children all right, and Isaac's too, and I wished that history could turn itself around and both of them could have been there with them, 'Tygers' all of them.

The weekly London entertainments guide, *Time Out*, which at the time had an editorial position close to the underground press, arranged an interview between three of their journalists, Lonca Rousseau — the teacher whose dismissal at Holland Park Comprehensive School in West London had provoked the school student strike at that school in December 1970 — and me. It was a real pleasure meeting Lonca, a deeply humane and committed woman whom I had never met before. The interview lasted for more than two hours in the West End offices of the journal, and was published with a wry Bash Street Kids-type cartoon on its cover. Lonca's experiences were not so dissimilar to mine. Holland Park was a huge school, profiled as a model comprehensive, yet most of Lonca's students had been in the bottom-most twelfth stream, where, as she attested, they felt a deep sense of rejection and shame, and were frequently faced with teachers who had very little else but contempt for them and hated teaching them. These had been the students who had led the rebellion when Lonca's contract was terminated, and had organised the strike headlined in the *Daily Mirror* as a 'riot'. The vicious streaming had shattered their hopes and self-esteem, and as ardent supporters of the principles of comprehensive education we were both shocked and angered that such deformed institutional structures were still conceived as part of a comprehensive school. I felt an intense empathy with Lonca's final published sentence and knew that it could have come from my own lips too, from my experience of my own students from the other side of London. Speaking of her students, she said that they had rejected 'the impulse to compromise. They haven't things to conserve so they haven't been very conservative. They have got the courage to say what they feel, because they feel that people don't take any notice of what they are saying anyway. So their honesty is devastating. They've got so much to teach.' When I heard her say that, I thought that she was also talking about the writers of *Stepney Words*.

Ron took me to Liverpool to visit the Scotland Road Free School, set up to care for and teach and learn from the truanting and excluded children of a large urban area that was being crushed and bulldozed all around them. As Ron's eternally snapping camera took his photographs of the crumbing terraces of Scotland Road and Everton Heights and witnessed their relentless demolition, we also spent some engrossing hours with the warmth, intelligence and humour of the children and talked to two of their hugely committed teachers — John Ord and Bill Murphy — struggling to keep all the positive fire of a community spirit burning through the life, learning and union of their school. It taught me much about what a school could become in East London too. Full of respect and admiration, I wrote a poem dedicated to the Free School and Ron, which was later published in the socialist teachers' journal, *Rank and File.*

And how could they so vandalise
these slopes beneath the Liverpool skies,
with human lives like broken teeth
to tear and break their hearts beneath?

Where brick lies crumbled, squirming, dead,
and dust and rubble find their bed –
can humans come from concrete blocks
that rise deformed from shattered rocks?

But teachers and children of the North
give themselves this new love birth,
and concrete, motored, mechanised hearts
cannot stop love's shattering shafts.

Chapter Six
Jewry Street Rag

As my case rolled on, I kept busy speaking at meetings held by NUT local associations and 'young teacher' groups, and the 'Rank and File' socialist pressure group within the union. From Wandsworth to Newcastle, from Brighton to Coventry and Birmingham, from Leicester and Nottingham and Liverpool to my old haunts in Leeds and Exeter, I gave talks on the *Stepney Words* saga and my own interpretation of it, which I called 'Divide and School'. The meetings gave me a keen sense of young teachers' thirst for progress, for the championing of comprehensive schools and mixed ability teaching and the end of streaming, and for huge teacher-led changes in the curriculum. There were also nationwide calls for democracy in schools, a unified pay structure and the end to the absolute power of head teachers. These meetings filled me with a high level of optimism about a new generation of teachers and student teachers and the real possibilities of progress as more and more of them entered teaching. These were young people who had lived and campaigned through the radical years of British university life, had experienced 1968 and all it meant, and were entering schools with deep commitments to the South African and Irish peoples, an end to the war in Vietnam and support for the trade unions and their resistance right across Britain. The isolation that I had felt within the anachronistic education establishment at Sir John Cass, I sensed, was well behind me now. I had also become active within the East London Teachers Association of the union and felt that I was part of a real vehicle for educational change.

I was still in the middle of educational struggles locally though, and when I went down the road to get a pint of milk one afternoon, I was confronted by a placard outside the local newsagent along Commercial Road: 'Blacklist threat to Stepney teacher'. When I bought the *Evening News* it told me that was me, and that almost all local secondary school headteachers had voted to refuse to employ me, should I decide to try to find a post in another local school. When I went to my next union meeting, the secretary of the local association, Walter Treisman — a maths teacher at the same Coopers' School in Mile End where I had failed the eleven-plus interview in 1955 — was almost delirious with joy. 'I've got proof. We've known about teacher blacklisting for years, but now we've got the proof. Here's a copy of their motion, look!' A progressive head had passed on a copy of the blacklisting motion, of which as a communist he'd been a victim of for years, and now he had the proof he needed! Usually a quiet and entirely focused man, I had never seen him so jubilant.

And there was another incident which seemed to tell me that other surveillance was going on at an even higher level. I didn't have a telephone in my Albert Gardens flat, so several times a day I would go to the end of the square, where it met Commercial Road, to use the red telephone box, often to organise meetings or to talk to other teacher-activists about upcoming events. These short walks to use the public telephone became a regular part of my daily routine. One morning I dialled a number of a trade union colleague and waited for him to pick up before I put in my coin. I pressed 'Button A' and I began to hear my own voice, recorded from a previous telephone conversation, speaking back to me from the receiver. It was a weird and harrowing experience: what, was I being tapped through a public phone box? Who was watching me, who was listening? I started using another phone box, further up Commercial Road, but the sensation of being observed and being heard by unwanted elements never left me.

One of the strengths of the powerful empathy that united so many of the *Stepney Words* poems was the ways they brought the young and the old together, and the sheer imaginative love that the young poets showed towards their elders in family and community. With the publicity that the anthology and the saga of the strike had generated, many poems were being sent to Reality Press, quite a few of them by pensioners about the hardships, loneliness and poverty of age. My friend Roger Matland, the Director of Dame Colet House, the settlement and community centre on Ben Jonson Road, invited me to run some poetry workshops with the pensioners who came for meals and social events there and I found that, as with the children, these elders had poetry within them and it was bursting to be released, words often compressed into short rhyming lines that held lifetimes of struggle, happiness and pain. Sitting at a table with her tea and Garibaldi biscuits, Julie wrote:

Life isn't funny
Without any money

It's a bitter end
Without a friend

It wasn't so bad
When I was young and gay

But it's a different story
Now I'm old and grey

And Sadie, sitting at the next table:

Life is happy
Life is sad
Life is complex
Life is glad
I woo thee oh sweet life sublime
For I am yours
And you are mine

These workshops put me back in the classroom spirit. I'd had a strong connection with Dame Colet House ever since I moved into Stepney and worked as a volunteer in its marvellous adventure playground. Roger and I had become close friends and he had been there, milling with the strikers on that May morning — as I saw when I examined the press photographs. Now, working in his centre among clients using the law centre, the claimants' union and the lunch club, I could see more and more of the young poets' world and that of their grandparents. And just up the road in a dark, unheated tenement block on Stepney Green lived Steve Hicks, ex-professional boxer, docker, factory worker and pensioner, now seriously afflicted by a dangerously ulcerated leg. But nothing could block Steve's poetical spirit. The *Stepney Words* strike at the bottom of his road urged Steve into poetry action, as he later described in his autobiography, *Sparring for Luck.*

> July of 1971 came and went and at the retiring age of sixty-five I became a state pensioner with nothing to do but write. I had been reading about the publication of a book of children's poems called *Stepney Words* compiled by local school teacher Christopher Searle. It was published without permission of the school governors, and for this 'wicked' deed Chris was sacked. During my lifetime I have heard some fantastic and weird decisions but this one excelled them all. Just imagine getting the sack for teaching good English poetry. I reckon if William Shakespeare had been around at this time he would have joined the school children's strike which ultimately followed. Seven hundred children came out on strike opposing the dismissal and the news media highlighted the event — it took a strike to decide whether or not poetry was for the good interest of the children. It was quite logical to me that with poetry in the news for a change I should send a few of my own to Chris Searle just for fun. A few weeks later I had a letter from him telling me that he was putting together a book of poems called *Elders* and all the writers would be pensioners, so therefore he had chosen two of my poems for the book. They were called *Economic Pensioner* and *Exit.* This was good news for me indeed, but I never expected for one minute that I would be reading them out at a later date on radio and television.

Steve's *Economic Pensioner* was the poem which prompted Ron, Linda and myself to compile *Elders,* for it

Cover photograph:
Ron McCormick©

told, lucidly, of the hardships of being old and poor, and the dire need of an increase to the national Old Age Pension. We had the funds from the sale of *Stepney Words,* so we swiftly got on with the compilation and publication of *Elders,* with poems sent in from all over the country. We also used it as a fundraiser, and its sale eventually raised several hundred pounds for the London Old Age Pensioners' and Trade Union Committee, who were campaigning for the increase in the national pension, for as Steve reminded us in *Economic Pensioner*:

> I have just turned sixty-five
> An uneventful day,
> But thankful to still be alive

To draw my first week's pay.
I have to really understand
Which food I wish to buy.
Because I cannot live so grand
With prices up so high.

So what I'll do with every hour
As I'll be so hard-pressed,
Is, rack my brains to find out how
To spend my money best.

I cannot live in clover
For I hardly have enough,
And there won't be much left over
When I've bought all my stuff.

So when my week's payout has gone
And my resistance too,
Alas, I'll have to struggle on
Just like the others do.

Steve's poem was a cue for fighting back, and we wanted the *Elders* anthology to be the same. Eileen Cowdrill's lines told of pensioners struggling with the new coinage of decimalisation and Prime Minister Harold Wilson's duplicitous assertion that 'the pound in your pocket is still the same':

Decimal money resting on the brink,
Decimal money going down the sink,
Decimal money gurgling the spout,
The sound of music, inflation beating out.
Now we are skint and haven't a dime,
Hurry on next week and pension time.

And Jack Dash's poem *Time* found protest and resistance at every point of the human being's story:

Time begins
with the ending of the embryo and the thrusting forward
from the vagina into a world of materialism and struggle.

Time is
the receiving of the maternity spank from the midwife,
that makes you cry out in protest.

Time is
when at the warm, succulent breast, you make your first
decision as a human, the rejection of the empty breast,
and reach out for the full one.

Time is
childhood, school, youth, adolescence, maturity.

Time is
night and day, industry, profession, punching the factory
   time clock,
productivity, shift-work, holidays, unemployment, poverty.

Time is
sowing, reaping, harvest, famine, love, marriage,
parenthood, pain, laughter, joy, tears.

Time is
The closing of the cell doors, marking the wall and counting
   the days
for actions political or criminal.

Time is
the seasons, the bursting of buds, the dawn chorus of the
   song birds in spring. Summertime, lazing in the sun
   autumn leaves, winter, cold winds, rain and snow.

Time is
our life's span, adorning of the last garment in nature's
   wardrobe
old age and death.

Time
is now! Use it!

And the final brief stanza of Jack's poem was as a rally-
ing cry to these poets. Milly Harris, another East London
voice, remembered moments of drama and courage in her
memories of the October 1936 Battle of Cable Street:

We stood at Gardiner's Corner,
We stood and watched the crowds,
We stood at Gardiner's Corner,
Firm, solid, voices loud.

Came the marching of the blackshirts,
Came the pounding of their feet,
Came the sound of ruffians marching
Where the five roads meet.

158

We thought of many refugees
fleeing from the fascist hordes,
The maimed, the sick, the young, the old,
Those who had fought the fascist lords.

So we stopped them there at Gardiner's,
We fought and won our way,
We fought the baton charges,
No fascist passed that day.

And in her poem *Tenement,* Milly wrote with a similar power of empathy that the *Stepney Words* poets had shown towards the old. Now the roles were reversed as she became a child suffering the cruelty of poverty:

Mummy don't hit me — mummy don't!
I'll give you — you little scamp!
Come when I tells yer,
Come when I call.
The things I do for one and all
Two flights up —
A wonderful domain.
Two flights up,
Must I climb them again?
Two scrummy rooms,
Cot, bed, table.
Nowhere to stretch,
Nowhere to look,
Nothing to see through the window pane.
Murky as hell — this wonderful domain.
Wet washing steaming! Kids screaming!
Mummy don't hit me — mummy don't!

But there was one very singular poem in *Elders* that became almost mythical in its effect and has been subsequently anthologised time and time again. It was sent to us by a Scottish nurse in a care home. She wrote that its author was a patient of hers who rarely spoke, but was seen to write from time to time. After she died with no relatives to take care of her few possessions, the nurse had cleared her bedside locker and found this poem, which we called after its poet, simply *Kate's Poem*:

What do you see nurses
    What do you see?
Are you thinking
    when you are looking at me
A crabby old woman
    not very wise
Uncertain of habit
    with far-away eyes
Who dribbles her food
    and makes no reply,
When you say in a loud voice
    'I do wish you'd try',
Who seems not to notice
    the things that you do,
And forever is losing
    a stocking or a shoe,
Who unresisting or not
    lets you do as you will
With bathing and feeding
    the long day to fill.
Is that what you're thinking,
    Is that what you see?
Then open your eyes nurse,
    you are not looking at me.
I'll tell you who I am
    as I sit here so still,
As I use at your bidding
    as I eat at your will,
I'm a small child of ten
    with a father and a mother
Brothers and sisters
    who love one another.
A young girl of sixteen
    with wings on her feet,
Dreaming that soon now
    a lover she'll meet.
A bride soon at twenty
    my heart gives a leap
Remembering the vows
    that I promised to keep.
At twenty-five now
    I have young of my own,
Who need me to build
    a secure happy home.
A woman of thirty,

my young now grow fast,
Bound to each other
    with ties that should last.
At forty my young sons
    now grown and will all be gone,
But my man stays beside me
    to see I don't mourn.
At fifty once more
    babies play round my knee,
Again we know children
    my loved one and me.
Dark days are upon me
    my husband is dead,
I look at the future,
    I shudder with dread,
For my young are all busy
    rearing young of their own,
And I think of the years
    and the love I have known.
I'm an old woman now
    and nature is cruel,
'tis her jest to make
    old age look like a fool.
The body it crumbles,
    grace and vigour depart,
There now is stone
    where I once had a heart.
But inside this old carcase
    a young girl still dwells
And now and again
    my battered heart swells.
I remember the joys
    I remember the pain,
And I'm loving and living
    life over again.
I think of the years
    all too few — gone too fast,
And accept the stark fact
    that nothing can last.
So open your eyes nurses,
    open and see
Not a crabbit old woman,
    look closer, see ME.

We launched *Elders* with Ron's brilliant photographs, including an evocative photograph of his own grand-mother standing in front of an aspidistra on the cover, at a commemorative reading at the Half Moon Theatre. Steve was there, Jack was there, Milly was there with many of the other contributors, and we presented the cheque to the trade union pensioners committee, who were astonished that poetry could raise such funds. Again, I reminded myself that it was the *Stepney Words* poets, and before them Isaac, that had started all this.

It had also caused me to suddenly be involved in a host of activities. I found myself as a speaker at a Children's Rights conference, called by a group which started the *Children's Rights* journal, where school students' trade unions were the main theme. Delegations from the Schools Action Union and the National Union of School Students made their pitches. I was also a main speaker alongside my favourite film director Ken Loach, whose brilliant film *Kes,* an adaptation of Barry Hines' Yorkshire novel, *A Kestrel for a Knave* had been released the year before. At a large meeting at Holborn Library, we both championed comprehensive schools, and school students' trade unions. It seemed very fitting, as the year before I had taken my class and many of the *Stepney Words* poets to the BBC Television Centre at White City, and we had watched a special, requested screening of Loach's television classic, *Cathy Come Home,* organised by my old school friend Terry Dixon, now a BBC News director, who had played the anarchic judge Azdak in our 1962 school production of *The Caucasian Chalk Circle.* Some twenty-five years later Hines came to visit my English classes in Sheffield when we were reading his *Looks and Smiles,* and he was friendly and very encour-aging to my mainly Pakistani students. My continuing legal struggle with the Sir John Cass governors meant that I was a few times interviewed on the Eamonn Andrews nightly news programme, and found Andrews both sympathetic and deeply interested in the case. When

Poilu was published I was invited on BBC's *Late Night Line-up* to answer questions about the genesis of the novel. I was also asked by the *Observer* to write some articles on children's poetry for their colour supplement, and then, surprise of surprises, the *Daily Mail* asked me to judge a national children's poetry competition with the author of *Cider with Rosie,* Laurie Lee. Thousands of poems arrived in the post, many were really outstanding. I spent days going through them, still amazed that such a right-wing newspaper would ask me to do such a thing. But what it showed was that I was not alone, and neither were the *Stepney Words* poets: children's poetry about their real lives was everywhere, as were the teachers who were nourishing and promoting it. Marjorie and Chiefie would be proud and pleased, I thought, and I wondered too if the young teacher of *The Star in the Mud* had submitted any of her students' poems, wherever she was.

I was invited to read my own poems at my theatre of theatres — Theatre Royal, Stratford E.15. And it wasn't just the venue, now sticking out of the rubble and destruction of Angel Lane, where I had seen Joan Littlewood's productions more than a decade before. I was asked to read alongside one of my East London hero-writers, the playwright and poet Bernard Kops. I had loved his plays, like *The Hamlet of Stepney Green*, his novels like *By the Waters of Whitechapel* and autobiographical writings like *The World is a Wedding*. He was one of the next generation after Isaac of epochal East London Jewish writers, and when he gave me a copy of his poetry collection, *For the Record*, from which he had been reading — including the incendiary words of his *Shalom Bomb* — and told me that he had been closely following my case and the whole story of *Stepney Words*, I felt hugely emboldened. I read some of my own East London poems like *Stepney Plane Trees, Swans in Blackwall*, and as I began *Isaac Rosenberg's Earth* there on that historic stage, I felt somehow that Isaac was listening, encouraging, criticising, ready to talk to me:

163

Remote from Stepney streets, you lie in French earth.
Your brothers are around you, all sides are full of men —
All the earth of foot-treads, end to end the tyrants'
     saving.
Some they called your friends, some they called your
     enemies
But all were the fount of your song
Of words and beauty, love-blasted from your heart.

Genius burst from you with the strength of flowers,
And trees that smoke and brick ground to the roots —
     How they conspired to contain you, to patronise you!
You died, making words for all our meaning, trampled to
     the mud.
But the earth and you thrive under concrete, under tar
For your children of poetry, walking these streets.

Then came another surprise. I was contacted by the director
of 'Poetry International 72' to see whether I could assemble
a group of the *Stepney Words* poets to read at what was the
country's most prestigious Poetry Festival, with readings in
the Queen Elizabeth Hall in South Bank and the Institute
of Contemporary Arts on the Mall, a hundred yards from
Trafalgar Square, which these poets had got to know well
through their own energies. They were sharing the bill with
poets like W.H. Auden, Stephen Spender, John Betjeman,
Edward Brathwaite, John Ashbery and Seamus Heaney,
and actors and intellectuals like Judi Dench, Dudley Moore,
Diana Rigg, Germaine Greer and R.D. Laing. They read
their poems with freshness and power in front of Ron's photographs at the ICA to an astonished and totally disarmed
'poetry audience'. Then they were invited to do the same in
front of television cameras at the Young Vic in between
future Nobel Literature prize winner Heaney reading his
poems and *The Female Eunuch* author Greer talking about
the poetry of Sylvia Plath. They made friends with them
both. The Austrian 'breath poet' Gerard Ruhm was so
impressed with our own poets that he insisted on coming
back with us to Stepney, and seeing their world. We took
him for a meal in our favourite Brick Lane Bengali restaurant, and he loved it.

The Guardian
22 June 1972.

Maxine Loftus reading *The Lonely Dustman* at the Institute of Contemporary Arts

A pupil of Sir John Cass School, Stepney, London, reading a poem at the ICA about life in the school's neighbourhood. Publication of a book of the pupils' poems led to a teacher, Mr Christopher Searle, being given notice of dismissal. The reading yesterday was part of Poetry International 1972. In the background were photographs of Stepney

Around this time I was contacted by a West End theatre impresario called Bob Swash, who said that he wanted to produce a musical adaptation of the *Stepney Words* story for the London stage. It seemed he was quite a powerful figure with a number of West End successes under his belt. He said that he had seen the success of a Broadway musical called *The Me Nobody Knows,* based around the poems of Harlem school children, and he thought that a musical founded on the *Stepney Words* story could be just as successful. I was very suspicious of his money-making motives, and said I would only be in any way interested if Joan Littlewood would be the proposed musical's director. I'd never met Joan, but she was one of my heroes. I'd been at the second night of *Oh, What a Lovely War* in 1961 at the Theatre Royal, Stratford E.15, and never been so intensely moved in a theatre as I had been that night. Her 'Theatre Workshop' — committed, community-orientated, full of song, criticism, humour and socialist-inspired drama — was to me the closest to Brecht that I had seen, and I loved her work. Swash arranged for us to meet in a pub along Shaftesbury Avenue: Joan, Ron, Swash, Gerry Raffles the co-founder of Theatre Workshop and with Joan was the Labour MP Tom Driberg, a friend of hers.

We started off talking about the Swash proposal. As he outlined it I could tell by Joan's face that she was not enamoured. She said that over her life in the theatre, she had seen so many young people let down and sometimes, destroyed by shattered expectations: actors, writers, directors. She spoke at length about the Irish playwright Brendan Behan, whose plays she had directed and whom she had known closely all through his life in the theatre. She knew the West End dream to be treacherous and fallacious, and she did not want to see any more working-class young people jeopardised by it. She didn't have to convince me: I could see exactly what she was getting at. I thanked Swash for his trouble and said no. So he left, and we got on with talking and drinking for the rest of the afternoon.

But there was a tailpiece. A few months later I was contacted by my friend, the Jamaican novelist Andrew Salkey, and told that there was to be a protest at the Institute of Contemporary Arts, where Enoch Powell had been invited to speak on poetry, a message which I received with some sense of irony, since that was the venue where our poets had read their work so beautifully a few months before. A large, multiracial group of us stood outside, while others gained entry. Adrian Mitchell tried to disrupt proceedings from the inside, but was soon ejected, while the external demonstrators held placards saying 'Poetry and racism don't mix' and other slogans. At the end of the meeting Powell left through the back entrance, but I was surprised to see Joan come out, beside Tom Driberg, who had apparently been a platform speaker alongside Powell. He recognised me and came up to me as I stood between Andrew and the Trinidadian poet, activist and publisher, John La Rose. Then he began abusing me, swearing and saying that we had disrupted free speech. Joan stood next to him, clearly embarrassed, and said nothing as his insults became increasingly contemptuous. Then he moved off with Joan. I stood there, somewhat perplexed, while Andrew said: 'Strange, he said all that to you — we're the usual targets.' And 'Free speech!' I thought; not very free for those being beaten up and chased around the estates of East London by the Powell-adoring 'Paki-bashers.' Not very free at all.

I was getting to know a little about publishing and publishers. By this time, with *Stepney Words* and *Elders,* we'd done a bit ourselves with Reality Press and even won the 'Young Publishers Award'. But as for publishing at the establishment level, it seemed like something of a detached and an alienating process. I was contacted by the international publishing firm, Jonathan Cape, to compile a national children's poetry anthology. I'd been sent so many poems since the strike, and I had a large pile in my bedsitting room from the *Daily Mail* competition. There were some gems, and they were coming in all the time, so I seized upon the Jonathan Cape offer. I went to meet their publishing director at their very smart offices in Bedford Square, and the experience was like a miniature of how I'd always envisaged business was done: a man with a flawless double-breasted suit, a pumping handshake and warm words of introduction, straight down to the proposition, a look at the watch, a rising from the large desk, another handshake and an open door. And all in about five minutes. Tom Maschler, the man's name was, and I looked at their current catalogue as I walked out of the elegant Georgian offices to the plane trees of the square: George Jackson's *Soledad Brother* and *Blood in my Eye,* the collected writings of the Colombian Camilo Torres, *Revolutionary Priest* and Neruda's great poem *The Heights of Macchu Picchu.* The best of company indeed for *Fire Words,* the agreed title of the new anthology.

Then, in mid-1972, I was contacted by Marion Boyars, to write a book on education for the Calder and Boyars 'Open Forum' series. When I looked at their authors' list it looked astonishing: Beckett, Sartre, Ionesco, Yevtushenko, Edward Bond — it went on and on. My book about schools, *This New Season*, came out in early 1973 with a launch in Dame Colet House right opposite the Sir John Cass entrance, and many of the students came to it.

The title appealed to the love of cricket still swilling in my blood, but it actually came from a mysteriously affecting *Stepney Words* lyric by twelve-year-old Charley Mason, who had written:

Give me a reason
This new season
Who I saw
I see no more

When I looked round
There on the ground

I found the question, Why?
And I saw a little boy cry.

168

The book was widely reviewed in the establishment and left press with the *Times Educational Supplement* surprisingly sending it to one of my favourite writers, Colin McInnes, author of such classic postwar London novels as *Absolute Beginners, City of Spades* and *Mr Love and Justice* with its Cable Street setting. McInnes liked the book very much, and wrote in his review (21/9/73):

> I have rarely felt so strongly, as in reading this book, the futility of all 'reviews', and the absolute necessity of the gentle reader's getting hold of the book itself, since the author expresses his ideas far more cogently and imaginatively than my bald summary might suggest. And apart from anything else, the kids' poems are often startling.
>
> Incidently, how often do we see a book in which poetry is restored to its primal function of revealing a social-spiritual situation to us? Books on 'literature' of course quote poets. But how often do social-political writers do so effectively? Sharon of 11, or Imtiaz of 14, often make the point better than Mr Searle (as he intended).

When McInnes wrote of poetry's 'primal function' as a revelation of our 'social-spiritual' condition, I realised something profound about *Stepney Words*. I also began to understand why Trevor Huddleston had loved the poems so much. Blake came back to me, with Donne and Whitman, all walking the streets with Isaac and his friends: no more 'feare' of poetry.

Calder and Boyars also published my first book of my own poems, *Mainland*, and shortly after there was a dispute in the company — which had only a handful of editorial staff — when the editor who had done an excellent job on both my books, an Irishman called Tim O'Grady, decided to mount a lone strike in protest at the firm's refusal to allow a trade union branch in their offices. I sent a long letter to Marion supporting his case and praising his work, and joined him one afternoon on his lonely picket of a publisher who a few months before had published a book with an introduction by Tony Benn, on the work-in by Glasgow trade unionists at the Upper

Clyde Shipbuilders! The contradiction was rife and absurd, and sitting sharing tea and sandwiches with Tim on a Brewer Street, Soho picket line next to the brothels and febrile customers of Raymond's Revue Bar, somehow made it all seem a little surreal. Tim was eventually locked out and never got his job back, but some quarter of a century on he became an applauded novelist himself, and I found myself reviewing his book. It wasn't published by Calder and Boyars, however.

In September 1972, fed up with not being in the classroom and still waiting for the outcome of my case, I asked the Inner London Education Authority, who were now supporting me and still paying my salary, if I could work for nothing in a London school until my case was resolved. They agreed, and when I said I'd like to work somewhere south of the river, the very supportive and poetry-loving Lambeth district inspector, Roy Waters, suggested that I visit the head teacher of Santley Primary School in Brixton, Ms Rebecca Crane. She said she would be pleased to have me working at the school as a supplementary teacher, even though I was untrained and had no previous experience of primary schools. For much of my time there, I became an assistant to a marvellous young teacher called Beverley Bryan, and simply observing her teaching taught me a lot about classroom work with primary-school age pupils. She was a Black Panther, and later co-wrote an important book called *The Heart of the Race*, a history of the struggle of black women in Britain. It was a fine and innovative school with a set of excellent teachers, and after Sir John Cass, I felt very fortunate to be there. I got to know well the music teacher, a jazz trombonist and pianist called Mel Robinson, and I moved into the communal house he shared with others, on Acre Lane. Many Santley pupils came from a grim estate next to the school in Ferndale Road, called Ferndale Court. The flats were unheated, so the council tenants who lived there in the main used the cheapest form of heating, paraffin stoves, to keep warm.

170

There had been a succession of fires started by these neurotic heaters, and some children had been seriously burned. A campaigning group had been set up to persuade Lambeth Council to bring central heating to the flats, but so far it had been unsuccessful.

One morning the children brought to school news of another fire, so Mel and I decided to do something. Mel was a superb visual artist, and he agreed to forge the illustrations for a small children's book on the fires. I wrote a short play-text which was acted out by the children, who wrote some poems, and these were incorporated into a narrative text, with Mel's powerful illustrations. We called the potential book *Ferndale Fires* but went to the other end of London to get it published. I'd had a strong connection with Centerprise Bookshop and community publishers in Hackney ever since they reprinted *Stepney Words* for us in late 1971. Glenn Thompson, the founder, had become a close ally and friend, and Ken Worpole, who ran the community publishing side, was a true pioneer of local publishing and a champion of working-class writing. The innovator behind 'The People's Autobiography of Hackney', he had produced many local books, and as an ex-teacher at Hackney Downs School, he had a singular interest in children's creative writing. Ken was later to become a major force behind the Federation of Worker Writers and Community Publishers, which sought to give a collective national voice to the many emergent local writers' groups breaking forth all over the country. *Ferndale Fires* was launched in Lambeth Teachers' Centre with poetry from some of the children, plus Andrew Salkey, John La Rose and a young and dynamic Linton Kwesi Johnson reading their poetry, with funds from the book's sales going to support the Ferndale Court Tenants' Action Group. The book wasn't so different in its content and objectives to *Stepney Words,* although it was certainly more explicitly wedded to community action. Yet the school and its head teacher welcomed it, helped its development and applauded its

171

FERNDALE FIRES A Children's Story. Text : Chris Searle. Illustrations and music: Mel Robinson. Poems: 4th year children (1973) of Santley Junior School, Brixton, London SW4. Published in January 1974 by REALITY PRESS. Distributed by Centerprise, 66a Dalston Lane, London E8. Printed by Expression Printers Ltd, London N1. Thanks to Beverley Bryan, Fred Corbett, Ken Worpole and Glenn Thompson. Text Copyright © Chris Searle 1974. Illustrations and music copyright © Mel Robinson 1974. Poems copyright © individual poets. Dedicated to children and teachers of Santley Junior School. Any profits go to Unity Centre Bookshop and Ferndale Tenants Action Group.

Ferndale Fires
Cover illustration
Mel Robinson

outcomes, contrary to the attitudes of the powers at Sir John Cass. I spent just two terms at Santley, but my experiences there filled me with a new hope and optimism.

Living with Mel and his housemates, I found that I had moved into a house of musicians. Three of us decided to form a poetry/song/jazz trio, which we called 'Two Fingers'. Mel, an ex-slideman of 'The Temperance Seven', played trombone and piano, our confrere Graham blew tenor saxophone and clarinet and played guitar and banjo and I banged a military bass drum which Mel found for me in a second-hand jumble shop. I shouted out Joe Hill songs like *Pie in the Sky* and my own lyrics to jazz standards. So *Pennies from Heaven* became *Crumbs off the Table* and *St. James Infirmary* transformed to *St. Katherine's Dockyard*, telling the tale of the huge profits being made by the Taylor Woodrow construction multinational in the docklands redevelopment. Mel caressed his keys and played *Lullaby of the Leaves* while I recited my poem to the beautiful grove of plane trees outside my flat in Albert Gardens, so close to the traffic and toxic air of Commercial Road. *Stepney Plane Trees,* I called it:

What nurtured you?
Some people say
The air which makes you beautiful
Is killing the world.

Your leaves are girls' faces
Your leaves soften London.
Your mottled trunk, peeling face
Tells of your stoicism.
Your itchy-backs make me laugh
Hanging like ear-rings,
And when they fall
Singing children kick them down the road.

How can you grow in this air?
How can you flourish while
Rushing artics, roaring engines
Give you your breath?
A city's beauty is a brave beauty.

173

British occupying troops in Belfast had begun going into schools to arrest and detain teenage schoolboys from republican families. *No Recruiting Song*, featuring Mel's quasi-tailgate trombone slides playing the *Galway Bay* theme and Graham's chinking guitar chords gave a powerful backing to this topical message:

Please don't go across the sea to Ireland,
Please don't go down Ballymurphy way,
Don't listen to the bullets flying madly
For British soldiers go where bosses say.

The Irish lads who walk the streets of Belfast
Come from the same world you know every day,
They're working class and struggling out of school-chains,
And looking hard for jobs to get their pay.

Why go and fight them when they live as you do?
Why go and fight your brothers from the Falls?
Why go and fight the boys who are your comrades
Around the bombed-out bricks of Belfast walls.

For Alex, Kevin, Seamus are your schoolmates
And they've got troops against them night and day,
So give them your support and free their people
And get the soldiers out their country's way.

But it was *David Oluwale* that proved to be our strongest piece, with a rampaging tune written by Mel, telling the story of the death of the homeless Nigerian immigrant, who for years was victimised, abused, beaten and finally killed by two Leeds police officers, his body retrieved from the River Aire in April 1969.

You made your passage through the seas
From Africa to Leeds,
You were young and dancing,
You never knew your knees.

CHORUS:

David Oluwale
Your blackness soon will rise,
David Oluwale
Your drums will pound the skies.

174

They threw you into doorways,
They kicked you in the balls,
They smashed your head till you were dazed,
From your mouth blood drools.

They hounded you for twenty years,
They saw that you were black,
When you were lame they gave you tears,
They kept you on the rack.

All along the River Aire
They chased you in their hate,
They screamed out 'UGGIE, UGGIE!'
With the power of the state.

Out of the cold black river
They dragged you in your death,
You couldn't even shiver,
The police thugs stole your breath.

Kitching and Ellerker
With the state bound in their fist
And all the blue-armed racists
Lied into the mist.

Justice Hinchcliffe frowned around,
He spoke out from his fright,
He said that you'd be scaring
To come across at night.

Justice Hinchcliffe called you
'A nuisance to the police',
But now our people's anger
Is never going to cease.

We performed *David Oluwale* at a solidarity fundraising event at Conway Hall for the journalist Paul Foot, the writer of *The Rise of Enoch Powell,* who was facing legal attacks for his exposés of the establishment; and at 'The Moving Left Show' at the Roundhouse in Chalk Farm, where we found ourselves on the same bill as some of Britain's finest and most audacious jazz musicians: saxophonists Evan Parker and Lol Coxhill (who I used to regularly hear busking by the Thames in Charing Cross), Mike Westbrook's Big Band with his orchestrations of Blake's poems, guitarist Derek Bailey and the revolutionary trom-

175

bonist Paul Rutherford. Also there was drummer John Stevens, who joined us at the Half Moon Theatre for another session with his alto-saxophonist comrade Trevor Watts and their friend the American trumpeter Bobby Bradford, who had played during the fifties with Ornette Coleman's first quartet in Los Angeles. John's drums were like thunder that night as we performed *David Oluwale*.

Calder and Boyars also published the influential book by the Austrian priest Ivan Illich, *De-Schooling Society*. I'd read it, and wanted to challenge him about his dismissal of state schools, and met him one morning in Marion Boyars' house. He told me that the main problem with education was schools and teachers — that the 'school' was a deformed institution and that teachers working within the state system were like 'good prostitutes', despoiling themselves while implanting a falsified and state-licensed version of knowledge within their students. There was much to agree with in these ideas, but much to take issue with too. I thought about his words. Was teaching in a school like Sir John Cass like selling yourself, serving an institution that was so clearly misconceived, unjust and full of scorn for its majority? Not if you thwarted it from the inside, impeded its reactionary objectives and made its learning spaces classrooms of resistance; for how else could you free the precious resources of school for working-class children? How could you be a 'good prostitute' then, I asked him. I said that I believed that the true comprehensive school system was an entirely different proposition, and that through it you could genuinely help children find their true potential with an end to streaming, division and exclusion in an embrace of mixed-ability teaching, democratic progress and the unity of education and real life that reached out to the communities that gave its trust and offered its children to the school's rich and diverse humanity in a collective and comradely setting. But this could only finally come to pass with a nation like England ridding itself of elitist, privately-funded schools that were such bastions

176

of class privilege. He shook his head as if I were a lost cause to him, and we shook hands and smiled at each other as if we were never going to fully agree.

And I left Chelsea and its fashionable, gentrified streets and came home to Stepney.

But there was another Chelsea story too. I was contacted by the Royal Court Theatre in Sloane Square with an offer of some free tickets for the play *Skyvers* about a class of disaffected inner city young Londoners and their experiences at school, written by the Jamaica-born dramatist and ex-teacher Barry Reckord. I turned up with a dozen or so Sir John Cass fourth formers, and we had a great night, really absorbing the play and its seemingly very familiar characters. And there, on the front of the programme, was the anonymous poem which had been left on a classroom desk, which prefaced *Stepney Words*, with its poignant opening lines:

I am just a boy
With a lot of dreams...

I thought about all the powerful plays and performances I had seen at this theatre when I was at school: from Beckett to Shakespeare, from Gogol to Osborne from Edward Bond's *Saved* to my play of plays — John Arden's *Serjeant Musgrave's Dance* — and I could only marvel at my unknown student's poem being read again by audiences in the other end of London. Strange and ever-surprising are the ways of poetry, I thought, as we caught the tube home, all the long way from west to east.

Meanwhile my case went on — and on. At the end of February 1972 there was a special, quasi-legal meeting of the Governors at the Sir John Cass Foundation offices at 32 Jewry Street in the City, with witnesses including the ILEA divisional officers and divisional inspector, the head teacher, deputy head teacher and three classroom teachers appearing for the governors, and Ron, Chiefie and two mothers of *Stepney Words* poets appearing for me alongside a very strong letter of support from Trevor

Huddleston. I was accused in different and contradictory terms. The militaristic ILEA Divisonal Officer stated that I had been dismissed army-style because I had 'refused to obey the orders of a superior officer.' To the Rev. Gibbs my offence was one of 'spiritual pride', as if I were the apostate in some medieval ecclesiastical dispute. Both reasons seemed archaic and absurd to me. The head of the remedial stream talked with fervour about his students being 'maladjusted in many, many diverse ways.' He went on to declare that 'it only needs one little tiny thing and it will spark off an eruption. To my mind, these children are now completely volcanic. I cannot always control them, neither can other members of my staff. They are actually trying to control us.' It seemed that the rejects were revolting but the school could still not recognise it, and carried on regardless. As for Huddleston, his prescient comments on the burgeoning influence of the 1968 generation were rejected by the governors, and my dismissal was confirmed: 'We live in a time when the whole concept of authority in society, in church and in institutions is in revolutionary change. It is quite unrealistic to expect either young teachers or their pupils to be unaffected by this situation.'

The divisional inspector, Mr Iles, had come to my classroom just three weeks after the strike. I was unforewarned of his visit, which I felt was unreasonable. He said to the panel 'It is significant that he is the only probationer I have known who has challenged the right of the district inspector to observe him without prior notice being given.' The class were fifteen-year-old fourth formers, and we were reading a Brian Patten poem from *The Mersey Sound,* a popular collection of poems by Liverpool poets, of which the English Department had a set. The poem was *The River Arse* which the inspector mistakenly thought was a student's poem, as one of them had copied it into her exercise book. It begins in this way:

> The rain is teeming
> across the river
> falling on the arse of
> > a nude girl swimming
> without even a splash
> > and O it's such a pretty little arse...

After the class and the departure of the students, he objected to the use of the poem, saying that he disapproved of it, even though it was a poem the class liked, and which had provoked a lot of interest. He had been reading through some of the student's notebooks while the lesson was in progress, and he picked out this poem by one of the boys called *Soldier*:

> I was a soldier
> A cockney soldier
> A man that was born to die
> Only cockney blokes get killed
> Stuffy officers stay back safely.
>
> I was a soldier
> A cockney soldier
> Before I died on the hill
> With a bullet in my heart
> I clawed my way to Hell.
>
> My brother was a soldier
> A bloody good soldier
> But he was also born to die.
> But he died by being shot
> Climbing over the wire back to our trenches
> We both met in Hell.

The poem was to be in *Stepney Words 2* and it provoked a lot of discussion. Why was his brother shot? Which side had killed him? It made me think of Isaac and his generation, and their trench agony. But this inspector's only comment was to highlight the use of the word 'bloody'. Should we be encouraging our pupils to use such words? Then he found another poem in an exercise book which he suggested was 'about drugs'. I have read this poem many dozens of times and its images of washing on a backyard line in the polluted city air, always seemed to me to be just about that,

179

unless the reader has a strange psychedelic vision of their own. Again it was to be in *Stepney Words 2,* printed on one of Ron's photographs of a Spitalfields washing line:

I have just seen my mother's washing,
They still look dirty though,
But my mother's nosing
Looking at the dirty washing
Hoping it might fade away.

She washed a white shirt,
She tried to make it clean,
But when she hung it on the line
It was the ugliest sight you have seen.

Mr Iles went on to assert that 'I see inherent dangers in the publication of this type of poetry,' and that the teacher's task is to move his students 'to transcend their environment and not dwell the whole time on its less desirable aspects.' And he quoted from his inspection report: 'I am profoundly disturbed by his outlook and attitude in his teaching.' And never, I thought, encourage your students to write about their mother's washing! It may hide a serious drugs agenda. Of course, if he'd bothered to read the whole of *Stepney Words,* he would have read more than one poem condemning the use of drugs by students in the same class, as, for example, *Gale is Dead*, which also sought to find the reasons why:

Gale is dead
We shed a tear
Nobody knew what she wanted
She wanted a mother

She could not live in just one place
They had to move her about
They didn't really want her
Nor did her real mother

In prison now she hears girls talk about drugs
And the way life would look
She thought it sounded better

Out of prison she is free
Has a job and
A place to live
Does not need to worry

But prison friends
They now arrive
They talk of things
That sound much better

They all go to Piccadilly
Gale goes along too
She takes some drugs
She takes some drugs

Gale is dead
We shed a tear
For she was not wanted
Not even by her real mother

Christine's poem was provoked by watching a television screening of the documentary with the same title. Lorraine saw it too, and wrote her poem, *Escape*:

Along the roads of the Dilly
People are sitting close together
Trying to find an escape from life.

They live and eat in dirt and rubbish.
In the crowds nothing matters.
Trying to find peace of mind
Love too much, or not enough

The escape will come soon
A needle, that's all it takes
A jab in the arm, the escape will come
At last... at last... at last
Reality is going, the fantasy world
Is appearing in their eyes
The dream of how they want the world to be
Will come to them soon
But their world is seen in a haze of dreams
It would never, never be true
But when you've tried to escape once
You will have to escape over
                    over
                        over
                            again.

Lorraine's last verse has stayed with me for forty-five years. So many times I have read it, and so many times the nakedness of its truth has stuck in my heart.

181

Chiefie's contribution to my defence in this inquiry was huge, and it made me feel so proud that my old teacher who had formed my love for poetry, for Isaac and for all the child-poets that I had ever taught, was standing up for me in such a principled way. When the NUT barrister asked him about the value of encouraging children to write poetry, he said: 'It is to talk about the things that are really important to them, deep down within themselves. These things are highly charged with emotion. In writing these things which are important and significant to them they are undertaking a struggle with language, and this is important. They achieve through the writing of poetry some kind of recognition, and for the pupils' development as writers this is important. Thirdly, it is important for the child to be able to write about things that are concerning him. Poetry is very personal, intimate and through it one can express in a legitimate form, attitudes, views, feelings and thoughts that one cannot so easily express in other ways. That is the great value of writing poetry, and poetry is just about the most difficult thing to get from children in any sincere way. One can get them to do exercises, rhyming jingles, but to get sincere expressions of feeling is one of the most difficult tasks I know for a teacher. It is based always on mutual trust between pupil and teacher. You cannot get that kind of writing in *Stepney Words* or any other creative writing, unless there is a real trust and respect between teacher and pupil. I can only say that this presentation contains the qualities of freshness and honesty and sincerity on the part of the children writing which is the most valuable thing about it.' And he quoted from Timmy's poem, calling it full of 'compassion, very poignant, very touching'. To me it was a children's blues, an East London children's blues, naked and searching:

I go to the park
To look at the view,
I see lots of people
But maybe they are lonely too

I go on a bus
There's such a lot of fuss
But I bet there's lonely people
Amongst all of us

I wish I was married
And had lots of kids
Maybe then I would not
Be as lonely as this.

Hearing Chiefie argue so powerfully for children's poetry reminded me how I had brought him my own poems all those years ago in Hornchurch, how he had encouraged and found faith in me, and was even doing so now. What it is to be a teacher, I thought, what it is to be a teacher for all your life.

The inquiry brought me other precious moments. The testimonies of two Stepney mothers, given in these intimidating wood-panelled city offices, in the midst of a host of grey-suited unsmiling men, was not easy for them and they were both very nervous. Maudie, the mother of Ramona, the twelve-year-old who had written *The Stall and Me* and other poems, was the first to give evidence. She began by saying how surprised she was when her daughter started writing poetry: 'She surprised me because before that she was all athletics — swimming, netball and things like that, you know, so when she started writing poetry I was absolutely amazed. I asked her if she was interested in it and she said it was because Mr Searle had told them that everybody could write poetry. He said that they were all capable of writing poetry and she used to sit down at home of an evening and write poetry.' She recalled when I called in to see her when I was thinking of publishing *Stepney Words*: 'I thought it was a marvellous idea because I mean, let's face it, kids in Stepney have not got much of a good outlook and to see their poems published in a book, well, I thought this was absolutely marvellous. Ramona has lots of friends and I know their parents. They were all in favour of it.' And she went on to talk about the strike: 'I had to admire the kids for doing it, I really did, because to me it seemed they had taken over the grown-ups' part. The grown-ups at the school were acting like children. This to me was the governors' attitude. They were acting like children. It was as though the kids had taken on the adults' part by going on strike. This is what it seemed to me. If I had not been at work I think I would have been down there with the kids.'

The sense of fear and anxiety these brave mothers felt was underlined when the mother of Lesley, the poet of *Autumn Morning in Stepney Churchyard*, asked the chair of the inquiry: 'Through my coming here like this, nothing can come back on my child, can it?' The chair gave his reassurances, but I remember well how worried she looked and how much courage coming forward to speak up for *Stepney Words* must have taken, as Mrs Samuels described the way in which her daughter consulted her about the poems she wrote, almost as if the writing were an act of the family: 'She used to go upstairs mostly, you know. She would come to me and say, "what do you think of this?" And well, when I went to school it all had to rhyme, but now apparently it does not have to rhyme, and that is poetry.' And this within a hundred yards of where Isaac used to live. I could only marvel. And I marvelled forty years later when I met these brave mothers' daughters again — now in their mid-fifties, at a *Stepney Words* reunion. Lesley worked as a senior administrator in the largest burns unit of the largest hospital in Perth, Western Australia. It was a long, long way from Stepney Churchyard. And Ramona had just finished qualifying as a primary school teacher in Essex, full of her mother's courage and ebullience.

And there were supportive fathers too. Among them was a local Tory, Tony Crowther, who I used to meet in his local pub in White Horse Lane, Stepney Green, for many a pint and discussion. When two hostile letter-writers to the *East London Advertiser* attacked me for daring to fight for my job, he wrote his own riposte which was published in the *Advertiser* on June 29 1973:

'I would ask K. Allvey where he thinks he would fit into today's liberalistic education system? I would like to ask did he conclude that Searle fitted into the class of people branded as wicked, evil, full of treachery etc., etc., which is how one immediately defines 'natural satirist'. Have you ever had the pleasure of meeting and speaking to the gentleman? For gentleman he is, Mr Allvey!

The majority of our population are working class – have working class cultures and speak their true working class language. Please let's not pretend to be other than what we are.

In reply to Louis Behr's criticisms that Searle tolerates no concepts of loyalties towards colleagues in his profession other than supporters of his doctrines. There are many things that Mr Searle believes in and too obviously has differing views to many people. This I believe to be his democratic right.

I was a supporter of Searle during the long drawn-out battle with the educational authorities against what I believed to be a true misjudgement of facts which brought about his suspension. I also have a daughter who was taught by Searle and she too knows what her mind and mouth are for, Mr Behr. Nothing would make my daughter and myself happier than for her to have Searle as her English master during her coming GCE course.

I am a Conservative, Mr Behr, and a very blue one at that. I also have a loyal friend in Searle.'

In May and June, I appealed to the Inner London Education Authority's Staff Appeals Committee to rescind my dismissal, which had been confirmed by the governors at the previous enquiry, and another long hearing ensued. References were made to recent strikes of the Schools Action Union, as the governors sought to move the focus of the hearing away from the poetry 'disobedience' to other emphases — in particular my 'spiritual pride' and 'disruptiveness' — and to articles I had written during my period of suspension from the school, and my perceived attitude towards school uniform. One of the most vocal of the governors, Mr Dromgoole, declared that, 'Frankly it is going to be a disastrous situation if he returns. It is going to mean trouble and it will put the headmaster in an impossible situation and it is going to mean trouble with the staff and trouble with the pupils of the school, and it really would be an impossible situation for us if he were at this stage to return, and it would be disastrous.' As for the Head of Business Studies supporting the governors, she said of the students: 'I think they might be led to believe if he did come back that it was mob rule that had succeeded as opposed to redress by a person they felt had suffered injustice.' Still the strike and its prodigious organisation by the students was being labelled as 'mob rule'. Hadn't the same been said when the Matchgirls made their historic strike at the Bryant and May factory in Bow in 1988? When the dockers made their pioneering mass strike and marched up Commercial Road for the 'Dockers' tanner' in 1889? When school children from all over the country, including Stepney, made their strikes in 1911? When East Enders stopped Mosley at Cable Street in 1936? When Jack Dash led his wildcat strikes of local dockers all through the Sixties? To admit the Sir John Cass strike as well-organised and humane as well as pre-cocious, would be, as another 'remedial' teacher attested, 'condoning their rioting, and this is what really and truly worries me... I don't want them to begin to destroy that world. I mean, we are here to help them into the world: we are not here to encourage them to riot, or to encourage them in such a manner, are we?'

In this context any teacher at the school who came forward to give evidence on behalf of the children, *Stepney Words* or me was going to be up against it, and my two ex-colleagues who appeared for my defence who were still at the school, showed immense professional courage. One was Beth, the PE teacher who was on the coach coming back from Fairlop on the Wednesday after-noon before the strike, who had overheard the fifth year girls' planning. She referred to the position of local parents: 'I feel the parents back Mr Searle to the hilt on this and if the decision goes against him, they, as parents, are going to think "Here's a teacher who taught our children, who had their interests at heart and he has been given the sack for it." Yet there are other teachers who they, as parents, don't feel do their jobs, who don't have the interests of children at heart and they can still have their jobs.' As she exposed the 'referendum' presented to staff immediately before the hearing and used as evidence at it, where individual teachers were canvassed by the Head of Business Studies to tick boxes whether or whether not they wanted me back, I could only admire her fortitude. As for my other colleague, Mary revealed to the hearing the pettiness of the school management in blocking my telephone calls out from the school, and how that had impacted on her: 'I think, looking back, I was not fully aware of what was going on sometimes. But there was one incident that did affect me personally and that was the time when the telephone calls were cut to Mr Searle. I can't remember when it was — sometime in the early summer last year — and I felt there and then; "This is my responsibility." I felt very angry that any staff member could not have their telephone calls taken through the office. On that particular day Mr Searle was trying to sort out a problem with the Film Society that night. The film had not turned up and he couldn't get a call out and it came to my attention. I remember him saying in the late morning: "I can't get this call out, I will have to wait until lunchtime," and then he came and told me he had heard that he was not to make any calls out at all, and it was left to one member of the office staff to tell him. I wondered then what was happening.' Shortly after one of the panel asked her: 'Does it strike you as strange that all the witnesses today, except one who is part-time, are all women?' 'Does that strike you as rather odd?' she replied, 'Yes', was the panellist's answer. 'Can I ask you why?' she asked back. 'No, I'm afraid not. You are here to answer my questions,' asserted the panellist, officiously. Her answer, after a pause, held real drama and almost had me, and others, applauding: 'Perhaps it is because women have something more to say than men.' I felt proud that she was there supporting me.

Perhaps the ILEA committee thought so too, because they decided that my case was the stronger and they refused the governors' recommendation to dismiss me. But it still wasn't over and the case went to the government level, to be considered and decided upon by the Department of Education and Science. I wasn't optimistic of the outcome as the Secretary of State for Education at the time was one Margaret Thatcher, not known for her affection for left-wing teachers and an open opponent of the ILEA. To schools she was 'The Milk Snatcher', the Tory minister who had in 1971, ended free milk in primary schools. So although I now had the largest local education authority in Britain on my side, I still wasn't hopeful.

Even so, the national press still broadly supported me. The Labour-supporting *Daily Mirror* had dedicated an editorial to my case, entitled 'The Good Teacher', praising the *Stepney Words* poems as 'lively and moving' and concluding that 'a stimulating teacher should be ungrudgingly offered the chance to return where he belongs – in the classroom. Quickly.' And more surprisingly, the very Tory *Daily Express* published a feature article the day before the final governmental decision was to be announced, under the headline 'The Man on Margaret's Mind Today', referring to me, photograph and all. Its author, the paper's Education Correspondent Bruce Kemble, frequently rang my father in his City office for the inside story, and they became quite friendly. It certainly didn't bother me and did me no harm, although what Mrs Thatcher thought of Kemble's article, I have no idea.

Carrying on at Santley, one astonishing classroom incident happened. I was teaching in an assistant role in a class of eleven year-olds, when I could sense that they were unhappy. I later understood why. Their teacher for that day, a middle-aged white woman, had said something to one of the Jamaican girls — the class was about ninety percent children of Caribbean origin — which was felt to be offensive and racist, and they were clearly upset about it. We were only a few minutes into the lesson, when a large Jamaican boy suddenly stood up on his table (each table had four students sitting at it) and began to chant loudly across the class, 'Black is power, White is flour!' Swiftly the other three children at his table stepped up on the table and joined him, repeatedly chanting the same rhyming words. Then in a virtual instant the whole class was doing the same. I was sitting at one of the tables with a group of pupils, and suddenly I was the only person in the room sitting down. All the class, including its four white children, were on their tables repeating the rhyme. The teacher tried to stop them but her raised voice had no volume over the children's collective repetition of the couplet. I sat there, silent and astonished while the teacher went to fetch the deputy head. By that time the class seemed to be satisfied that it had made its point, and by the time the deputy head arrived the children were quietly back in their seats. I felt I had been witness to something not only dramatic, but prophetic. I had no idea then that eight years after, when these children would be in their late teens, Brixton would be alive and resonant with their protests on its streets, confronting the police and the racist underbelly of the state.

Chapter Seven
Cable Street Strut

In May 1973, almost two years after my dismissal from Sir John Cass and the children's strike, I heard that the governors' appeal had been unsuccessful and my dismissal was invalid: I could return to the school. I had wanted to demonstrate to my students that trade union action could be successful as it had been so many times in East London from the Matchgirls onwards. The outstanding work and loyalty of the National Union of Teachers had won that day for me — also creating a precedent for all other probationary teachers, that they could not be summarily dismissed, that there had to be a properly constituted hearing and an opportunity for them to put their cases before their employers. I was sure without the children's strike and the publicity and solidarity that it generated, I would have suffered an unexposed hole-in-the-corner sacking, which has been the fate of many teachers over the years. But the children's action, its sheer spectacle and the precious brilliance of its organisation meant that my case could not be ignored. And for many of them it was an essential educative moment which taught them, at such a young age, a lesson they never forgot. Jimmy, the eleven-year-old poet of the lines that began 'I'm old, I need rest', said to Alan Dein, a BBC interviewer nearly three decades later, as a part of his BBC radio documentary about *Stepney Words,* which he called *The Fire is in Our Hearts*: 'I can't explain it. I can feel it now, it was brilliant. The power and the collective commitment and strength, it was something I've never experienced since. The energy — it was just unbelievable.' And others, including another *Stepney Words* poet who was a fireman for over three decades, have told me recently how much those hours on the green outside the school and the march to Trafalgar Square apprenticed and prepared them for the struggles they had at their workplaces over many years. As for the long-awaited Thatcher intervention, the *Daily Express* of April 14 quoted me verbatim: 'The meanest, most retrogressive and class-biased Education Minister for generations has been pressurised to decide in my favour because of the support and solidarity shown to me by classroom teachers, local children and parents and the National Union of Teachers, who have stood up and fought for me.'

During the afternoon of Christmas Eve 2014, I had a telephone call from an ex-Sir John Cass student who I hadn't seen since 1971. He'd got my number from David Bishop, an ex-Stepney Green schoolboy who had watched the strike from a high classroom in the school, and seen senior boys from Stepney Green scaling its tall iron gates to join in solidarity with the Sir John Cass strikers. Bishop was now writing a book about the strike and had contacted many of those who took part, like Leroy. He still sounded like the same boy who had been in the low-stream third year class I used to teach drama to once a week — full of life, energy and laughter, with a number of Caribbean and mixed-race students, like he was, who were sharply intelligent and imaginative but not seen as academic by the school in any sense, and allowed to wallow in the school's lower streams. They loved reading the playscripts that I gave them — particularly those which had songs, which they sang with a rich gusto and humour, like *Oh, What a Lovely War* and Peter Terson's story of the life of a disillusioned football supporter, *Zigger Zagger*. On the phone some four and a half decades on, he reminded me how one of his classmates had told me they'd never been to a theatre, never seen a live performance and how I'd got them some tickets for the musical adaptation of *The Canterbury Tales* in the West End, and a dozen of us went to see it one night.

He told me how much the visit had meant to them, and I remembered how they had responded with so much fervour to *The Miller's Tale* and *The Wife of Bath's Tale* with all their Chaucerian bawdiness and shenanigans. 'It was great!' he said, 'and that's why we came out on strike for you!' and I thanked Chaucer too. As for Leroy, he told me he'd also had a memorable night because he sat next to one of the girls in his class that he'd liked for ages, and he'd found the courage to ask her out too. He also said that the experience of the strike had served him in good stead for forty years as a local council worker and trade unionist.

But now I was back. I also moved back into my old Albert Gardens flat, which I had lent to a friend while I was in Brixton, and returned to Sir John Cass for the final term of the 1972–73 school year, agreeing to take groups of 'remedial' students for the rest of the year, on the basis of being given a full English timetable for the upcoming school year and being treated like any other member of staff. As I wandered around the school again and saw many familiar young faces, I knew that many of my old students had left, but there was still the same vitality, humour and dynamism springing from the class-rooms and corridors. Many of the old staff faces were there, and although the Head of PE, a lively Welshman, who had been a strong opponent during the months of the dispute, made a public, staffroom event of shaking my hand, announcing that although he didn't agree with me, he wanted to look forward to a new era within the school, I found this wasn't typical. I was virtually ostracised by many of the other teachers, particularly those who had openly supported the governors. But there were some very friendly new members of staff, particularly two new colleagues in the English Department (one of whom had been my replacement) and we soon became friends. At lunchtime on my first day back I wandered over the green to Stepney Churchyard, and further over to the adventure playground where I used to spend many a lunch break with the younger students and where we would go directly after the last morning class with my science

192

colleague, the Melbourne-born Rob, a dear friend who had resigned his Sir John Cass post in solidarity with me after I was sacked, and who now taught in a school in South London. I also remembered David's exhilarating *Stepney Words* poem, *The Rolling Rope*, which he had written in an afternoon class immediately after such an adventure playground session:

As you run up the ramp
You've got to be fast
Or else you'll slide back down again.
When you get to the top, you can see the tops of people's heads
Then you walk along a thin, half-burnt log —
You've got to be careful or else you'll fall off,
Then you come to the rope, the rolling rope
Somebody swings it up
You grab hold of it
Then you jolt
You're on, you're on the rolling rope,
You feel like Tarzan falling through the trees.
You look at the post,
It's coming nearer and nearer
You think you're going to crash,
But the rolling rope is slowing down
As if it knows you're in danger...
Then it stops.
You get off and start again.

Walking home through the Mountmorres Estate, I thought of the poem that Maxine had written during the dustbinmen's strike in the weeks before the *Stepney Words* events. She had been earning some extra pocket money removing some garbage from outside her neighbours' front doors, and had composed this one evening after she had finished her work:

I, the lonely dustman, go walking along the dusty streets,
    my only truthful friends are the rubbish.
They come rushing against me, so that I can throw my
    only friends away into the world of rubbish.
Every day my friends are thrown into the streets and put
    into iron cages,
And they rely on me to take them out of a dreadful, dirty
    and awkward world of horror.

Then along comes a different world.
It's a dust-cart.
Then once more my friends rush against me and I throw
   them into a world of darkness.
But now we are on strike, I see my friends wherever I go.

Amongst the millions of people who read this when it got published in the *Daily Mirror* was a Devonian dustman who wrote a warm letter to Maxine's mother; 'I saw Maxine's verse in the *Daily Mirror,* and I think she has a real understanding of people like the dustman and his world of the dustcart, and the bins full of rubbish. As a dustman myself I can see the love and hate that go with the job, up early in the morning in all sorts of weather, and thinking who will be my best friend today? The dust-cart really is a different world, for people are glad to know you once a week and then forget all about you until the day comes around again. Some say hello, but most prefer to keep a safe distance. I think all the verses of the children in the *Mirror* showed understanding of the world they lived in, and that what is missing is true friendship between people.' Many miles and years separated these two writers, yet they had met and begun to understand each other across them.

It wasn't only dustbinmen that were reading and appreciating these poems. Poets, academics and critics were having their say too, sometimes emerging from any-thing-but-progressive journals. *The Times Educational Supplement's* reviewer, Richard Burns, had described *Stepney Words* as 'a commentary on Blake. These are the real children of Albion.' In the journal *Encounter* (later directly associated with the C.I.A.) the poet D.J. Enright, whose poems I had studied at school with Chiefie, wrote: 'What is inescapably painful, and frightening, about these laconic verses, and finally most impressive, is the children's clearsightedness, their unwavering gaze — or, at any rate, the total absence of illusion.' And I wondered if he was thinking about 15 year-old Sandra's poem, *Facts and Fantasy*:

194

Fantasy is so unreal
but it's nice to dream.
Fact puts the truth to you
so it's quite cruel.

People escape to fields of fantasy
because they can't face the truth,
But, never mind, the time will come
for them to see the facts.

Life flies past in a world of fantasy
but in fact it goes quite slow,
So why dream of fantasy
when you have to see the truth one day.

And in an extraordinary essay in the journal *Books and Bookmen* (women writers were still considered exceptions in a man's literary world, even in 1971!) the educationalist and critic David Holbrook, whose early career as an English teacher in a Suffolk secondary modern had given rise to his innovative study, *English for the Rejected,* compared the *Stepney Words* poems to Yeats, Solzhenitsyn, Shakespeare, Joyce, James Baldwin, Heaney and Arthur Waley's translations of Chinese poetry. He wrote of their 'skill and existentialist passion' and said 'they speak of the human predicament at its deepest level of suffering and aspiration. For children to be trained to mean what they say is a great gift to their humanity — not least in a world which is so full of the trivial, superficial and meretricious.' Reading this, I thought: and this all happened in a Stepney classroom, and in the streets and the very few open spaces that surround it. And in Isaac's streets too, what would he have thought? And weren't my classes full of new Isaacs, for the children of Blake these children certainly were, but weren't they also children of Isaac, with each poem they wrote a determined shout that they would live so much more than 'the half-used life'.

My national anthology of children's poems, *Fire Words,* had appeared in late 1972, with *The Times* devoting a whole page to it. As I read through it, the poems coming from everywhere in this, my country, I thought to myself

'Yes, this is Britain, this is what we have to change!' and my attention turned again to a poem which to me was about all those boys I had left behind in Hylands, and all those struggling in the low streams of Sir John Cass who had rescued my job for me. It was written by a seventeen-year-old boy called Peter Gresty, who was from Greater Manchester, a city where I was going to end my teaching life in 2012. It had no title: it didn't need one:

I am one of those secondary moderners,
The ones that the future holds nothing in store for.
Don't anyone tell me I have a future,
Because I am one of a million fleas
Trapped in a land of giant bees.
When I left school my heart was set on writing,
When I left school I didn't know that all my life
I'd be fighting
Something called a working man's ditch,
Where the poorer get poor and the richer get rich.
Already my bones begin to ache
And my mind is drugged to hell with all the trash of life, my life
Already at seventeen my soul begins to stretch and awake,
And I wish with all my brain I could go back to sleep again.

Future, bah!
What future have I?
I'll tell you what the fruitful 'Garden of Eden' has for me,
To exist in a ball of confusion and constant delusion, and die.
But if I could choose my destiny,
If but, by a little bit of luck, I could see where I'm going,
My eyes would see a class of writer, like that of Mark Twain,
I would paint for the children of the earth such colourful figures
My pen would paint, and for all people I would create.
Such dreams my mind does weave
My hands do feel, my heart does grieve
Never to write such stories.
My future, is long drowning years
All made up of eight hours, five days and holidays of one week or two.
I must go on, plodding on with the broken spirits,
The wild and the meek,
    the strong and the weak,
This then is my future.

When I read his poem now, I realise he's sixty and probably approaching the end of a working life. What did he do for more than forty years? Did he ever become a writer? Or did his poem in *Fire Words* correctly chart and prophesy his life? Perhaps one day I'll know.

The anthology created all sorts of waves. At the National Theatre, the revolutionary dramatist Edward Bond had quoted one of its poems in the programme notes of his translation from the German of Frank Wedekind's play about adolescence and sexual repression, *Spring Awakening*. It was the precociously worldly-wise lyric, *My Parents* by a ten year old boy from Ashford, Kent, Mark Vinten.

They gave me life
Can it be that what I am
Is theirs?
They cannot know my thoughts and hopes
And fears.

They gave me life
Yet all I am is mine
Not theirs.
I've lived within my self alone
For years.

They gave me life
To run and think and grow my way
Not theirs.
Now I can give to them my happiness
Not tears.

Then one of my hero-actors, Colin Welland – the future screenwriter of the Academy Award-winning film *Chariots of Fire*, sent me a message about the anthology and asked me to meet him. As we sat and talked about *Fire Words* in a West End cafe off St Martin's Lane, I remembered well that this was the man who had played Mr Farthing, Billy Casper's English teacher, in Ken Loach's film of *Kes*, who had encouraged Billy to tell his classroom story of the kestrel with all the boy's raw South Yorkshire eloquence and figurative power. When I had seen the film, his lesson had been an exemplar to me of how to teach. I was thrilled to be talking to him – an ex-teacher too, and especially as he had played P.C. David Graham, one of the squad-car Liverpool policemen in *Z-Cars*, my favourite TV drama from my schooldays. *Fire Words* was leading me towards meetings and treasured experiences like this, provoked by *Stepney Words* and Isaac, moments I had never dreamed of.

Two incidents at Sir John Cass confirmed the kind of culturally exclusive and fearful institution it truly was. One day, from the classroom next to mine, I heard some beautiful and totally unexpected sounds as my students were writing their poetry. It sounded like the perfect accompaniment. It was the tune of *Blue Monk* tapped and blown out on sticks and whistles by a first-year class taken by two innovative and revolutionary free jazz musicians, drummer John Stevens and alto-saxophonist Trevor Watts from the Spontaneous Music Ensemble. They had been invited into the school by the progressive music teacher, all paid for by the Inner London Education Authority. I knew the tune well, and had a record of the great pianist, Thelonious Monk, playing a solo version of his deceptively simple tune. Then the lesson ended and I went down to the staff room for morning break. When I went for a walk at lunchtime, I found the two musicians on the pavement outside the school, and approached them and thanked them for the sounds they had conjured. 'They've just stopped us!' said an irate Stevens, 'and they've told us they don't want us anymore, even though we were booked with different classes for the whole day. What's the matter with them — somebody complained and we've been shown the door.'

I could believe it: Monk excluded and expelled, just like *Stepney Words*! I sat talking and commiserating with John and Trevor all lunch hour on the green and something positive, for me anyway, came out of it as I got to know them and their music, and even read my poems alongside their marvellous improvised sounds. But how stupid it was that the students were robbed of another brilliant opportunity with two nonpareils of their art.

And another sinner like Monk was the Marxist Italian film-maker Pier Paolo Pasolini. When I heard that his classic portrayal of Christ, *The Gospel According to St. Matthew*, was being screened one afternoon at the local Limehouse Library, I was the first in the queue for the tickets, and got enough to take my entire fourth form class. As there were more than twenty, I had to have another teacher with me, so the Head of Science, a close colleague of the head, was chosen for the task. Being a Church of England priest, I thought he might be genuinely interested in the film, but when he began to take in the actions of Jesus the young revolutionary, in particular his passionate overturning of the tables of the moneylenders in the temple, and the altogether human orientation of his character and preaching, it was too much for him and he walked out of the library, returning to school and going directly to the head to report his disgust. It was too late though, and the students had sat through the film — black and white, inexperienced and unprofessionalised actors, subtitles and all — with concentration, absorption and deep interest, for this wasn't Jesus as they had been taught and as they thought they knew him.

I soon found that my new students loved writing poetry, and it became as much an integral part of my teaching as it was before my dismissal. There was no way the governors or the head could prevent that. There was the same concentration upon local issues, except that over the two years of my absence, consciousness about the future derelict docklands in the neighbourhoods surrounding the school had grown powerfully. The London Docks in Shadwell and Wapping, those at the Thames entrance of the Regents Canal in Limehouse and the West India and Millwall Docks of the Isle of Dogs, had all closed, largely through the corporate embrace of containerisation. In the oldest of these docks and those closest to Tower Bridge and the City, St. Katherine's Docks, the huge new Tower Hotel was being constructed by the building firm Taylor Woodrow. In September 1973 the *East London Advertiser* reported that the firm was due to make two hundred million pounds profit out of the development, which the local 'Homes before Hotels' protest lobby, the East End Docklands Action Group, declared could create new homes for some thousands of homeless people. If this were to become the model for the docklands future, how would it serve local families? My first-year pupils became deeply engrossed in this question. Some girls brought to school the recently completed Tower Hotel's tariff with its outrageous prices completely out of the orbit of local people's lives, and the class began to write. Some made poems of the old days, talking to parents and grandparents of how they remembered life before the containers. Peter wrote:

Wapping

Wapping is nice
    and you can smell
that spice.
Big ships
    small ships
        all kinds of ships.
Little sparrows
    flying like arrows
    through the air
        landing nowhere.
Sailors have mynah birds
    shouting out dirty words,
That's what it's like in
    Wapping.

But now they wrote portraits of desecration, as in Tracey's *Derelict Dock*:

Silence moves through the dock,
No one around but an old dog.
Cranes all rusty, dirty and old,
Engines broken down, long ago.
The river moves quietly,
Not a boat to be seen.

No people anywhere near now,
Drinking beer, near the canal.

But there was also a new spirit of defiance and indignation entering into their words. What about their futures? First there was eleven-year-old Lynn and her *Rich Luxuries*:

Why did Taylor Woodrow build the hotel?
When there are so many people who have nowhere to dwell?
The Tower Hotel is for millionaires,
There is nowhere for us to live and play.
In the Tower Hotel they have waitresses
While we have to slave for ourselves.
They have luxuries galore
Our homes are just a bore.
They have 836 rooms in the hotel
Where we are scrambled up in about four.

And her classmate Kym made it even clearer in her poem *Houses for People,* as if the Matchgirls were back in town:

What is to be done
With this land that is left?
Will there be at last
Nice houses for people to rest?
Why don't we build houses
So clean, neat and bright
Instead of these shabby things
People dwell in day and night.

This new place they have built
Called the Tower Hotel is not for us,
But for rich people to dwell.
And with what land there is left
They want to build more,
All for the rich
None for the poor.

We will fight to stop them building,
And we'll build just what we like —
Just for the less rich people
We will make a happy sight.

And if they still try to stop us,
We will fight and not give in,
Until we get our houses built
We will fight until we win.

For both Lynn and Kym it was call-and-response, poems made of questions and answers, like many a folk song and ballad, direct from popular tradition. And when cuts to the local health services caused the closure of Poplar Hospital, a community hospital that had served the people of Stepney and Poplar for generations, the same class studied reports in local papers and struck out with their own indignant poems. First there was Sharon:

Poplar Hospital is closing down
And people start to gather round,
Screaming, shouting, waving banners
And saying that they will be winners.

They say it is understaffed
But the nurses say 'that's a laugh!'
They lie and cheat the public so,
They say the East Metropolitan Regional Board should go!

All those beds lie empty now,
Why, some half-dead person could be cured.
So people, people, come out and support us,
Or that dead person could be you!

And Beverley saw the closure in terms of the privatisation of the health service:

Poplar Hospital is going down
With no beds in the town,
Government say it's understaffed
But the people round here are not so daft.

With the people signing petitions
In their thousands everyday,
On Saturday perhaps the government might say 'O.K.
Have your own way.'

81 beds going to waste —
That is not enough in this place,
To the government that's their way,
To let the people die on the street.

And on a windy day.
But if they are ill
They have their private wards so that they get well.
They must say:
'Let them die in Poplar, we are OK,
In our private wards
Living like lords,
Everyday.'

Looking back at these spirited poems again now, when the National Health Service is being attacked and privatised by central government in ways that it has never been before, they seem strangely prophetic, like vibrant messages from the past. They are neither transitory nor simply momentary about far-gone past events, but they read like commentaries on now-times. They tell us how everything precious that has been won by British working people is vulnerable, easily liable to be removed like so much actually has been, and forty-plus years later these Stepney children are still telling us how we must campaign and fight to save them. As for Tracey's *Derelict Docks,* looking from the very same place on the top floor of Latham House now, where Ron took his photograph for the cover of *Stepney Words* with its wilting cranes and gleam rising from the stagnant dockland water, where are they now? When you look over towards Limehouse, Poplar and the Isle of Dogs you see the world of high finance, the towers of greed of Canary Wharf — not Kym's 'houses so neat, clean and bright' for local people. For there are still 'these shabby things, people dwell in day and night,' all over the borough, as if everything has changed, but nothing has changed.

For the people of Chile, everything changed on September 11, 1973 when a military junta took power in a brutal coup d'etat. We had been back at school but a week, and very quickly the British government had gone ahead with the sale of frigates to the new dictatorship. 'The thought of them warships makes your blood boil' wrote eleven-year-old Richard in a poem, and very soon the students were using their powers of imaginative empathy to reach the people of a nation the other side of the earth. They looked at the flag of this previously unknown country, and Frances wrote much in four lines:

The flag of Chile represents
The blood of death,
The star is the star of freedom,
The white is the emptiness of lonely people.

But these were people who could be reached through the imagination, through the exercise of Marjorie's 'creative-critical principle' and over the following week they became Chilean mothers, fathers and children dealing with effects of cruel and murderous military rule, and a group of Chilean dockers who sought to resist it. In the very same week British papers were full of the massacre at Carletonville in apartheid South Africa, where eleven black miners had been massacred by police while striking for higher wages at the Western Deep Levels Mine. It was an entry into an investigation of the laws and realities of life in the country, and the narratives and short plays written by the students explored the lives of South Africans enduring and resisting the apartheid system. The students were enthusiastic about both the subject matter and methodology of empathy. Even more so when we considered a Belfast story of four Catholic fifteen-year-old boys, who had been arrested at school by British soldiers and taken to the infamous Long Kesh Prison, where they were interned. Now this wasn't faraway Chile or South Africa, this was Britain in 1973. The students took different positions and many opposing arguments were made among them — some were from local Irish families, others had elder brothers or cousins in the Army who had served in Northern Ireland — but when it came to soldiers coming to schools, there was a powerful unanimity. Perhaps Kym crystallised this with her lines;

Everyone should share this sacred land.
Run children, run before the bomb hits you,

Run children, run before the soldiers get you!
You think we're unlucky, well look at them, this is misery.

The spirit of humour-in-resistance came out sharply in the children's depiction of working lives. They wrote dramatic sketches and poems about those (like some of their fathers) working on the assembly line of Ford's in Dagenham, or (like some of their mothers) working day-in day-out in a metal box factory in Bromley-by-Bow, staffed by rebellious and striking women. We read some of the work-narratives in Hugh Beynon's brilliant account, *Working for Ford,* and reports of building workers in the UCATT union organising against the 'lump' system of casualisation. They also studied the lives of miners, whose strike brought down Edward Heath's Tory government in 1974. What impressed me was their grasp of detail about a miner's life, such as this extract by John, a thirteen-year-old East Londoner, imagining the daily experience of a Barnsley miner:

> Some people say 'the miners are greedy. Why not settle within the Stage Three limits. They have been offered 16%, it's the best offer they've ever had.' But do they know how much it really is? Is £2.50 the best offer?
> Say our shift begins at 8 o'clock. We have to be in at 7:30 to get our safety equipment (just so that they know who is down the mine) helmet, batteries and light. By now it's ten to eight. Ten minutes lift journey and then seven minutes to the coal face then we can start. Two o'clock, we rise to the top in three quarters of an hour to have a wash. We work five days a week (many don't, they have to work seven days to get the money) that is six and a quarter hours without pay. By the time I'm 54 I won't be able to work anymore. A fair offer? How do they know? How do they know?

Or there was their fascination with the high-rise crane operator John Fontaine, who, wanting to support his construction workmates at ground level striking against the system of casualised labour called the 'lump', refused to come out of his tiny cabin for several days, marooning himself one hundred feet above the site. Eleven-year-old Chris was up there with him:

> I try to get the workers to strike
> My name is John Fontaine,
> I climbed right up to the top
> Of my big 100 foot crane,
>
> Look at all those people
> Standing on the ground,
> I'm so high up in my cockpit
> I cannot hear a sound.
>
> I'm up here in my crane,
> My hungry belly is like a bump,
> But I'm up here fellow unionists
> To go against the lump!

In studying stories from local histories as stimulus for the students' writing I came across the story of Daniel Mendoza, told in his own *Memoirs*. He had been born in 1764 in Aldgate, into a poor Portuguese Jewish family, and largely due to an apprenticeship in street-fighting as resistance to the racism and bigotry that he faced, he developed a 'scientific' skill with his fists, eventually becoming all-England boxing champion and hero amongst his contemporaries, particularly his Jewish contemporaries, becoming a role-model as a proud Jew who would never accept insult or discrimination. Now, nearly two centuries on, East London was plagued with so-called 'Paki-bashing', with its victims predominantly the new refugees and immigrants arriving in large numbers from the war of independence in Bangladesh. The week that we were studying extracts from *Mendoza's Memoirs* a fourteen-year-old Bengali boy was brutally assaulted in a neighbouring school in Whitechapel. The *East London Advertiser* described the attack in this way: 'A 14-year-old boy was savagely beaten with chains and sticks at Robert Montefiore School, Whitechapel, on Friday. The brutal attack by ten other pupils lacerated the lad's skull and stripped the skin from his left cheek. Incredibly it occurred openly in a school corridor thronged with pupils on their way to lessons — and no one tried to break up the fight or report it. "There isn't a kid in the place who doesn't know what Paki-bashing is," said one teacher. "They have no chance.'"

As we read Mendoza's story in his own words, it seemed sharply and lucidly relevant. In an incident in Northampton he tells of being 'accosted by a bully of the place, who observing two Jew lads, strangers to him, thought proper to show a little consequence on the occasion, observing that he supposed "we were after no good," that "he hated to see such fellows strolling about the place," that "it was a pity we were not sent to Jerusalem," and using many other expressions equally absurd and insolent... and he threatened to kick me out of town.' Not so different to what the Bangladeshis, the most recent newcomers to East London, were facing every day in the streets and in the schools. And I thought again of the boy Isaac, the son of a Lithuanian Jew and a newcomer to Cable Street. What were his experiences, his mother tongue Yiddish, but moving into his second language, English, at St. Paul's School, Wellclose Square in Stepney? Was he bullied, threatened with being kicked out of London, by rampaging members of the British Brothers' League and told to go back to Jerusalem, or any other place that his insulters seized hold of? Did he know about the life and struggles of men and women like Daniel Mendoza? And did he ever write schoolboy poems about him, like Joe, with his own Eastern European parentage:

Born in East London in 1764
When times were hard and Jews were scorned to the
    floor —
Daniel Mendoza was the little baby's name
But to the English, Jews were all the same.

He had to learn to stand on his own two feet,
Because fighting in them days wasn't very neat.
His family starved, for they had nothing to eat,
He learnt to fight out in the street.

When fighting one day out in the street,
The opponent laid in on him, kicked him off his feet.
Mendoza fought hard, on concrete, on tar
And then was spotted by a star.
Richard Humphries was the man, his nose like a fox,
He thought, 'that lad's good, I'll teach him how to box.'

He had to fight Humphries three times to win,
He lost the first, won the second and the third too —
He was now champion, Humphries was through.
Mendoza died in 1830,
He died loved by all,
By his scientific boxing knowledge
He made his opponents fall.

I was becoming more and more involved in trade union work during my year back at Sir John Cass. I was still getting invited to be a speaker at a lot of NUT local association and 'Rank and File' meetings around the country due to the wide publicity around my case. I found myself on the same meetings circuit as Michael Duane — another hero of mine, the ex-headteacher of Risinghill Comprehensive in Islington, North London, whose school had been closed by the Inner London Education Authority in 1965. They had disapproved of Duane's non-authoritarian and libertarian approaches to school life, despite strong support from students and parents. So he was known as the sacked head of Risinghill, whereas I was the sacked teacher of Stepney, and we both traversed the country, holding dozens of meetings with young teacher trade-unionists. But now I decided to concentrate more time within my own local association, the East London branch, where weekly meetings were both powerfully stimulating and intensely frustrating. Stimulating because the debates were conducted with skill and articulacy by highly intelligent young teachers of my own age, who constantly informed and educated me about vital professional, national and world issues; and frustrating because despite the huge significance of these matters, the scourge of left sectarianism dominated almost all the discussions. They were depressingly inter-combative, and some evenings, after a long and mutually hostile meeting, I used to walk home through Poplar, thinking that some of these colleagues seemed to have more contempt for each other's hardly different politics than they did for our common enemy, capitalism. These febrile differences created a lost opportunity for broad teacher solidarity. As we engaged about subjects like democracy in schools, the hugely divisive and variegated teachers' pay structure and the necessity to abolish wage differentials and the absolutism of head teacher power — or the creation of a truly internationalist curriculum with knowledge and perspectives which served and vindicated working class families, there was almost complete agreement in principle. The same was true in our discussions on internationalist campaigning around South Africa, Chile, Vietnam or Ireland — or the Portuguese colonies fighting for independence and a socialist-orientated society: Angola, Mozambique and Guinea-Bissau. There was unanimous support too for the striking miners, the Shrewsbury Building Workers' Campaign, the arguments of socialist feminists in many informative and brilliantly-conducted debates. Yet too many of them seemed to end in bitter sectarian rivalry between teacher members of the two predominant Trotskyist groups of the era, the International Socialists (who sold the *Socialist Worker*) and the International Marxist Group (who sold the *Red Mole*). The Communist Party was simplistically reduced to and caricatured as 'Stalinist' and the long experience of individual communists in international, local and trade union struggles was summarily dismissed. Labour Party activists were repudiated as mere 'reformists'. The meetings became gladiatorial contests of impressive brainpower — even more so at meetings of 'Rank and File' which was an uneasy alliance between the 'IS' and the 'IMG', with other non-aligned elements like me involved — but too often they missed the essential ingredient of unity, despite the often inspiring and educative contributions of many members. One of these was a young New Zealander called Blair Peach, once a fireman but now a teacher in a special school in Bow called Phoenix, who in defiance of his stammer, made his points with militant fire, skill and humour, and was always the first to volunteer for any task. Blair had a powerful impact on me. I was a nervous and reluctant speaker at union meetings, but with the brave example of Blair fighting his stammer in his every intervention, he inspired me to get up and speak whenever I felt the urge.

I was frustrated at Sir John Cass by not teaching some of my former students, so I was looking for a way of regularly meeting them again and continuing the writing and publishing projects. When a friend and local community worker, the secretary of the local trades council, who was also a powerful socialist artist, Dan Jones, told me about the space in the basement of St. George's Town Hall in Cable Street, it seemed like too good an opportunity to miss. We could use it free, he said, as a venue for a local writers' group. So we put the word around, and at the first meeting an impressive cohort of young writers turned up, including several ex-students now in sixth form at Sir John Cass, and two school-phobic friends, Billy House and Leslie Mildiner, who had written a book about their experiences of school called *The Gates*, which was later published as a unity project between 'The Basement Writers' (which we decided to call ourselves) and Centerprise Publishing Project in Hackney. Other attendees at that first meeting were Tony Harcup and Alan Gilbey, two Sir John Cass students. Tony was the son of a beefeater, and lived in the Tower of London, where he returned after every session to his parents' flat and the spirits of Boleyn, More and Raleigh within those walls. Looking back now at his remarkable life, he went to Leeds University but dropped out and became one of the pillars of the campaigning and 'underground' *Leeds Other Paper*. He later exchanged alternative journalism for a university life, becoming a Senior Lecturer at Sheffield University, the author of a clutch of books on ethical journalism and the editor of *The Oxford Dictionary of Journalism*. But his first published work was *Never Had it So Good,* published by the Basement Writers in 1974. Alan started off shy and reticent — he says he walked backwards and forwards up Cable

Street past the Basement steps maybe a dozen times before he found the boldness to come down. Once down, he never looked back. He'd been one of the original *Stepney Words* poets with his poem of the jiggery-pokery of Watney Street Market with stallholders selling broken plates, half-rotten bananas and stolen purses, but alongside his writing was an astonishing skill with drawing and cartoonery which later developed into animation. His vibrant comic on the future of the docklands (he lived in a block of flats facing onto the Shadwell Basin) which he called *Up the Docks* and which featured a battle royal between 'Taylor Woodrow Slater Walker Profitgrabber the Third' — an arch-developer — and the caped and Y-fronted 'Will of the People', was one of the Basement's first publications and was sold and left anywhere where East Londoners walked and sat, from the underground, local doctors' surgeries and the buses ploughing up Commercial Road and Mile End Road. His prodigious skill-base grew into television animation (for which he won a BAFTA award), local history presentations and organised historical walks around the 'back passages' of Stepney and Whitechapel.

During the first Basement meetings, the members read their poems and stories and we discussed how we would set about publishing. The sense of history in that dark room coursed through us all as we took over the space every week from a judo class. Outside and up the steps was where people of East London — Jews, Irish, communists, labourites, factory hands, children, black people, dockers and rag trade workers — had combined in October 1936 to stop Mosley and his blackshirts. We were reading our own poems in a venue of heroism, in a place of history and unity. When we talked about what we would publish first, two projects immediately shot to the forefront. The first was, as everybody agreed, 'Stephen's poems! Let's publish them!' Tony and Alan had been visiting Steve Hicks regularly, and he found difficulty in getting out with his sick leg. But he was an honorary Basement writer, and used to send his poems for us to read almost every Tuesday night, and they often made us laugh, and almost cry with their contradictions of wit and pathos. Tony had written a poem to him and it crystallised the deep feelings these young people had for the elders all around them:

The Fighter (for Stephen Hicks)

Searching for satisfaction all his life,
Unemployment, poverty and strife.
Living alone, now, in one small room,
The old age pension don't lift the gloom.

His friends pop in to speak a while,
And when he sees them coming he's happy and he smiles.
He talks about past times, both good and bad,
And seeing him so lively makes his friends so glad.

He shows his friends certificates and old school reports,
Photos and press cuttings of the boxers he has fought.
He thanks his friends for sparing the time and he talks
    about his poems,
He smiles and laughs, but must be a bit sad when his
    friends are going.

But we love going to see him, and we're always glad we do,
He's a great bloke and poet; I know you'd love him too.
It's really great for us to see his big blue eyes alight.
Even though he's finished boxing, he'll never end his fight.

Searching for satisfaction all his life,
Unemployment, poverty and strife.
Living alone, now, in one small room,
The old age pension don't lift the gloom.

And Stephen became a living symbol of poetry and the poetic spirit to these young poets: he had to come first. So when we published *The Boxer Speaks* (it was paid for, like the other Basement publications from the money that showered in from *Stepney Words)* it was if we were simply doing what was natural, what was right, just giving exposure to a voice of millions. As he wrote:

212

It seems that somewhere within me
A silent voice, now and then says,
'Hurry please, let everything be,
And pick up your paper and pen'

We all listened, and like Stephen, did just that.

The second project was a poems poster. East London was full of wallspace — on the walls of derelict houses, on fences, hoardings, vacant shop windows, and all ripe for poetry. Cheap too, just the cost of printing an A3 sheet which could hold about fifteen poems — one from each of us and some of our friends. The first one went up all around Shadwell and Cable Street. There was Tony's piece, reflecting on the changing docklands as he sat, the beefeater's boy, on Tower Wharf; one from Stephen about East London sporting heroes, and one inspired by him by Alan, putting new, critical lyrics to *Maybe It's Because I'm a Londoner*. Keith from Wapping, a Cass boy, looked at national politics, and wrote:

> We're heading for a confrontation,
> The Tories introduce new legislation:
> 'Put the troops on red alert,
> Give those workers a bit of Tory dirt.'

And Costa, from a Greek Cypriot family and another Cass student, looked at his despoiled heritage in his poem called *Birthplace*. It began:

> It was the land of free thinking and elections,
> The home of poetry and speech,
> The land of beauty and song,
> The cradle of humanity,
> The birthplace of the word 'Democracy'.
> But what has happened to this beautiful land?
> It's now under a military hand.

And Billy Colvill, a young playwright writing from Stepney's own Half Moon Theatre, set down the agenda for all of us, and all those sometimes bemused readers who found poetry on the corrugated iron and hardboard spaces that were nailed up all around them:

213

That Means Something

I see
A woman at the Social Security
With two kids, screaming for money;
That means something.

I see
In the paper
That the miners
Won't give in;
That means something.

I see
Lovers laying on the grass
Like barbed wire;
That means something.

I see a drunk
Looking down the road;
That means something.

And when I know what it means
Then I'll mean something,
And when I mean something,
Then I'll hit back.

For that's what the Basement became for its members young and old: the endless struggle for their writings to 'mean something'.

I say 'young and old', for out of all the surprises of the Basement, that's what it became, and empathy with the elders became, not without tension and argument, an alliance with them. The first to manifest this was an extraordinary woman in her fifties called Gladys McGee. Her much quieter daughter, Kim, wanted to come to the Basement but was too shy. So Gladys pushed her, and the only way she would come was if Gladys came too. In his book, *Everything Happens in Cable Street*, Roger Mills, another Basement writer and author of the skillfully observed school memoir, *A Comprehensive Education*, interviewed Kim, who told him: 'I told Gladys I wanted to go but was too nervous. She said, 'Oh Kim, don't be ridiculous. Just go. It's only over the road.' So I said, 'Right I'm going.' I got dressed up, got to Cable Street, got to the bottom of the stairs and thought — oh no, I can't go in on my own! And I came up the stairs and went all the way home again. Gladys said, 'Did you go?' I said, 'No I didn't I'm too shy.' She said, 'Oh for fuck's sake Kim!' I said, 'Can't you come with me?' and she said 'I don't want to go down there, do I? It's for youngsters.' But when Gladys finally did come she broke the ice. She had the gift of the gab. She was the first non-young person to join the Basement Writers.'

And she brought a four-line poem with her that became the group's unofficial watchwords:

> Please read my poetry,
> Don't let me write in vain,
> Because it's only in the last few years
> I found I had a brain.

After Gladys came other elders — Jim Wolveridge, who ran a bookstall in Whitechapel Market, a veteran raconteur and authority on the cockney language, whose book *Ain't it Grand? A Stepney Autobiography,* and his remarkable study of East London speech, *The Muvver Tongue,* written with Robert Barltrop, were published during his tenure in the Basement. And then there was Sally Flood, whose beautiful lyrical poems were inscribed and hidden from her supervisor on paper patterns placed under the materials she was working on while sewing as an embroidery machinist in a Brick Lane factory. She was another John Clare of Spitalfields, her poetic observations of urban birds, again comparable to Clare's fenland descriptions:

> A magpie sat on the garden wall
> Then slowly flapped its wings,
> Displayed a breast of black and white
> Rotated round on springs.
> His claws were stuck as if with glue
> So tightly wrenched were they,
> Then suddenly, he raised his back
> Before he flew away.

I had first seen Gladys at the school gates on the first day of the *Stepney Words* strike. Kim's own poem in *Stepney*

Words 2 was another bird poem, written when she was eleven, and when I read it I saw a person more than a bird; but it wasn't Gladys:

The Old Bird

The old bird has broken wings,
The old bird can hardly sing,
The old bird can only stare,
The old bird cannot bear
The hot weather nor the cold.

What sort of bird is the old bird?
What sort of things can it do?
What sort of things can he say?
Can he fly, can he cry?
I sometimes wonder this as I walk by.

Gladys was eternally playful — her poetry was racked with laughter and the absurd, always laughing at herself while satirising the pompous, the affectatious, the smug and the reactionary. She could look back at her own distant childhood and remember the nonsense of her schooling, as in her *Empire Day* which she would hilariously act out as she read it, dressed in a grotesque Britannia costume:

I've been picked!
I've been picked!
My arms were a-flinging
And my heart was a-singing
'cos I'd been picked!
It was Empire Day, I'd been picked,
My teacher said I was a good reader
And could dress up as the leader of the empire we had then.
And I'd wear a bronze helmet
And be draped in a red, white and blue flag
And reign over all other lands —
That's what an empire meant then.
The day came nearer, I was getting excited
Then my teacher spoke to me,
And my day was blighted,
She realised I was too small to reign —
She wanted someone tall and striking

216

Who looked like a Viking,
Holding a shield and looking across the sea.
I was already weedy
And felt rather seedy
And asked if I could go home,
Because I was in pain.
She said I could do the part when I was older,
How could I, silly old cow! —
We aint got no empire now!

Yet inside this hilarity and boisterous satire was the soul of a true poet, intense and poignant in her language, which she was struggling to release from herself. I remember the night she first read her poem *Winter* in that rough and echoing basement room. When it came to her turn to read, we were prepared for the customary laughter, wit and elements of farce, but this was what she read. The room was suddenly covered by anguished surprise:

Winter,
The feeling is gone
Something, somewhere
Is dead.
Also I knew
that something was wrong.
It was a long time ago
since I sang a song
with love and feeling
which should go
with maturity and love
of life.
But my love and feelings
have died in the winter
of the year.
So now something has turned
my feelings into a sorrowful spear,
which I am ready to use
to cause others tears.
The thing that is within me
that is so dead
is withered and dried
and does not care
what it says.

217

> I hate it, but it is myself
> that is in the winter of me
> that is so cold.
> But the rages which
> are within
> shout loud and embarrass
> everyone who is listening;
> I sometimes notice this.
> Then the anger and hurt
> disappears again
> and are ashes of the fires
> that die in the cold
> of the same old winter again.

There were many memorable moments, and longer, during the years of the Basement. I have called it 'poetry's open door' and it was that, certainly. There was the drunken Glaswegian who staggered down the steps and into one of our sessions, mistaking the basement entrance for that of the vagrants' hostel further up Cable Street. 'Wha' is this, is it poetry?' he muttered, then gave us a drama-soaked rendition of a long narrative poem in powerful Scottish dialect. Or there was the quietly-spoken old man who entered the downstairs room very carefully, asked if he could say a poem, and when we welcomed him he declaimed by heart the entirety of Browning's *The Pied Piper of Hamelin,* thanked us politely, and left. But Gladys' intensely moving reading, so unexpected and poignant, was a moment of poetry which was unsurpassed. Alan called her 'the Bard of Stepney' (barred from pubs and betting shops all over the borough), but there, reading this poem in that dim underground room, she was sublime, unforgettable. If Isaac had come down those steps in that same street where they had both lived, he would, I'm sure, have recognised a true kindred poet.

As the Stepney months rolled on, we published a host of small poetry books. There was Alan's *Inkslinging*, Gladys' *Breaking Through*, Leslie Mildiner's *Sometimes You Can Hear the Birds Sing*, and a collection of short pithy poems by a young woman called Debbie Carnegie who wrote all her poems in bed — hence her title *Bedwritten*. The next poetry poster had a powerfully urgent community theme, with Debbie's poems stopping readers in their urban tracks, as they encountered:

> Silence, they tell me, is golden.
> Is that why we don't speak
> Now I wear your ring?

Poems of love and struggle, bread and roses were all over this A3 sheet posted up all over Stepney. There was the chicken story by songwriter Dave Swift, whose contacts in the print meant we could typeset and print up to 400 copies of our basement poet collections for around £40:

> 'Once upon a time was fine,'
> The chicken said.
> 'I scratched the ground
> And I picked up the crumbs from where I stood.
> It wasn't much, but still...'
>
> Now I'm just a battery hen.
> The farmer said it's cheaper
> To have us live in blocks of ten
> With ten next door
> And ten times ten
> Below.
>
> Can't turn my head to see my friends;
> Although he says we're only hens,
> We're all we've got
> In this tower block.
> What you gonna do about it.
> Chicken?

This sense of challenge to passer-by readers was the bloodstream of these poems. Keith saw the dockland speculation from his Wapping Council flat, and wrote:

> When I look from my door, on the fourth floor,
> I can see a shore which is now bare but once was there.
> It was the Eastside of the London Docks,
> I remember it well when I was a lad
> Because I could count the cranes and ships

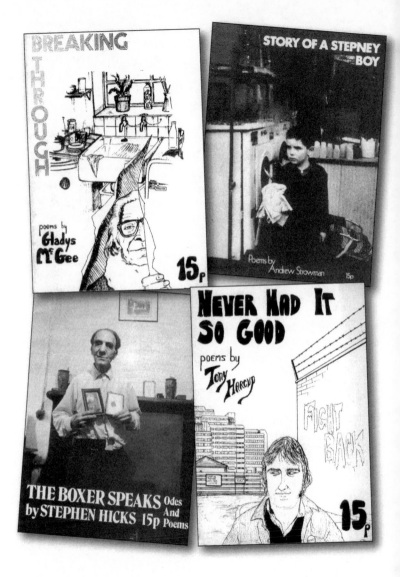

Basement book covers:
photographs, Ron McCormick,
drawings, Alan Gilbey.

And the variety of goods come out of their dips.
But now it's all gone because a certain group of
   businessmen
Have brought a sun to shine for their own kind.

But alive the water is still
Though it's gradually being filled with dirt.
The warehouses are bare,
The ones that are still there
Except for a guard dog.

When I look from my door on the fourth floor
I can see in the distance the Tower Hotel,
Where the rich dwell on land and we did not sell.
But, dear folks, we shall not stand there like jokes
And see our homes go under the speculator's bulldozer.
But we must stand and fight
For the right of our own homes
On land which belongs to the East Ender.

And from the black teenager to the pensioner who fought
in the war, there was a sense of proud unanimity against
racism, in the face of Powellite hatred and the emergence
of new fascist groupings like the National Front. Eddie's
life told us what we must remember:

Have you read Mein Kampf?
You should. It tells you why
So many of the world's young men
Were marched, and forced to die.
They started with a slogan,
'Our nation first', it said,
Then 'Tainted blood must be cleansed'.
They left six million dead.

Not dead in patriots' honour,
Not dead in a soldiers' fame.
Dead. Gassed in multitudes,
Of six million, not a name.
To purify the nation
Secret searchers were installed.
They murdered Jews and Gentiles,
The whole world was appalled.

A national front was unified,
Jubilant in their quest,
The pall of death lay heavily
All over Europe's West.
Swollen with their victories
Over the helpless and the small,
They marched beyond their boundaries
To purify us all.

At last the outside world took heed,
Their rifles made of wood,
Dummy guns, planeless skies
Ready for battle stood.
One by one they were beaten down,
The blood of their souls ran red,
A conqueror had purified
Another million dead.

The burning house, the bleeding child
Held, as its mother died,
The legless man, the blinded boy,
These were the purified.
So many paid the final price
Who wished to see men free.
They left their trust with us who lived,
Their folk, like you and me.

Not the usual words you read on an iron hoarding, but for a few weeks they were there, plain and lucid. And I wondered too if the teachers of Sir John Cass noticed and read Alan's poem on their way to and from school, as they walked up to Stepney Green station. *Second Year Defeat*, he called it:

Rude words on the blackboard,
Crushed chalk on the floor.
Books out of the window,
Run out, bang the door.

Teacher's depression
Me and my class,
Football in the playground
Connects with school glass.

From *Up the Docks*
by Alan Gilbey

Cigarettes in the toilet
And nudie books too,
When I leave this dump
Then what will I do?

Work on the railways?
A stall down the Lane?
Empty the bins?
Or clean out a drain?

I'm nothing special,
The school's told me that.
I aint got no brains
And my prospects are flat.

Can't hit back at the system –
It's blank, has no features.
So while I'm at school
I'll take it out on the teachers.

223

The Basement Writers were establishing themselves across the community and their words were everywhere, not only on their books and posters, but in poems in local newspapers, in taking an active role in community festivals — particularly the E1 Festival in the summer of 1974 and following years at Bigland Green in Stepney, in local schools, at the readings at Half Moon Theatre which began around the same time, and at events organised by the Federation of Worker Writers and Community Publishers, which sometimes took them far and wide. The defiance-of-generations attitudes of these writers was exemplary and profoundly unusual, and in their rejection of 'leaders' and hierarchy they began to hold a new model for writers, so often seen as individualists, supermen and loners. This was undoubtedly the literature of the ordinary, and as such, the stuff of potential excellence.

Chapter Eight
Dod Street Stomp

At the end of the school year in July 1974 I parted company from Sir John Cass, to take up an English teaching post in Langdon Park Comprehensive, a mile eastwards in Poplar. It was a split-site school, and I was based in the Limehouse annexe, in charge of teaching English to the second and third-year students also based there. Just off Burdett Road in a back road called Farrance Street, it was sited in an old nineteenth-century board school, and cared for with the utmost pride by a group of cleaners who had a real love for the building. Two of them, Ruth and Nancy, became my special friends, and as they cleaned my classroom after a day's teaching, they loved to talk about their families and hobbies. Ruth loved the voice of Frank Sinatra, and would rhapsodise about the time she heard him live in London. She lived in the highest of the high-rise apartments, Balfron Towers in Poplar, right next to the Blackwall Tunnel approach road. She loved it there, and out of her windows could look over the whole of East London. As for her workplace, she and Nancy kept it gleaming and pristine. You could see yourself, dark and angular, in the waxed floor of the assembly hall.

From my classroom window I could see the huge stone lantern of the church of St. Anne's Limehouse, just over the East India Dock Road, conceived by Nicholas Hawksmoor and referred to by Charles Dickens in *Our Mutual Friend*, protruding out of the London mists, his symbol for the Law's unconscionable delays — something that I felt that I knew a little about. On the school's northern side was another apparently insignificant road called Dod Street, but one with a powerful history. In 1885 it used to be the prime assembly point to hear speakers of the Social Democratic Federation, England's first revolutionary socialist party, with their featured speaker, the poet and artist William Morris. The police would frequently break up these meetings, until one Sunday morning the assembly became so huge and determined that the police met their match and had to give up their harassment. So the right to mass public protest was won in the street next to our school, and as a group of English teachers, we were going to make sure that our students knew all about that! And much more too.

I couldn't believe the difference between two staffrooms; Sir John Cass and Langdon Park. As for their headteachers, they were polar opposites. My new head, Peter Andrews, was to support and defend our work, and had created an open, welcoming school with a strong community outreach. Here in Limehouse I found myself among kindred teaching spirits. The teachers were almost all progressive, left-orientated and libertarian in their methods. There was a well-established approach of team-teaching within mixed-ability classes and no frozen philosophy of streaming. Group teaching was much more the norm, and as English teachers we decided to develop a methodology of bringing two, sometimes three classes together for theme lessons, then breaking back into classes, with further divisions into working groups. We also decided on two main curriculum themes for the year. One would be 'Stories from Local History' and the other 'Internationalism'. Each teacher selected subjects for the theme lessons that they would teach, and undertook to provide the curriculum materials and activities relating to each topic. My first one was the Dod Street episode, followed by the conditions that led to the 1889 Great Dock Strike, and the conduct of the strike. My colleague Irene Payne covered the 1888 Matchgirls' Strike at the Bryant and May factory in Bow, and the struggle of the East London Federation of Suffragettes, led by Sylvia Pankhurst. Our oldest colleague, Bill Foot, by then semi-retired and an ex-deputy head at my old school Hylands (he took up his post after I left, but was there when I went back to teach the last few weeks after my Leeds University year had ended), had lived through as a boy the General Strike, so he enthusiastically took that as his preferred topic. He remembered how he and his friends from the East London neighbourhood of Leyton had all come to school wearing red ties in 1926 to support the strikers (some of whom were their fathers) and he wrote a poem which he read to the students during his theme lesson:

May 4th, 1926

May 4th 1926 — morning
East End classroom crowded
With youth and feeling unconfined,
Crimson ties proclaiming oneness
With the workers — red flags fluttering
In the corridors of the mind.
To bull-like masters red rags,
Well-worn beyond those cockrow years,
Beyond betrayals and disasters;
Remembrance that the battering shower
Of time, its storms can never nip.
Among her festivals and bitter tears
Comes home this memory
Like a well-laden, triumphant ship.

I felt proud that Bill, also a strong NUT member and born where my own father had been born, showed me his poem. What — a Hylands teacher from my old secondary modern, had written this, and here we were teaching together in an East London comprehensive school, teaching children whose roots were from all over the world, from the Caribbean and the 'isles of the southern seas', from Ghana and Nigeria, from Burma, India, Pakistan and Bangladesh, from Malta and Cyprus, all here, all with us. Bill was in his seventies then and I was thirty, but we were together again in the same classroom, with the eleven-plus gone, for our students anyway, although the East End grammar schools — Cooper's and Central Foundation, Raines' and George Green's — were still there, blighting and complicating the educational cityscape.

Throughout the early Seventies, large numbers of Bangladeshis, particularly from the Sylhet region, came to join families and settle in East London, their greatest density in the Spitalfields neighbourhood, along the same Brick Lane corridor where Jewish refugees from the late nineteenth-century Tsarist pogroms had come, and before that the Huguenots from seventeenth-century France, fleeing religious persecution. Many thousands of Bangladeshis were seeking refuge from the tumult of war in their own homeland, now a new nation and a separate polity from Pakistan, whose soldiers had sought to suppress Bangladeshi nationhood with violence and oppression. Some of our

New students from Bangladesh:
Langdon Park School, Poplar 1975.
Photograph: Ron McCormick©

new Bengali-speaking students, tense, uneasy, anxious and bearing terrible psychological scars of conflict, had also been very close to it, and were now targets of violent racism in local streets and estates, threatened by Powellite sympathisers and the organised stirrings of fascist groups, the most venomous of which was the National Front.

These students were keen and quick to learn English and frequently prompt to express their memories of their people's resistance in the world they had left. Ouhidur Choudry, from my English class, was from Chorisoppur village in Sylhet and remembered his friends' part in his people's struggle:

After a while I went to our old village where there was the civil war. I was not sure about escaping from the soldiers of Pakistan as soon as the war was starting. Our countrymen began to call our country 'Bangladesh'. We could not walk in towns like Sylhet after four o'clock because there was a curfew by the Pakistan soldiers. It was known that Bengalis would be shot after that time. They even killed Bengalis anyway. I always wanted to see the Pakistani soldiers. One day we saw some smoke, it was from a bomb dropped by a bomber. A few days later at home, our house was shot at by a fighter plane. Then lots of Pakistani soldiers were killed by lads as young as me, or older than me. The easy way the lads attracted the soldiers of Pakistan was to shout 'Joy Bangla, Bangla joy!' (meaning 'Long live Bangla!') When the soldiers came and asked the lads 'who said that?' or 'shut that up!', they said, 'a group of people going that-away!' When the soldiers moved away from them, they started shooting them, getting guns from their belts or throwing grenades. They were trained to do that and I hoped to join them, but I never. After the war, I went to the town and lived there until we came to this country in November 1972.

Another student, Nazrul, lived at the end of the street where I lived, in an unkempt council block, with his older brother Muhammad, a university-educated young man who was an activist and poet whom local racists had targeted. Their flat was broken into, defaced and daubed with racist slogans. Shortly after, Muhammad visited the school and read his poems to his brother's class and others. I remember this one poignantly. He called it *How Do You Feel?*

'How is it? What is it like?' asked the friend in his letter.
'I shall be delighted to hear about that,' he added in a manner
That showed his profound faith and solemn hopes in the matter.
So I wrote to him first thing next morning, surviving the engine clatter.

'It is like truth as I never tasted before,
It's like the ultimate thing
That makes you not to ask for more,
It is a feeling that had 'no' more.

Like an unforced wave which fades before the tide,
It is like the traumatic agony, scrambling to hide,
While you conquered the lofty terrain of youth
And are hounded by the stony ghost of a minor truth.
It is like being demoted to the lowest nursery class
For your failure for keeping up with the aged perverse.

Looking like a beggar in the pavement of Calcutta bazaar,
While wearing the best-available attire.
It is, like an infamous convict, released after ten years inside
For the severest crime committed against all the neighbourhood.
It is a perpetual effort, a struggle with a life assumed
In the borrowed fantasy of humanity, subdued.

It is like being dead
Before the destined dread of death.
Everyday
It is like breathing your last
While saving some breath,
Like an abused effigy of a hated caste
You appear alive, never to last.

For from all the rest of fellow beings
You are aware
You are undeniably different.
You are an immigrant.'

Muhammad's poem prompted me to wonder, did Isaac ever have thoughts like these as he wandered the same streets as Muhammad with his friends, as they shared the same age, the same part of the city, the same hostility, the same estrangement? What was it like for him sixty years earlier? He had written in his poem *The Jew*:

> The blonde, the bronze, the ruddy
> With the same heaving blood,
> Keep tide to the moon of Moses.
> Then why do they sneer at me?

And I thought: Jew or Moslem and other millions in the world, those who escape, those who are hounded, is this how they feel, every founding moment, every day of their lives in East London or in thousands of other places of arrival that nobody writes about?

But there was much hope too in this school, with many of its students making good-humoured, warm and close friendships across religions and cultures, and caring, looking after each other in difficult circumstances. So we had much to celebrate. One cold lunchtime, Mark and his friend Ashok were playing along Limehouse Cut, a grimy canal that runs through Poplar into the Thames. Their classmate Denise took up the story in her poem that was read out in assembly a few days later.

> They threw stones into the canal,
> that was deep,
> They stood on the bank that was
> High and steep.
>
> But Ashok slipped and fell in
> Mark jumped in to save his friend —
> If he had left him
> His life would have been at an end.
>
> The water was cold in Limehouse Cut,
> Mark might have lost his own life, but
> He still jumped in
> To save his friend's life.
>
> He took Ashok back to school
> They were both dripping wet —
> But he saved a boy's life
> So he deserves the reward that he'll get.

These children had much to contend with and they did so bravely, and they were unafraid to write about it. Here are Giash Uddin and Halal Uddin writing together and pooling in their lives in their poem *We Want to Live*. They were writing in the murderous wake of the deaths of their Bangladeshi brothers like Altab Ali and Tuslim Ali, cut down by racists in the streets of Tower Hamlets.

> We walk down the road,
> They call us 'ugly toad',
> The NF are full of hate,
> They beat us up
> because we are brown.
> The NF have killed Bengali men
> Just because we are different to them.
>
> They call ugly names
> We are scared to walk the streets
> Never knowing who we will meet.
> Will we see the National Front?
> Will we see a knife shining in the dark?
> Will it be stabbed through my brother's heart?
>
> We cannot do our shopping
> Without a backward glance.
> We will fight them back one day,
> When we get a chance.
>
> The NF say that they are strong,
> They think they are the best.
> I think we are all the same,
> We want to live, like all the rest.

But it was Tabassum, thirteen, proud and conscious, whose poem touched me the most. It moved her class-mates too, as she read to them: *A Dream*. I'd heard similar words from Martin's men and women six years before, but never so real and poignant as this:

> I say
> Open our hearts
> Like a new flower.

Let the hatred in us
Flow away like a stream.
Let justice be sat in our hearts
Like a stone standing
Straight and firm.

I have a dream that one day
People all around the world
Shall eat from one plate of peace,
And say together,
'We shall stay so always.'

One day
A tree will grow high and strong
In the garden of justice
And live forever.

As our course moved ahead, I was constantly in the local history room of Tower Hamlets Library at Mile End, searching out resources for our classes. Helped by the brilliant librarian, Bernard Nurse, I went through issue after issue of the old turn-of-century socialist journals like Sylvia Pankhurst's *Woman's Dreadnought* and *Lansbury's Labour Weekly*. These had bold local poems in almost every copy, and the back page of the *Lansbury's Labour Weekly* was always the sheet music of a socialist song. Every poem I found was like a discovery, and when we used them in the classroom as texts of both history and literature, I knew that we were bringing living words from generations of struggle and there was more and more of 'excellence in the ordinary'. From the *Woman's Dreadnought* came this *Lullaby*:

O hush thee baby, thy sire was a slave
Whom overwork thrust in the dark early grave;
The gloomy grey streets from this den which we see,
Are hungrily waiting, dear baby, for thee,
O hush thee my baby.

O sleep whilst thee may babe, by night and by day
Thy pale mother rests not, but stitches away;
There's no one else to guard thee from hunger but she,
Her tears flowing silently all for thee.
O hush thee my baby.

> O hush thee my baby through the days dark and wild
> Stream sun-shafts of glory that can't be defiled;
> The marching of myriads is borne to our ears,
> And we will march with them, and sing through our tears,
> O hush thee my baby.

Or like our own students, there were the poets of *Lansbury's Labour Weekly* who, with their proud empathy, extended themselves in the nineteen-twenties to pit families, as in T.D. Coughlan's *Pit Fields*:

> The face of earth is smiling, pranked in state
> With green of hope and garlands of the spring,
> Her breath unlaboured, scented, fills the air
> With promise of her beauty fostering.
>   A thousand feet below, the coal pit's core
>   The jinny rings for more and yet for more.
>
> Her smile will change to laughter with the joy
> Of June's rich mirth of melody and praise:
> Her glade and field, the haunts of bird and bee
> Resound the level of her richer days.
>   A thousand feet below the keen pickers swing
>   And putters stripped to pelt both sweat and sing.
>
> On summer eves the nightingale will thrill
> The dusk in calling to the dew-moist rose.
> The moon will mount her realm and argent light
> Will make the earth's night pageant full disclose.
>   A thousand feet below the night shift strive
>   To save a comrade, trapped in number five.

These were remarkable poems, published in working-class journals by working-class writers, never republished or anthologised, never breaking through into the established and elite world of 'poetry'. Coughlan's poem, with its powerful evocation of the beauty of the natural world above and the hellish jeopardy of the pit world below, is such a jewel. And it wasn't so far removed from Sally Flood's 'Basement' poem of contemporary garment workers in a Brick Lane factory. She called it *Man's Hell*:

> Szzzsht! Szzzsht! The sound of steam
> Escaping
> Brrroom! Brrroom! The Hoffman Press

234

Awakening.
Clank, clank, power released
By the touch of a treadle.
Clang, clang, the top rises
To expose the knife edge
Of a freshly pressed seam.

On the factory floor
Machines! Are coming to life
Squeak of unoiled engines,
The crash! As feet meet steel.
From the office
Phone bells ring,
Feet rush to and fro,
An unending string
Of energy,
Released by a clock.

On Earth, is this Hell?
The working class
Know too well,
To be ruled by a clock,
At Dawn! To rise.
At Night! Shut out by lock.
Deafened! By the sound of noise,
While the pious sing
'All men on Earth rejoice'.

Of whose creation,
This civilisation?
All men! Equal to one?
While! Some just laze and relax
Others! Work is never done.
Perhaps someday it will be revealed,
Why birth alone should separate the classes.
Poverty! Known only to the lower masses.

Just a few share the riches
Of man's sweat and labour.
The whole earth laid bare,
The fruits of work turn sour.
One has not the energy to spare
For relaxation.
The steam of labour pollutes the air,
God help the coming generation.

If this is living
Where does Hell begin?

Reading this poem again in now-times, my mind went back to Mr Clarke at Hylands, and everything that he taught us about metaphor, about rhetorical questions and his introduction into our lives of that weird and unforgettable word so explicit in this poem of a working life — onomatopoeia! So this was what he meant, this is how naked sound inhabits the words and world of the factory and of poetry, and using Sally's poem read out at the Basement, I could use it in my own classroom, where the Basement Writers themselves arrived one afternoon to read their poems like this.

And many of the poems hidden within the stacks of old journals and the microfilms of the Bancroft Road library and the local history room were by working-class poets who were the contemporaries of Isaac and his friends. One of Isaac's few poems that explicitly names his home streets, *A Ballad of Whitechapel*, telling of the poet's encounter with a young woman of the streets, has infernal images close to those invoked by some of these poets. Then, reading through some of his brother poet Wilfred's earlier work, I came across his poem of the dockside written about a place at the back of Albert Gardens, *Shadwell Stair*:

> I am the ghost of Shadwell Stair.
> Along the wharves by the water-house,
> And through the cavernous slaughter-house,
> I am the shadow that walks there.
>
> Yet I have flesh both firm and cool,
> As eyes tumultuous as the gems
> Of moons and lamps in the full Thames
> When dusk sails wavering down the pool.
>
> Shuddering the purple street-arc burns
> Where I watch always; from the banks
> Dolorously the shipping clanks
> And after me a strange tide turns.
>
> I walk till the stars of London wane
> And dawn creeps up on the Shadwell Stair.
> But when the crowning sirens blare
> I with another ghost am lain.

I thought of Isaac and Wilfred's sharing and walking through those same streets at night, conceiving of those kindred loathsome and stygian images, and I thought of the same world of trenches, another hell entirely, which they were both going to inhabit, one as an officer, the other as a lowly private, physically small and weak and vulnerable with his wheezing lungs. And yet they both walked these streets and found poetry there.

In my classroom, I used the high Victorian walls to celebrate poetry. By the end of the first term almost every reachable space was covered by my students' work, and above all I climbed up to attach large white sheets, one with a giant quotation from Morris' *March of the Workers*, sung to the theme of *Glory, Glory, Hallelujah!* at Dod Street just down the road by the victorious assembly, and sung now in our classroom by young East Londoners with their origins from all over the world:

> What is this, the sound and rumour? What is this that all
> men hear?
> Like the wind in hollow valleys when the storm is
> drawing near,
> Like the rolling on of the ocean in the eventide of fear —
> 'Tis the people marching on!

Looking at them from the front of the classroom, above the blackboard were the lines in large letters from the poem *Looking at Your Hands* by the Guyanese poet Martin Carter, who, within less than a decade, I was to interview in Grenada. But for now, his words were written across a classroom wall in Limehouse as a teacher's watchwords:

> We do not sleep to dream,
> But dream to change the world.

As for the young writers, they seized these narratives, poems and texts which dramatised the lives of their forebears, with verve and enthusiasm. Just as we had the sites of epochal events on our doorsteps, we had the descendants of some of their protagonists studying and writing alongside us. When we were discussing the mass events of the Great Docks Strike of 1889 and the role of leaders like Harry Tillett, someone called out, 'Hey, that was Harry's great-grandad!' and the thirteen-year-old Harry Tillett had a moment of glory. The events were that close to us: the students suddenly realised the proximity of their heritage and their heroes. There was Jackie imagining herself as a child in 1857 roaming too far from home and seeing in the distance a monster being built in the shipyards. What was it?

> I am a kid, I live in Millwall.
> One day when I went out to play
> I wandered a little too far away.
> I went through fields and marshes bare
> And to my amazement I did stare —
> Standing high above the houses
> It looked like some kind of iron man.
> I could see the people standing there
> Looking up to stare.
> I asked a man who wasn't in a stare
> What the iron was doing there.
> 'It's the *Great Eastern*', he replied.
> I said, 'Thank God, I thought it was a monster in disguise.'

Or there was Trevor from Barbados, now a Matchgirl afflicted by the terrible disfiguring disease 'phossy jaw':

> I've got an onion
> With my bread.
>
> I know what I've got in my bread
> PHOSPHORUS!
>
> Every day we eat it
> Every day the same.
>
> We don't have to buy it,
> Every day it comes free.
> But not long now for me,
> I've bought a brand new oak tree.
>
> Goodbye Mum, Goodbye Dad,
> What do you know?
> Getting buried tomorrow.

Or here was Tony imagining himself as Sylvia Pankhurst, enduring force-feeding at Holloway Prison in 1914, as a part of the struggle in Bow and Poplar for the woman's vote waged by the predominantly working-class East London Federation of the Suffragettes:

> Their feet came stamping on the stone floor,
> Their feet banging like the sound of war.
> The pipe in my throat ripped and tore,
> They left my cell, I fell to the floor.
> I wish they wouldn't come any more,
> They'll come tomorrow; it's their kind of law,
> I wish they wouldn't come any more.

Many of the students lived in council flats and houses on the Lansbury Estate, right next to the school, but they didn't know who George Lansbury was and knew nothing about the imprisonment of the Poplar Council, which Lansbury led, in 1921 for their refusal to raise the council rates. But they soon learned about it, even more so when Dawn read out loud the poem she wrote to the man who gave the name to her flats:

> George Lansbury made speeches
> Through the prison bars,
> Although he was a councillor
> He did not drive posh cars.
>
> For he was just a working man
> And upper class he hates,
> For he was put into a cell
> For preventing rising rates.
>
> He spoke to many people
> Although he was in jail,
> He told them not to worry
> For they would never fail.
>
> He said quite soon the government
> Would have to set them free,
> For they had many people
> And public sympathy.

Just as George predicted
The government gave in,
And George and all his councillors
Were 'forgiven' for their 'sin'.

He said they had a meeting room
And keys to their own cells,
As everybody listened
To what he had to tell.

He said to many people
That he was not ashamed —
The man proud to be guilty,
George Lansbury he was named.

When Bill told the story of the red school ties, the students were amazed that one of their teachers could remember as far back as 1926. Philip listened very carefully, and afterwards wrote his own version of the events in his poem called *Playing Truant*.

I woke up in the morning,
Everything was bare,
I went to get my breakfast
And to comb my scruffy hair.

I looked out of the window,
I could not see a moving thing,
Not even a big dirty dog
Clattering on a tin.

I put on my school clothes
And a red tie,
It dangles all about
From my neck down to my flies.

When I hear my mate coming
Walking in the road,
He knocks at the door, I let him in
And he shouts at my pet toad.

We set off on our way
And try to hitch a lift,
Then a coach of posh people going,
Oh, what a whiff!

They stop and pick us up
And then we move again,
We come to Gardiner's Corner
Where there's not a single moving tram.

Then we see hundreds of people
And they won't let us pass,
They try to rock the coach
So we get off it fast.

Then one posh person gets off the coach,
'Let us get to work, you stinking filthy dummy!
You pigs may be striking
But we want to earn some money!'

Then a big strong worker
Whose muscles are like steam-rollers,
Stretches the man's hat over his head
And makes it five bits of a bowler!

I don't think Bill expected that reinvention of his childhood, but young poets like Dawn and Philip had a similar kind of poetic spirit to Stephen Hicks — the use of rhyme, metre and balladry, soaked in emotive power and wit, and with a striking sense of picture: the stuff of generations of people's poetry pouring out of them. We studied the causes and events of the Battle of Cable Street — now commemorated by the huge mural depicting the heroism and humour of East London defiance on the bricks right up the steps of the Basement and on the end wall of St. George's Town Hall, directly facing the shell of St. George in the East Church, another Hawksmoor creation, its innards ripped out by Nazi bombs — and the humanity and unity of these children's words shone right through. This was Christine's poem, *They Shall Not Pass*:

They shall not pass, I swear to God.
They shall not pass 'cause Mosley
Thinks he's the great dictator,
While Mosley lives with his blackshirt army.

They shall not pass — we'll not let them —
For all they've done, so why should we let them?

They shall not pass
We also have an army,

> But our army has a difference,
> We fight for the Jews and our families.
>
> We're going to win, I know we shall,
> Because Good has power over the Bad.

Cheryl's frank and lucid rhyming made couplets of clarity in her *Memories of Cable Street*:

> They blamed it onto the Jews,
> They said 'Put them in the zoos!'
> They were fighting in Cable Street
> And a little Jewish kid got beat.
> The working men would not let them in,
> They said that Mosley should be put in a dustbin.
> They made a fuss,
> They turned over a bus,
> They kept the blackshirts away
> And that was how they won the day.

And Allison's poem contemporised Cable Street, made it a part of 1974, in the face of the National Front hatred, calls for repatriation and violent attacks on Asian families. *Our Black Brothers* was the name of her poem:

> Brown, black, white or red
> We must all go to work to earn our bread.
> Either day in a factory
> Or night in a train
> In boiling hot sun or freezing cold rain.
>
> We can't afford to make a fuss
> Who works on our roads or drives a bus,
> 'cause if we do
> They'll all go back
> And England will be useless, and that's a fact.
>
> England called, and thank God it did
> 'cause they've helped our country to earn a few quid.
> In East End and West End
> And country too,
> The black man's our hero, who made our towns new.

A short poem from a 1926 issue of *Lansbury's Labour Weekly*, shining out of the brown-edged pages in the local history room, seemed to crystallise poems like Allison's and hundreds more by these young poets. Anonymous

and precious, its two verses held an urban truth I have
never forgotten:

> Along the streets of cities drear
> The stones line heavy: but I know
> That prisoned under pavements here
> The good brown earth is still below.
>
> Beneath the stony lives of men
> Grown hard and loveless, still I find
> That whoso digs in faith again
> Comes on a heart that's warm and kind.

But there wasn't much 'good brown earth' around
Limehouse and Poplar, except in the churchyard and
around St. Anne's. Next to that was a Victorian pile of the
Limehouse Town Hall, whose entire ground floor had
been claimed by the National Museum of Labour History,
and filled with trade union banners, placards, books, documents and exhibits denoting the years of formations and
struggle of the early organisations of Labour, so many of
which had begun and flourished in the neighbourhoods
around our school. The museum loaned us an expressive
photograph of a parade up Commercial Road, East India
Dock Road and Poplar which had rallied entire local communities around the dockers in 1889, and we used it for
the cover of our anthology of our students' poems 'reliving' the history of East London 1860–1940, which we
called after Morris' poem *The People Marching On*. One of
the museum's pioneers was Ivy Tribe, a veteran of the
Socialist Sunday School Movement early in the century,
and together with the director, Terry McCarthy, she
asked us whether we could bring some students to the
annual History Workshop Conference at Ruskin College
in Oxford, and demonstrate a Socialist Sunday School
meeting at one of its sessions. I went to meet the socialist
historian Raphael Samuel, the organising genius behind
the conferences, who lived in a Georgian house in Elder
Street, Spitalfields, and we worked out the session, involving the singing of classic socialist hymns like *God Save the
Workers* and *England Arise*. I wrote a contemporary

version of The Good Samaritan parable, where an East Ender is mugged in the street by some thugs and a local Bangladeshi finds him and cares for him after he is passed by and ignored by city bankers slumming it up Brick Lane. It was a tremendous day out for our students: everything was paid for including the coach, food and an introduction to Oxford colleges. Our cosmopolitan band of young East Londoners seemed to have a vibrant and engaging time. It was strange though. Our school was quickly gaining the reputation of being a left-wing institution. Some parents humorously referred to it as the Kremlin, but they were always very supportive and laughed off its reputation, largely because the students were happy there and worked very hard and with a potent enthusiasm: they saw the school as their own.

But there were disputes too. A fourteen-year-old girl in my class called Tina, who was keen and industrious as well as being deeply imaginative, was also worried about the themes we were pursuing at school. We had a talk about it one afternoon after classes, and she invited me home to meet her father. He was honest and up-front and told me he was an English nationalist who didn't appreciate the internationalist and anti-racist emphasis of our teaching perspectives. This surprised me, because a few weeks before, in the wake of the work we were doing on Cable Street, Tina had written this piece, giving it the title *All the People Together Again*:

> I had a strange dream last night and there were black people, white people, yellow people and all kinds of people. They were all talking and laughing together.
>
> Then a great big piece of paper was passing around the room and on the paper they signed their names and said they would never fight again. When the paper was all signed and a million copies made they all bowed down and shook hands and prayed and prayed and prayed.
>
> And in the streets below, the people were dancing round and round while guns and uniforms were scattered on the ground.

244

I showed it to him, but he had read it before. 'Surely you don't object to this,' I said, and praised its prescience. He was polite and friendly and made me a cup of tea while his daughter looked on anxiously. 'Yes, I like that,' he said, 'but you've got to promise me you'll never undermine England in your classes.' I said I maybe have a different idea of England to him, one which was close to his daughter's in her prose-poem, but I certainly wouldn't undermine that — it was what I wanted for England. He laughed and shook my hand, and thanking him, I was gone. One of our sons now lives near the street where he lived, and I have to walk past his house on the way from Bow Road Station. And I think about Tina and her father as I pass and wonder what happened to them, and if she still clings on tight to the vision of her poetic spirit.

Isaac's memory had come hurtling back in the autumn of 1973, when Alec Ayres, the librarian of Isaac and his friends' old haven, the Whitechapel Library, had agreed to host an exhibition of the paintings and poems of one of the *Stepney Words* writers, Imtiaz Malek. Isaac, of course, was a poet-painter and so was Malek, a fifteen-year-old born in India, whose enigmatic *Time and Distance* had been the *Stepney Words* closing poem:

Time and distance
They both travel equally
Waiting for no one
Time is sometimes wasted
Time is sometimes fastened
The green grass is taken by time
As time goes into the future
And makes it present and the grass
    is polluted.
Sometimes people are left behind by
Time,
When people are old the time leaves them.
The world and people get old
But time goes on and on.

He had a whole page of short poems in *Stepney Words 2*, including this extraordinary lyric he called *The Cells*:

Among the crimes there is innocence
Among the bad there is good
Through injustice justice stood
Through the dark Hell
Brightness shone,
Dimness of space
Brightness of earth
Darkness of death
Brightness of light

He span these brief poems out with paintings of planetary conceptions and striking colours: the young Blake of the tenements of Royal Mint Square. Alec printed a four-page leaflet with biographical information and some further poems to consider while looking at his pictures, including *The Watcher*:

The white clay face
Expressionless, feelingless
Watching the white path through the universe
Into the distant abyss
Watching the clusters of turquoise blue
Watching the pulse stars
Watching eternity

Watching the judges, priests, kings, queens, ants, apes, snakes, books, plants, planets, colours mix into a meaningless mass of nothing.

Watching civilisations mix into smoke of a fiery furnace of nature.
Then vanishing onto the eternal darkness.
The watcher watches on.

I lost touch with Malek for thirty-five years. We met again in Toronto in 2006 when I was a visiting professor at York University there, and he had become a nuclear physicist, with a major role at the Pickering Nuclear Power Station close to the city. As we sat and talked about what we had been doing for the previous four decades, he revealed to me much of what, as a teenage schoolboy, he had been reluctant to tell. How he had been targeted by racist bullies in his year, how they had waited for him outside school and had set upon him as he walked home, how he had devised endless different routes to reach his flats after school so that his attackers could never predict how he would get home. I wondered how much of such experience was implicit in his poems, and whether Isaac had ever known similar moments. And I thought of one of his short *Stepney Words 2* poems:

Look skywards
The sun is going red
It's old now,
Cold and lifeless,
A lone person
Shouts,
Nobody answers.
Everything is still
Tranquil like it used
    To be.

Back at Langdon Park, we delved into our curriculum programme on internationalism. The most obvious place to start was ourselves, the histories of all the young people in our classes, their families and their myriad places of origin. So the students were asked to talk to their parents and find out about their provenances. It was revelation after revelation when they discovered that the world was in their classroom as they read out the stories of their families. St. Lucia, Jamaica, Antigua, the Greek and Turkish sectors of Cyprus, Burma, Pakistan, Uganda, Barbados, Guyana, Bangladesh, India, Gibraltar, Kashmir, Hong Kong, Nigeria, Ghana, Kenya, Scotland, Ireland, Sierra Leone, Malta and Italy: now it was all East London, proud and cosmopolitan in this old nineteenth-century building that had known the footfalls of thousands. We studied the process of immigration, what provokes it, what it leads to. A key text was the book by John Berger, *A Seventh Man*, which through Berger's words and Jean Mohr's photographs examines the lives of migrant labourers of Europe. We projected Mohr's photographs through slides onto the classroom wall and the daily moments of these workers came alive. In December 2014 Berger, now in his eighties, wrote in *The Guardian* about translation, and the task of the translator: 'True Translation,' he wrote, 'demands a return to the pre-verbal. One reads and rereads the words of the original text in order to penetrate through to reach, to touch, the vision or experience that prompted them.' Reading these words now, they also seem to tell what these young people were achieving in their poems — penetrating, reaching, touching and experiencing the lives, the excitements, the pain and most importantly the quotidian moments that filled the lives of migrants. Staring at Mohr's photographs of Yugoslav workers in hostels in Germany, Philip wrote about one of them, 'penetrating' his life; the life of a 'guest worker':

Drajon, The Migrant Labourer

He left Yugoslavia
Prosperity he tasted,
He headed for Germany
With a smile on his face.

Munich was his destination,
He wanted to work with cars,
To find some good friends
To drink in the bars.

But when he got there
The sight was so sick,
Ten to a room
And the maggots were thick.

Eating with other people
He did not like,
Sleeping with them,
Oh, what a fright.

His wages were low
His humour was poor,
He wants to go back
To kick his front door.

His posters are high
Up on the wall,
But he's made a mistake,
He feels a big fool.

Back he will go,
He hates the Express,
They're all cramped together
He just wants a rest.

He will go abroad again,
He has no work here,
Goodbye to his family
For another long year.

It was kin to what Stephen wrote uncomplicatedly in his introduction to *The Boxer Speaks*, telling how he first started writing poetry on a building site 'to break the monotony of the work.' He added, 'If you can understand rhyme and rhythm, then you can write poetry.' Yes, but the further dimension of true poetry is also the power to become others in the constant provocation and 'penetration' of revolutionary human empathy, which is what Stephen did in his poems and what these children did too as their imaginations travelled the world.

We went from studying events in Spain and Portugal — the anti-Franco resistance in the former to the revolutionary events of 1974 in the latter. We read the words of the imprisoned Spanish writer Eva Forest, who wrote in her memoir *From a Spanish Jail* that 'it seems to me now that the imagination is a kind of motor — that it moves, and it moves other things. It is what collects up the accumulation of past experience, and changes it into new forms and "dynamises" it and propels it into the future.' Our students were doing just that as they considered events in the Caribbean, Chile, the world of the Chicanos and the United Farm Workers' Union in California, and the Sioux in their occupation of Wounded Knee in South Dakota. We studied African life and resistance in South Africa, Namibia and Zimbabwe, and the RAF support for the corrupt and tyrannical rule of Sultan Qabus in Oman. Some of these nations were entirely new to the students, and the teachers too learned much from the materials we used and particularly from the poets and speakers who were constant guests. Poets like the

Barbadian Peter Blackman and the Jamaican Andrew Salkey and the brother of one of our Bangladeshi students, Muhammed Haque; 'Steel and Skin' — the drummers from Africa and the Caribbean; American folk singers Peggy Seeger and Jack Warshaw who gave free concerts at the school; the 'Third World Troubadours' led by Malaysian poet Cecil Rajendra and composed of a pianist from Sierra Leone, a Jamaican guitarist and percussionist Helio from Brazil, who set the students' rhythmic urges on fire by sharing his drumming skills with them. Elaine Nicholson, the London representative of the United Farm Workers of California; and George Johannes from SWAPO, the liberation movement and later the first government of Namibia — and old friends and students like the Basement Writers and Lyle Alexander of Tobago, who was in England for a year. Peggy, whose brother Pete I had heard sing on the steps of the Lincoln Memorial in Washington D.C. at the Poor People's Campaign in 1968, sang her beautiful praisesong to immigration, *Hello Friend*, and set the girls' ambitions throbbing with her feminist anthem, *I'm Gonna Be an Engineer*. A compelling contribution came from Trevor Huddleston, who in June 1976, just days after the massacre of hundreds of school children in Soweto, the township outside Johannesburg, visited the school, gave an assembly and talked to the students about the scourge of apartheid, something he knew well after his years of service in Sophiatown. He spoke with a moving eloquence, telling the students how some of those shot down were the children of his own ex-parishioners. He later wrote in his preface to *The World in a Classroom,* my book about anti-racist teaching at Langdon Park: 'It was a great privilege to be asked, a short time ago, to speak at the school... a privilege because the subject chosen for discussion was South Africa and the violence in Soweto. A privilege also because it was obvious from the response of the children and their questions afterwards that the background situation was well understood.'

250

But for me the most precious moments of this year, and a lifetime in teaching, was the visit of Joan Jara to the school in December 1975. Joan was the wife of the Chilean folksinger Victor Jara, who had been murdered in Santiago Football Stadium, which was being used as a jail, by soldiers of Pinochet's junta shortly after the coup. He had been a popular force all through the campaigning and government of Allende's *Unidade Popular*, and a powerful guitarist and singer, who as one of our poets, a boy from a Jamaican family, expressed it: 'knew how the people's heart beat'. Before Joan's visit we had studied translations of the lyrics of several Victor Jara songs, and also read Adrian Mitchell's poem, *Victor Jara of Chile*. We had also spent classes explaining the lead-up to and events of the coup, and read James Watson's novel of the times in Chile, *Talking in Whispers*. Joan was due to give an hour's session about Victor in the morning. She talked about his life and played some of his records. In the event, she became so engrossed and moved at the response of these classes of twelve and thirteen-year-old Poplar children that she stayed all day and didn't want to leave. After her morning session the students who had heard her got to writing, so by late afternoon we had several of them keen to read their poems to her. I'd read them and knew what to expect, but for Joan it was something deeply human and 'penetrating' that was happening. First there was Julie, reading her poem *Victor Jara's Hands*.

Victor Jara's hands played music like an angel's hands,
He played the strings like silver bands,
Until one day it came to be
That a new government came and the old did flee.

He was captured and placed in a cell
As they pushed him he fell,
And he played his guitar,
Yes he played his guitar.

He sang about the freedom that he once had,
The golden leaves
On winter trees,

Cold springs and streams flow by
And the animals so shy.
And he played his guitar
Yes he played his guitar.

Then the guards came and took him
And tortured him until his hands were no good,
And he could not play his guitar,
No, he could not play his guitar.

So instead he did sing till night-time fell
And his cell began to smell.
So they took him away again
And with his hands behind
So for himself he could not fend.

They hit him so hard that he screamed
And they shot him next day at dawn.
But he still sings and plays in the heart of his wife,
Yes he still sings and plays in the heart of his wife.

I was watching Joan's face as Julie read her poem. Deeply moved, she said nothing but stood up, moved over to her and hugged her tight. Then Denise read her poem, which she called *Victor Jara's Wife*:

Victor Jara's wife
Would have lost her life
If she had stayed in that cruel land,
But she got out of Chile and was England bound.

People said he was a hero
But he only did what was right.
So when people say that to me
I say, 'all he did was fight.'

At night I leave the light on,
Waiting for him to come in.
But deep inside me I know
That he'll never walk through that door again.

It's hard being a widow
When you're only young
Our life together
Had only just begun.

> I keep his records to remind me
> Of the man I loved so dear,
> And every day I play his records
> The ones I loved to hear.

It is the ordinary actions that make this poem so compelling — leaving the light on at night or playing the records, and the woman she is writing about is right there in front of her, listening intently. I saw Joan to the bus stop at Burdett Road. She got on the bus to Mile End Station, and waved. It was the only time we met, but I still have the records and photographs of Victor she gave me.

Just this week, as this book is nearing completion, I showed these same poems and others on Chile to my friend Pedro, a Chilean activist who had been arrested after the coup and imprisoned for two years before being released on condition that he left Chile, and removed himself to England, where, through the work and contacts of the Chile Solidarity Campaign and Sheffield trade unions, he found work and another life. He had arrived in England, in Sheffield at exactly the same time that Joan had visited our school. I showed him the poems that Victor and Joan had inspired and others about the events of 1973. 'What imaginations, eh?' he said. 'That these London children could transport themselves in this way to Chile, and in this, our people's time of agony, is astonishing — and in language that is so natural. Yes, this is the imagination of children at work, how they move beyond barriers and use their imaginations to transcend themselves and find unity with others so far away, on another continent.'

As the National Front rampaged around East London, racism and fascism were taking a more organised form, building on Powellism and violent attacks on Asians, particularly Bangladeshis, whose arrivant numbers had been growing in Tower Hamlets since the war in East Pakistan had created the new nation. There was no organisation in the borough specifically established to organise against racism and fascism, so a group of us decided to set one up. We called it Tower Hamlets Movement Against Racism

To all of you who
have written about Victor.
5/12/75.

254

and Fascism (THMARF). Initially formed by teachers and community workers with most of the organisation done by the Poplar community worker Pete Thorpe and chaired by myself, soon we had a vibrant group of activists and trade unionists involved. We set up meetings, put on cultural events like screenings of key films such as *To Die in Madrid* at Dame Colet House, which was followed by a presentation by veteran International Brigaders about their experiences of the Spanish Civil War. We organised poetry readings — such as the one with a 'They Shall Not Pass' theme, to commemorate the Battle of Cable Street — and fundraising dances with soul and reggae bands including one featuring a Jamaican band called *Blooblo*, led by the father of Kelvin, a *Stepney Words* poet. We mounted an anti-racist bookstall on Sunday mornings at Club Row Market at the top of Brick Lane, where National Front members regularly sold their papers. And we organised local trade unionists, youth and residents to march with us on anti-NF demonstrations across London where they had made inroads, like Haggerston, Lewisham and Hoxton. Disgusted that the ILEA was allowing the NF to use the Haggerston School for a public meeting, with hundreds of others we mounted a strong picket at the school gates, and Blair somehow got in and tried to disrupt the meeting from the inside before he was violently ejected by NF stewards.

One Monday night in September 1974 after a union meeting a group of a dozen or so teachers went, as we usually did, for a drink and discussions, to the Railway Tavern, a pub in Grove Road, Mile End. It was usually a friendly, multiracial pub, but we noticed that there was a new landlord and a distinct absence of the usual black customers. When one of us asked the landlord where the black clientele were, he snarled at her that they 'were all pimps, queers and prostitutes' and he didn't want their custom anymore. When we heard this, we all poured our drinks back over the bar and walked back to an alternative pub near Mile End Road, where we found many of the black

255

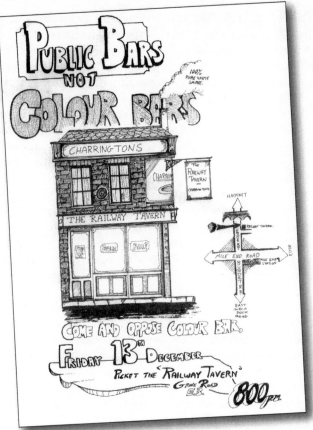

Poster by Alan Gilbey

ex-customers of the Railway Tavern. They told us the landlord there was operating a colour bar. So after a drink we went back to the Railway Tavern and mounted an instant picket outside, persuading quite a few people not to go in. The irate landlord called the police who tried quite summarily to move us on. When Blair Peach refused, he was taken to Bow police station and charged with 'threatening behaviour'. His case came up in the West End at Bow Street Magistrates Court, and a succession of us stood

256

up in the witness box and attested to his integrity and very teacherly behaviour at all times, and he was acquitted. As we all walked out of the courthouse, laughing and jubilant, one of the arresting police sidled up to Blair and whispered in his ear: 'Don't worry. We'll fucking get you, Peach.' Nearly four and a half years on, on April 23, 1979 on the streets of Southall where he was demonstrating against the National Front, they did just that, and our dear colleague Blair was killed by a police truncheon to the head.

Another time we had a narrow escape on the streets of Poplar. We had organised an anti-fascist public meeting at Limehouse Library. But when we arrived to arrange the hall, the place was locked as the booking had been mixed up. So, disappointed, we crossed the road for a pint in The Star of the East, a regular haunt, and sat at tables at the back of the bar. We had been in a few minutes when a large group of National Fronters, several of them carrying flagpoles with spear ends, entered the pub. They were irritated too, for their intention had clearly been to break up our meeting. We were soon recognised, and in a minority, we knew we were very vulnerable. So we edged towards the door, broke out and scattered running towards the Burdett Road traffic lights, where my colleague Bob Brett and I jumped on a bus going up East India Dock Road. A large group of National Fronters saw us and jumped on the bus immediately behind, pursuing us. We jumped off the bus at Upper North Street and ran up the road, with our pursuers, who jumped off their bus at the same place, chasing us with their pointed flagpoles. As we ran, I remembered that the old people's home where, every Wednesday after school, we took some students with us and showed the film that was used in the school film club, was close by. We had shown the beautifully crafted and moving Bo Widerberg film *The Ballad of Joe Hill*, the story of the immigrant Swedish revolutionary singer in the U.S. and martyred militant of the Industrial Workers of the World, just a few days before. So when we reached it we ran in the gates, puffing like mad, and walked, as casually as was possible, into the lounge where we used to show the films. We could see our hunters hurtling past outside, thinking we had continued further up the road. Some of the residents recognised me, welcomed us and made us a cup of tea. Still breathing hard, we sat down and laughed, thanking the gods that we had fixed up this weekly film show with the elders. For the NFers were after our blood that night, and it was our pensioner friends who had saved our bacon!

The next morning on the way to assembly, a boy called Freddie, who had seen two of his teachers being chased up Upper North Street near his home the night before, came up to me. The brief conversation as we walked into the hall, went something like this:

'Hey, sir, why was you and Mr Brett running from those men last night?'

'They were the National Front, Freddie, they were trying to catch us and beat us up.'

'Why, what's their game, sir?'

'They're racists, Freddie. They want to send our kids back to where they think they came from. They want to send you to Jamaica.'

'Me, sir? But I come from here, I'm from Poplar. My mum and dad came from Jamaica years ago, not me.'

'That's the point, Freddie, that's exactly the point.'

'Yeh, this is where I live sir. I'm staying here.' He was giving me the lesson that morning.

In June 1975 we invited Rosie Davis, the wife of the imprisoned East Ender, George Davis, into the school to give an assembly, with her husband's loyal friend and arch campaigner, Peter Chappell. Davis had been convicted and sentenced to twenty years for armed robbery on flimsy and contrived police evidence. All over East London and beyond, the Davis activists had painted their signature slogans, 'George Davis is Innocent OK' on hoardings, bridges, underground stations, derelict houses, corrugated iron and yellow brick walls. The words had become a part of the daily lives of our students.

258

In August, Chappell and some companions were to enter, at night, Headingley Cricket Ground in Leeds before an Ashes test match against Australia, pouring oil on the pitch and scuffing up its turf. The Half Moon Theatre had performed the play with the inevitable title *George Davis is Innocent OK*, written by Billy Colvill, one of the original Basement Writers — which we had taken our students to see at a special matinée. The campaign, vibrant and relentless, led to Davis' eventual release in May 1976.

The Rosie Davis assembly connected powerfully with our students, many of whose families had been on the end of some bad policing experiences, and they needed very little encouragement to prompt their writing. A boy from a Polish family, Joe, wrote four lyrics dedicated to the Davis campaign. This was one of them:

George Davis

Davis is in prison on the Isle of Wight,
He was convicted of armed robbery
    but I know it's not right.
His friends demonstrate, march, write on walls,
But the judges and the coppers think,
    'What a load of balls!'

They streak in the park
From dawn until dark,
But one thing I know is
There will be justice for Davis!

His wife Rosie cries, I can tell
While her innocent husband is locked in a cell.
You could eat as much as cows go to slaughter,
But poor George Davis has bread and water.

No one knows, only time can tell,
But George cries he's innocent as he sits in a cell.

Rosie Davis wrote to me a week or so after the assembly: 'I would like you on my behalf to thank the children who wrote the poems about George, they were really terrific.' And as the campaign continued and Davis was finally freed, several students who had been closely following the case spontaneously wrote follow-up poems, like this one from Andrew, born in Ghana:

Last night the cell door opened.
        'You're free!'
Davis was stumped, he couldn't believe it.
        'Who, me?'
'Whose orders? What happened? Why?'
'Home Secretary. Lack of evidence'
        Davis started to cry.

On his way to Waterloo, to meet
        the Press and his wife,
A free man again, out in the world,
        to start a new life.

I hope this goes on for people
        convicted wrongly,
From this day on, Davis will
        remember strongly,

For two years at Langdon Park I had a wonderful class of thirteen and fourteen-year-olds: vibrant, growing fast in mind and body, ever-creative, full of enthusiasm, friendliness and endless humour. I lived amongst them in a terraced house in a street off East India Dock Road in Poplar and saw them regularly in out-of-school hours. Amongst them were Jamaicans, St. Lucians, Bangladeshis, Indian Sikhs, Turkish Cypriots and a Ghanaian boy called Andrew. They all responded to and wrote poetry, but Andrew was a poet in his blood and in his bones and would write about being a SWAPO guerrilla in Namibia, a Republican prisoner in one of Franco's Spanish jails, a Trinidadian in East Dry River, an apartheid-afflicted Johannesburg worker, a striking Californian chicano grape picker, a Sioux protester at Wounded Knee in 1973, an antifascist at Cable Street in 1936 — and George Davis. The world was truly his classroom and he was unstoppable in his creative writing, like many of his classmates.

He lived in Bow with his mother, who was a regular visitor to the school and was constantly checking that he

260

was happy and working hard. He was at the centre of his class's energy, boisterousness and commitment to learn through the power and empathy of their insurgent imaginations. But already in his short life he had known sadness and hostility, as he revealed in one of his autobiographical acrostic poems, which he named after the shouts he had heard aimed at his family when they first came to live in London:

I n 1963, when I was two in Ghana
M y mother came here to England.
M aybe it was because of her colour
    that three white boys nicked her purse.
I t was hard to find work at first –
G hana High Commission bank is where she first worked,
R eally it's because she had lots of friends there.
A t that moment my mum was expecting —
N ations of all kinds must learn to live together —
T hen in 1970 I came over to join her.

I n my brown skin I walked the streets.
M emories flash by of my time at home —
M isery in this place called East London,
I nsults shouted after me everywhere I go,
G roups of white kids gang up on you,
R unning here and there hiding,
A nyone I see, my heartbeat grows louder.
N eglected by other people —
T errible things are done to Immigrants.

In 1976 I left the school in order to work in Mozambique, and after this I never saw Andrew again — for thus is a teacher's life. You become sometimes as close to your students as it is possible for two unrelated human beings to be. Then they leave school or you move on and the bond is broken; and all you have is memory.

Recently, I was sent a book to review, published by the Institute of Race Relations in King's Cross. Called *Dying for Justice*, it details deaths in custody of black prisoners, detainees and asylum seekers in British prisons, police stations and deportation centres over the last two decades: some 509 in all. Among the cases quoted described was the

suicide of a Ghana-born inmate in Swaleside Prison on the
Isle of Sheppey, Kent. When I read his name, my blood
shivered. It was Andrew's name. I hadn't seen him since
1976, but had often thought of him and read his poems. It
was him. The book referred to an article in February 1993
in *The Guardian* which reported:

> The death of a mentally-ill man found hanged in prison
> despite his condition being known to the prison medical
> service was 'aggravated by lack of care' a jury decided
> yesterday.
>
> Andrew Ohene, a Ghanaian-born man who suffered
> bouts of illness since returning from a visit to Africa, was
> found hanged on June 13, 1991, in the hospital wing of
> Swaleside Prison, Isle of Sheppey.
>
> Lionel Skingley, coroner for north Kent, told a jury: 'At
> no time was there any real assessment of this man's con-
> dition. By the time he died he had still not received any
> medical or psychiatric treatment.'
>
> Mr Ohene, who had a 'relevant and significant history
> of mental illness' had been isolated in a cell despite a
> deteriorating condition.

It was the boy I used to see, early before school, every
morning, who came and sat in my classroom with the
other early birds and talked, joked and laughed out loud;
the hard-tackling young footballer who was the scourge of
playground matches with his classmates; the startling
young poet with a huge gift of empathy; the boy I took
with me and a dozen of his classmates for a week on a
Thames barge owned by the Inner London Education
Authority, up and down the East Anglian coast, in and
out of the estuaries of Essex and Suffolk and the coastal
towns like Aldeburgh and Felixstowe, or in the tidal
mouth of the River Orwell outside Ipswich where we
anchored and swam off the mudbanks at sunset; where
we played football on the beach at Walton on the Naze
and hauled on the rigging as the sails opened every
morning. Andrew was there, fully involved, always laughing. Yet it was he who had killed himself in jail during his
thirtieth year, and on the same Isle of Sheppey where

every year, when I was a boy, we would have our family holidays; where I first learned to swim on the pebbled beach at Warden Bay, getting stings galore by the Portuguese men-of-war jellyfish who swarmed along the Kent coastlines in the late fifties; where we played cricket in the hard mud road; where I had my first kiss on a Leysdown levee with a girl called Nicky. How could it all be, how could it have happened to Andrew, my student, my friend, for two years almost my son? How much had those early years that he wrote about when he was thirteen in *Immigrant, Immigrant* carried their weight of pain through his life? What had he suffered? How much had he been hurt? I felt and still feel in agony about his loss. A photograph of his class is on my wall and he is at its centre, surrounded by his friends, his mouth wide open as he throws a beaming, joking V-sign at Ron, who

Langdon Park School, Poplar 1976.
Photograph: Ron McCormick©

took the picture. How could it have ended for him in that way, with the state giving him nothing but neglect and agony? It put me in turmoil, a turmoil I still have, which haunts me as I write these words, some twenty-five years after the end of his life and four decades since I knew him so closely as my student.

Chapter Nine
Best Friend Blues

I've been a lucky man, working with some fine and progressive publishers in my writing life, but the most dynamic and audacious of these was Glenn Thompson, a man who created innovation everywhere he looked. Glenn was born in Brooklyn in 1940 and grew up in Harlem. His mother died when he was eleven and his father was imprisoned shortly after. It was a tough boyhood, partly redeemed by the power of books. Through an adventurous and absorbent consciousness of reality, particularly street reality in New York and East London, which was to preoccupy his life, his agency was in reading and his ability to imagine a million other realities through the power of the word. After active struggle in the Civil Rights Movement and freedom rides in the US southern states, through the second half of the sixties he travelled to North Africa, India, Nepal, Afghanistan and Israel, where he worked on a kibbutz. In the late sixties he found himself in Hackney, and became a youth worker and a book worker too, setting up the Centerprise Bookshop with other activists and with local teacher Ken Worpole, establishing the bookshop's publishing arm. That's where I met him, when he offered to mount the reprint of *Stepney Words* as one of many projects of young people's writing which he and Ken commissioned, which resulted in young Hackney people being reborn into books.

Then in the early seventies he joined the pioneers of paperback publishing at Penguin Books, as a part of their progressive Education Books Department. Through his advocacy the works of the Brazilian teacher Paulo Freire first found thousands of readers in Britain, in particular

Freire's classic text *The Pedagogy of the Oppressed*. He also set my book on Tobago, *The Forsaken Lover*, into paperback. Then in 1973, with his partner Sian Williams and the Canadian writers Lisa and Richard Appignanesi, he set up the Writers' and Readers' Cooperative, which I joined in 1974. It was a bold enough enterprise, combining libertarian ideals and collective decision-making directly involving writers, with an understanding that mainstream publishing could also be combatted on its own terrain. Glenn's huge energy and subliminal pragmatism were both fully exercised. In the morning, he might be besuited, sitting in an office of the City bank Coutts, seeking ambitious lines of credit, and in the afternoon with his shirtsleeves hitched up, packing books for

Life of seminal black publisher

CHRIS SEARLE remembers the luminous innovative bookworker Glenn Thompson — 1940-2001.

WHEN you hear the word publisher, what kind of a human being do you envisage?

A man in a suit behind a desk, with a pumping handshake who gives a writer at least four minutes of his money-laden time? A smoking woman, feigning pleased to see you, but her eyes only half on yours and even suspicious of her own strong schedule?

Or Glenn Thompson?

He published four of my books. The first one that I took to him was entitled *Classrooms of Resistance*, which was about the teaching of English in an inner London classroom in the early '70s and included many examples of teenagers' creative writing.

Glenn took it, reconceptualising it as a visual anthology with the poetry laid out across evocative photographic images and made it twice the book that it was.

And he did it with such a storm of creative enthusiasm and empathy with the children's work that I was swept into his imagination and consciousness.

That was how he worked and it owed so much to how he lived his life.

He was born in Brooklyn New York, in 1940, his mother died when he was 11 and his father was imprisoned shortly after.

Glenn grew up in Harlem. It was a ...

DOCUMENTARY TIMING: Glenn Thompson's (above left) publication of Grenada: The Struggle against Destabilisation in October 1983 first came out in the week that Maurice Bishop (clapping right) was murdered.

Morning Star
19 September 2001

mail order, working the stamping machine and carrying sacks of books to the post office up the road from the Co-op's warehouse premises in Kentish Town. Whenever I could find the time, I went up there to join him.

Glenn's relentless commissioning work meant that the Co-op published some of the era's most significant and progressive books. He got to know John Berger, living in the France-Switzerland Alpine region, published his memorable *Pig Earth* and then his entire backlist. He took the risk in publishing the cartoon book *Cuba for Beginners* by the Mexican cartoonist Rius, then *Marx for Beginners* and *Lenin for Beginners,* which provoked a whole new genre of the demystification of politics. He put more and more of Freire's work into English print — *Education for Critical Consciousness* and the *Letters to Guinea-Bissau*, and the Brazilian's dictum about 'reading the word and the world' became the Co-op's watchwords, as he went ahead publishing the works of the Bolshevik witness Victor Serge, the Cuban novelist Alejo Carpentier, the struggle in El Salvador in the photographs of Susan Meiselas, the novels of the Turk Yashar Kemal and important feminist texts such as Dale Spender's *Invisible Women*. When the Chilean exile and democrat Orlando Letelier was murdered by Pinochet's agents in the US with C.I.A. connivance, the Co-op published Saul Landau's account of the crime, *Assassination on Embassy Row.*

Glenn published four of my books during the Co-op's decade of existence. The first was *Classrooms of Resistance*, which focussed upon my teaching and the children's work when I returned to Sir John Cass — the writing about the Docklands speculation, Chile, South Africa, working at local factories and Fords, the closure of Poplar Hospital and the experience of Belfast school children. I remember his reaction when I first showed the texts to him. 'We've got to do it, Chris,' he declared, almost in a whisper, 'we must do it, we will do it!' Then he reconceptualised it, as a visual anthology with the

267

children's writing laid out across evocative photographic images — rather like Ron had done with the *Stepney Words* poems — and he made it twice the book it originally was. When it finally emerged it was greeted by howls of hostility by the establishment press. The pink newssheets of the *Financial Times,* well-attuned of course to the neo-liberal economies of the 'Chicago Boys' who were directing Pinochet's 'model' Chilean economy, gave over one of its pages to the dangers of the ideas within *Classrooms of Resistance* under the headline 'Teaching Revolution in the Classroom', discussing where the line should be drawn against teachers such as I. 'If the present danger to democracy in Britain is not to become overwhelming,' wrote their correspondent Joe Rogaly, 'we must first make up our minds about where this line is to be drawn and then cast aside inhibitions in defending it.' The *Daily Telegraph* was even more direct: 'There is no doubt that *Classrooms of Resistance* is clear indoctrination,' it declared, with the *Times Educational Supplement* attesting that I was creating nothing but 'mindless replicators' in my classroom. But it was the television commentator Peregrine Worsthorne who had the most demonstrative say. Also Deputy Editor of the *Sunday Telegraph,* he wrote in that paper in an article headlined 'Get class out the classroom', referring to me: 'the sooner he is sacked, *pour encourager les autres* — of whom there are far too many — the better,' after all, as a teacher I was showing 'a degree of intellectual meanness, not to say sadism, far more outrageous and unforgivable than the worst excesses of Mr Squeers.' Yet strangely enough, while the reviews section of the *Times Educational Supplement* lambasted *Classrooms of Resistance*, its editorial writer seemed to have a different perspective:

> Mr Searle is a lively and combative exponent of an approach to education which bears a close resemblance to that of Paulo Freire, the Brazilian philosopher and adult educator, who argues that the key to learning is to

be found in giving the learner insight into the social, economic and political realities which dominate his existence. It is Marxist in its assumption that the ownership of the means of production, distribution and exchange determine the consciousness of children in school, and their families. Hence, opening their eyes to a Marxist analysis of the distribution of power within society is the first step on the road to learning.

The motive force for education, according to this view, is found in the desire to change the society by radical criticism and action: this is the guiding light which can generate an effective desire to learn in children who otherwise are likely to feel helpless and impotent.

When I first read this I was astonished and felt that I couldn't have put it better and more lucidly myself, and this was the *TES,* one of my most powerful foes! But it was my Co-op colleague John Berger, writing in the *New Society*, that most truly understood the function of both the book and the teaching that generated it:

> Chris Searle teaches English in a London East End secondary school. His pupils are working class. Around the school the docks are being closed down, social services are being cut, unemployment is increasing and the poverty of the permitted choices is becoming more and more obvious. Nearby, a luxury hotel of over 800 rooms has been built, warehouses are being transformed into luxury flats and a mooring 'port' has been opened for private yachts. All this outside the classroom. Inside, what should the kids be studying and writing about? Wordsworth, A Walk in the Country, My Favourite TV Programme?
>
> Searle allows them to think and feel what is happening outside the classroom and what is likely to happen next — given who they are. I say allow, because if not discouraged, it is what they might begin to do for themselves. I say given who they are because the first principle of his lessons is self-recognition. All the kids have been born into an exploited class. If they don't resist they will be worse-paid and worse-housed. By encouraging such self-recognition, a sense of justice and the will to fight back, his English lessons arm the adolescents for the lives already allotted to them as adults by a class society.

As often, Berger's words became deeply prophetic. A year ago I returned to Poplar to see how our old Limehouse School was doing. It was closed, the steadfast nineteenth-century edifice converted into a block of gated luxury flats. I looked up at the windows where my classroom used to be, forty years earlier, and saw velvet curtains. The playground, where we played football and cricket with the students, now had Porsches parked within it behind high iron gates. I thought of Ruth and Nancy's translucent tiles and immaculate staircases. Now only half a mile away from the giant bankers' tower of Canary Wharf, I could only guess who lived there and creamed off the labours and years of education of those who, as Sally Flood had put it in her Basement poem, were 'generations of the exploited'. I turned away, saddened and angered.

Another kindred book that Glenn published, and a 'brave vigorous protest' against the treatment of elders in Britain was a book by 'Gladys Elder OAP', which was how she named herself, called *The Alienated*. Gladys had written to me after she read the *Elders* anthology, and eventually sent me her manuscript from Cheetham Hill, Manchester, where she lived. She also developed a loving, faraway relationship by letters with Stephen Hicks, although they only met once, face to face. In his autobiography, *Sparring for Luck*, Stephen called her 'a wonderful woman and a learned one as well,' and in the final poem of his story, *Up the Hill*, he writes:

I'm thinking of her more and more,
I don't know why it is, I'm sure...
And when composing verse and rhyme
I'm thinking of her all the time...

I passed the text of her book on to Glenn, who was deeply moved by its descriptions of the treatment of the aged, in particular, the aged of the working class. Again, he enriched words with photographs, this time by the photographer Mike Abrahams, and sent a copy of the manuscript to the veteran playwright J.B.

270

Priestley. Gladys died while her book was in the process of publication, and Priestley, 82 himself, became its champion. In his introduction he wrote:

> In the endless campaign waged by the old against poverty, neglect, insensitive administration, this book is a report from the battlefield. Even in her very title *The Alienated*, she shows her understanding of the central problem of old people today.
>
> Quite rightly we are spared no disturbing facts in this book, for it is not intended to be pleasant light reading, and is indeed a brave, vigorous protest.

The powerful cover photograph of an old woman surrounded by fellow shoppers and peering into her purse, was Glenn's idea, and it crystallised Gladys' indignation and insights. It also took me back to *Stepney Words*. I knew that its poets would have understood Gladys, and I remembered:

> I am old and frightened
> In this darkened world,
> I'm shut behind bars...

And

> I live on my own
> Have no friends
> It's damp and dark
> I've got voices in my ears
> But they're all in my mind.

Or Jean's defining lines from *The Lonely Man*:

> The man walked across the grass
> With a fag in his mouth,
> The leaves fall down on the old man's coat,
> He don't have a care in the world
> Except to walk in the park all
> Alone.

Yes, the alienated, the alone: Gladys and the Stepney children knew its meaning in the elderly lives all around them, and Glenn knew it too.

Back at the Basement the Tuesday nights had become even more full of life and imagination, with new members and books of poetry being published almost on a weekly basis. Even I got in on the act with the publication of my classroom play, *Mendoza for Ever*. One of the most stimulating sessions was when we had a visit from Adrian Mitchell, who walked down the steps and immediately sensed he was with comrades of words, and talked about his poetry, reading poems from his most recent collection, *Ride the Nightmare*. The Basement Writers had adopted one of his dictums as their watchwords: 'Most people ignore most poetry because most poetry ignores most people.' It resonated hard, and down those steps we all resolved to create its contrary. The Basement Writers were also getting more and more involved with the Half Moon Theatre, in Alie Street, near Aldgate. The Half Moon stalwarts had moved into and converted an abandoned synagogue, and transformed it into a 100-seater theatre, while Ron had taken on its lobby and staircase and made a photographers' gallery out of it. One of the actors, Maurice Colbourne, who later became a prominent film actor, and the Canadian director Guy Sprung, seemed keen on the Basement being more involved in using the theatre. We grasped the opportunity and the Half Moon, particularly on Sunday nights when there were no performances, became our venue for very lively and surprising poetry readings. The first one commemorated *Elders*, with Stephen taking centre stage, and we had others celebrating the Battle of Cable Street and supporting the struggle of the Shrewsbury Building Workers. There was a reading called *Black Words*, when we invited a number of black poets including John La Rose, Andrew Salkey, Mustapha Matura and Cecil Rajendra and the Third World Troubadours, to help publicise and raise funds for imprisoned black activist Tony Soares. There were other more lighthearted performances, and a dramatic adaptation of Alan's comic, *Up the Docks*. All these readings took place in the sets of whatever plays were

272

Poster by
Ron McCormick©

being performed during that week, whether it was Brecht's *The Mother* or *St. Joan of the Stockyards*, Steve Gooch's marvellous *Female Transport*, Shakespeare's *Henry VI Part I* or Billy Colvill's *Soft Like a Girl* or his dramatisation of the 1911 children's school strikes, *Fall in and Follow Me*. The Half Mooners would give us their keys, ask us to drop them back through the letterbox as we left, and we never paid a penny for any of the many, many times we used the theatre. Their generosity was exemplary — they just wanted their theatre to be the cultural hub of the community. Stephen loved it there, and wrote this poem as a tribute:

If William Shakespeare walked again
He'd make for this place, I'm sure,
But though he possessed a poetic brain
In here he could learn even more.

He'd think it was grand
To spy out the land and learn all the secrets therein.
But when he was done, away he would run
And make out he wrote everything.

He'd loosen his joints to pick up more points
And no one could pick them up better,
So we'd come very hard and the bard would be barred
For life, from the Half Moon Theatre!

And he read this on the set of *Henry IV Part I* with more than a single twinkle in his eye. For the Half Moon was truly the Globe of the Basement Writers.

It was around this time that I met a teenage poet called Andrew Strowman. He had grown up in Stepney and was profoundly and ironically proud of it: it seemed to define him and his poetry. He showed me a collection of his poems under the title *Story of a Stepney Boy*, and told me that he too, like Isaac three of four generations before, had grandparents who were Jewish immigrants from Russia and Poland. He seemed very much a loner — he never came to the Basement Writers — and many of his poems were deeply introspective, yet contradictorily also

274

powerfully outward-looking even though they seemed to come from a ruefully pessimistic heart. Using the Reality Press imprint and continuing the localised tradition of *Stepney Words,* we published his collection with an evocative cover photograph by Ron of an anxious dark-haired boy holding some washing and looking from the window of the launderette at the bottom of Princelet Street, four houses down from Ron's flat. Perhaps he was a thinker of Andrew's *Young Boy's Story of the Slums*, set in powerful Blake-like rhymes:

Under the chimney pots
Under the sky
I wonder where in the world am I?

My voice is unison
My story is one
My hopes, my destinies
I must have some.

I have seen
Begging looks and tired faces
I have stood alone
In empty places.

Heavy I am in thought,
Little am I in age,
Stupid am I in sums,
And yet I know
The story of the slums.

Like Blake too and the *Stepney Words* poets he identified with the people of the street — the old, the vagrants, the disabled, the mentally ill — making his readers marvel again at how the young can know so much, empathise so fully, as Isaac did with his fellow-soldiers, with a trilling lark above the battlefield or a rat scurrying between opposing trenches. Something about Andrew took me directly back to Isaac; his naked words, his exhausted people, his startling images — as in *A Strawberry and an Onion*:

Once
I heard a blind man say
God, give me my eyes again
But no-one came.

Once
I heard an old tramp cry
Please, Lord, do not let me rise tomorrow
But he did, and was overcome with sorrow.

After we published his little book, I rarely saw Andrew again. I eventually went to teach in Mozambique, but his dedication was to Stepney, its people and its images. But I still wondered about his life and words: where did they go?

In 1975 I made contact with a biographer of Isaac — Jean Liddiard, a lecturer at the London School of Art and Design, who was, as a part of her research, looking for anyone who had known him or written about him. One of my father's Jewish clients had seen her advertisement in the *Jewish Chronicle*, and knowing my deep interest in Isaac's life and work, had shown it to my father, who passed it on to me. I telephoned her and we spent a fascinating day together, talking about Isaac's art and life. She borrowed the thesis I had written in Canada on his poetry, and generously acknowledged it in the preface to her fine and humane study: *Isaac Rosenberg: The Half Used Life*. She also told me that his closest friend, the poet and translator Joseph Leftwich, was still alive and living in North London.

I was overjoyed to hear this. Leftwich was now in his mid-eighties, (he was born in 1892, two years after Isaac) and my first reaction to hearing of his survival was: Isaac could still be here too without that grotesque war and those politicians and generals who killed him, or even if he'd managed to avoid death in the trenches for just a few more weeks of 1918, until peace was declared. Joseph was lucky — his Dutch passport saved him from the British military. I was determined to meet him and ask him about his friend. I knew I could never speak to Isaac, even

276

though I thought I was closely inside his mind and life, but I could at least talk to his dear boyhood friend. Leftwich was one of the young men who called themselves 'The Whitechapel Boys', who would meet in Whitechapel Library where sixty years later the spark of *Stepney Words* had been lit, and go on their long nighttime walks in those same streets where I had walked with Ron and my students. As Joseph had written in one of his own poems, *Imminence*:

> Midnight struck, then one o'clock, two,
> We still talked of what things we would do.
> Down Hannibal Road, Jamaica Street,
> Then back again, with untiring feet
> We talked of our hopes and of our fears.

Jean gave me his telephone number, and when spoke I to him he responded warmly, inviting me to his Highgate home where, he said, he would happily be interviewed.

In 1939 Leftwich's anthology of poems translated from Yiddish, *The Golden Peacock,* was published and received much attention, but he was also a fine poet in his own right, as his collection *Along the Years: Poems 1911–1937* attests. He was born in Zutphen, Holland in 1895, the son of a Polish Jewish cobbler, and arrived in Stepney in 1900, when his family emigrated. When I walked into his spacious house in a fashionable north London neighbourhood, it somehow seemed another world from Whitechapel, but his friendliness soon made me feel at home, and I marvelled that this was the man who had been the closest confidante of the poet I loved and who had died so young. I began by asking about what life was like for young Jewish men and women in the years following the racist 1905 Aliens Act and the growth of the British Brothers' League, the National Front of their day. He spoke quietly but with a profound assurance, telling me of streets and places which I knew well:

> Our life was mostly centred around our own families and our own people — the Jews of the East End with whom we lived in daily contact, with whom we had fights and

277

disagreeable relations sometimes because we were on top of them and they were on top of us.

We didn't have much dealing with non-Jews. Our streets were almost one hundred percent Jewish streets, the factories and workshops and the shops were all Jewish and the occasional non-Jew who lived in the streets amongst us was on the whole friendly. I remember some buildings called Dunstan Houses in Stepney Green which had two shops at their entrance, a grocery shop and a leather goods shop. The grocery shop was a Jewish shop but the leather goods shop was a non-Jewish shop run by a very formidable woman, who was extremely boisterous, stood on her rights, knew exactly what she was doing and was a very demonstrative disciple of the Anti-alien Movement which campaigned against the Jewish foreigners who had come to live in those streets. Yet, strangely enough, in her personal relations with her Jewish fellow-residents she was the best of friends. The reservation about disliking the foreigner did not include the people with whom she lived and with whom she dealt. I think that was fairly typical.

In Hannibal Road where we lived there was a dairy. The cows were driven to London from the valleys in Wales, and then driven back at the end of the week, the drivers used to come into my father's house next door to the dairy, in order to spend an hour or two talking in the most friendly way. We also had a gas fitter who came to us from the Commercial Gas Company in Ben Jonson Road to install a cooker. He became very friendly with my father and my mother, to such an extent that he used to come with his wife regularly to our house and we used to go to their house, and when I put in an application for naturalisation, they were my witnesses. So this was the peculiar situation that has always been impressed upon my mind, that public feeling and private emotion did not go together and were, in fact, very, very separate.

The only occasions of violence that I remember were during the Sidney Street Siege of January 1911. I remember the crowds that hung around Stepney and its outskirts because of the sensational developments. The papers were full of reports that aroused many fears that the government might take steps to deport aliens, particularly Jewish aliens. I remember meeting in the street Mrs Winsten, the mother of my friend Samuel Winsten, who was almost weeping with fear. 'Do you think they're going to deport us? Will they send us out?' She was terribly afraid. They were all socialists, the entire family, and had emigrated from Russia where her eldest son had been one of the leaders of the Bund, the Jewish socialist party, most of whose members later switched to the Bolsheviks. So she was afraid of yet another move, yet another tipping out into another country.

I asked him about the influences of socialism among Isaac and his friends during those pre-1914 years, and he was very explicit.

We all belonged to the Young Socialist League and we were very active in it. I can remember that in my diary I have a note that our non-Jewish comrades, our fellow young socialists, were just as anti-semitic as the people around them in the East End except they made an exception in favour of us, their Jewish comrades!

The League had a deep influence upon us. First there was the theory; there was Marxism, the criticism of capitalism. We heard this at open air speakers' corners at almost every street corner. We had some remarkably good speakers — I remember one in particular called Fineberg, who went to Russia as soon as the revolution broke out. We held meetings continually and organised discussion groups. Again in my diary, I wrote about going to a Social Democratic Federation meeting in Bethnal Green, where one of the women organising the meeting was amazed that youngsters like us should know so much about what the party stood for. I remember that once I wrote to the great socialist artist Walter Crane and told him that we, the Stepney and Whitechapel Branch of the Social Democratic Federation and the Young Socialist League wanted to organise something on our own to put into the May Day march. We were very much attracted to that idea and we wanted to know if he would help and support us. He responded in his beautiful handwriting and gave us a lot of his thoughts and ideas.

The influences were all around us. There was, for example my friend Morris Goldstein in the Stepney branch of the League. He found his socialism in pity for the poor vagrants of the embankment. He used to drag us all along with him to talk to the tramps and the homeless and to give them sixpences which we could not afford ourselves, all to show them our understanding and solidarity. For us our whole lives were to go here, to go there, to see people, to hear people like we used to hear the speakers and hecklers at Mile End Waste. At our meetings we discussed everything, but mostly literature. Isaac used to read his poetry to us and his essays. We walked the streets until one or two every morning, talking in the darkness or under the gas light, talking all the time down to Aldgate and back again to Stepney Green. Or we met in one of our houses and jawed for hours about socialism and how we would spread its ideas through our literature and the pamphlets we had by Hyndman and others, and of course, the League's journal started by William Morris, *Commonweal.*

Then there was the influence of Rudolf Rocker and the Anarchist movement that he led. Although we were unemployed we found that we had no time for all the places open to us and all the things we wanted to talk about. We had Toynbee Hall, we had South Place, we had the People's Palace, Victoria Park, Mile End Waste — we had no time for all the things we wanted to do! When the war broke out in 1914 we were in command at Toynbee Hall, I was almost running it that time. We had many meetings and discussions about peace, and one of the people that I invited to speak was Bertrand Russell. When he finished and caught his train back to Cambridge he was arrested and spent the rest of the war in prison.

We had strike marches through the East End. In 1906 and earlier we had strikes in the tailoring workshops and the workers' groups of fifties and hundreds marched through the streets with a brass band. We had the big May Day marches that went to Hyde Park from Mile End Waste, some of them big, straggling marches. We listened to the speakers as they declaimed from coal vans, carts and shire horses and we met old and new comrades. We had the great meetings in 1911–12 of the dockers and transport workers. I remember the great speakers in Victoria Park like Ben Tillett. I knew Tillett, and like many others he didn't like the dilution of, as he saw it, 'Englishry'. He thought the alien immigration was doing harm to the economic position of the English working man, and he was opposed to the introduction of an alien language. But again, he held no antipathy to the people whom he knew who belonged to the other ethnic groups. Again, he made that public and private distinction.

As these words poured out of Joseph about his and Isaac's world, I found myself constantly comparing East London then and now. The cultural ferment he lived through was still simmering in places like the Half Moon and the Basement and in the big community festivals, but the heat of revolutionary and socialist politics had certainly cooled, almost frozen. When he talked about his night walks and meetings with vagrants I thought of the now-times pitches by the Spitalfields fire outside the fruit and vegetable market, or where the homeless cooked their potatoes and swedes in jackets. I thought of our friend Banjo, or Banjo Scouse, as he was known. Ron, a fellow Liverpudlian, knew him well, sitting with him and photographing him as he played his banjo, kazoo, cymbals and drum outside Christchurch Spitalfields with a white dog called Suzie. Banjo found his 'skippers' and sleeping places in dark places and basements around Puma Court

Banjo Scouse and Suzie
Ron McCormick©

and Fournier Street. Ron and I once took him with us to an education seminar that I was speaking at, held in a smart college in Weybridge, Surrey in the stockbroker belt. As we walked into its main hall, Banjo saw its grand piano. He made a beeline for it and started playing it like a master. Ron and I marvelled at his skill and the music and beauty that was coming from his gnarled and battered fingers as he caressed the keys. He was suddenly in another world, a million miles away from the flames of the Spitalfields fire. For a short time we had an act together with me and my poems and Banjo's one-man-band. We did a session at the Half Moon with another Liverpudlian, the poet Adrian Henri, one of the founders of the new Mersey poetry. But then Banjo disappeared, somewhere — who knows, after giving me his usual farewell: 'Be lucky!' I'm not sure that he ever was.

But all this came back to me as I listened to Joseph, and he told me more about the conditions that he, Isaac and their friends lived through:

> There was the hard grind, the poverty, the hours of soulless work, the being thralled to the slave system, and for us as writers and artists, not being able to write or paint as we wanted because those hours were the master's. But in addition to being there, in the home of the new immigrants many of us were very largely dependent on the Jewish Board of Guardians for charity and social help. For there was not only poverty but a juxtaposition of many sharing a common fate, a common language and a common semi-alienation from the world around them.

And then he found his focus on his friend Isaac:

> Rosenberg had very little contact with non-Jews, like me. He went to a school where ninety per cent of the children were Jews, and then because of his drawing ability he was apprenticed, through the Jewish Board of Guardians to the Jewish firm of photograph engravers, Karl Henschel. He prayed for his deliverance from this apprenticeship so he could go out into the world and do something else and find a place for himself as a poet. I was working in a furrier's workshop at the time and I

had the same feeling. When his apprenticeship finished, he reacted in his growling, grunting way. He had no money; he hadn't a penny to dress himself with. He couldn't contribute to the family at all. His mother had to struggle hard, the same as all our mothers did, and eventually Isaac ended up in the Army in order to get a separation allowance for his mother to enable her to run the home. It was the only way he could contribute to the family income. That is what led him to be killed — why they ever enlisted him, God only knows. He was the last man who should ever have been in the Army.

Joseph shook his head several times, reliving his friend's financial agony. I asked him more about his family:

He was brought up in a traditional Jewish home, a fairly religious home. I knew his whole family and they all spoke Yiddish at home. His father was a very silent man, his mother very vivacious, a bubbling, self-assertive woman who was much given up to her family and home. So Yiddish was his mother tongue as it was for me. Later I introduced him to a number of Yiddish writers and poets in Whitechapel, which at that time was still abuzz with Yiddish culture.

Isaac often had to drag himself along to our Socialist League meetings. For although socialist ideals were a part of our lives, he was never, like the rest of us, committed to socialism in the sense of talking or writing about it. If it came into his work it came in unobtrusively, there was no proclamation, 'I am a socialist!' Moving with us and around us, the socialist dream must also have been a part of him. Our group was open to all the winds around us, some penetrating to a certain depth, others like the socialist wind, very profoundly. We didn't choose as much as we were chosen.

In my foreword to my first book of poems I talk of Rosenberg as taciturn, mooching along behind us. He wasn't a talker. He would read his poems to us but he would rarely talk. An idea would possess him and he would work upon it. He would rewrite a poem a dozen times and it was the wording that moved him. He didn't talk to me about what I wrote or bother about the work of any of us because we were all writing well before we met each other. He was too self-absorbed to do that. But we all had a conviction that Rosenberg was a genius.

Knowing how so many of my own students were bilingual — in their case mainly in Bengali and English, from the families that now lived in the same streets and houses in Whitechapel and Stepney where Isaac, Joseph and their friends had lived, I asked Joseph about how he thought that the spanning of two languages influenced Isaac in his writing of poems in English.

For all of us who grew up in Yiddish-speaking homes, then inevitably something must have adhered to us from that particular influence as we learned and then spoke fluently in our new language, English. How far it permeated and yeasted out of the life we expressed in our new language is very difficult to say. It must have given some advantages to the way we spoke English. There is a famous Yiddish poet who speaks of this particular question, and he says that this is a Yiddish poem in English words:

It does not repeat,
The land does not come again
The angel is not always near.

I don't know. Many poets in all times in many languages have pondered this and there are those who will come with a ready-made theory who will work the subject to it. But with Rosenberg, I don't really know how the language of his poems was affected by his Yiddish mother tongue. Here or there I will detect something, a spot perhaps. But he lived not upon Yiddish poetry, he lived on English poetry. He saturated himself with it, he was reading and repeating it all the time. Isaac felt no restrictions in the English language simply because it was his second language. He thought of himself as very free in English, that he could move around, that he could swing and fly in the language. He was an *English* poet, and that is one of the things that in my anger I always insisted upon. He was an *English* poet. A poet! That's all he wanted to be.

I asked him about the patronage that Isaac felt forced to accept because of his poverty. How did he, as a socialist and a poet, feel about being known by his patrons as 'impoverished little Rosenberg', the East End boy with no money and no smart clothes?

He didn't resent patronage, he resented *condescension.* He resented being taken to task for not spending more time at his work, for being told to do things and how to live his life, for being regimented. You see, right from when he would come with us on summer trips to Epping Forest, he would bring his paint box with him and paint. He was desperate to become a painter at that time and it was a miracle that brought him to the Slade School of Art. He was picked up in the National Gallery by two Jewish ladies, and the cousin of one of them called Mrs Cohen paid for him to go to the Slade. They were women from families who were prosperous but also idealistic. Mrs Cohen's mother was a suffragette who had been to prison many times — and they sought contact with Art, Culture and an ideal world. They too were socialists of a kind.

Then there was Sir Edward Marsh who was Churchill's secretary. He took up Rosenberg's artist friend, Gertler, who dragged him to meet Marsh. Any help in the direction of becoming either a poet or a painter was welcome to him. So he didn't object to the help itself, but to the way it was exercised. But he shrugged off the condescension. He could be very outspoken in his language to Marsh. When he told him, for example, that he didn't care for the poetry of Marsh's friend, Rupert Brooke, he told him so in no uncertain terms. The last time I saw Rosenberg he was walking along Mile End Road and he jumped off a bus and shouted to me. He was on his last leave and showed me a letter from Marsh about Brooke's death and how it had affected him, as if the sun had gone out, he had written. Rosenberg was very angry that Marsh should be concerned about someone whom he considered to be a very inferior poet. He showed that anger in very definite terms, yet it was not an anger of class. He never felt out of place anywhere, none of us did. We were all aware of the difficulties that such differences in class and wealth brought, and of our own impoverishment compared to the likes of Marsh or Brooke — and we were all socialists and believed in a class war. But it was to a certain extent theory and like the racism it did not always affect our personal lives. As far as people like Sir Edward Marsh were concerned, they might give you a leg-up.

I wanted to know, more than anything from him, what his assessment was of his friend's poetry, what he thought of him now, nearly fifty years after his death. He was silent for several seconds, then he said, very quietly:

> I wouldn't dare say. I wouldn't dare to pick him to pieces.
> Just read him. He was in the tradition of great visionary
> poets, like Blake. He loved the simplicity of Blake and it
> was allied to his admiration of Blake the draftsman and
> artist. Like Blake he tried to rise to inaccessible heights
> in his language, but he worked to be understood and he
> worked to be appreciated. All his articulacy came out in
> his poetry. He was not a speaker at all, he was a
> mumbler, a fumbler and he needed poetry to articulate
> himself. I can't remember him once speaking at a public
> meeting, yet the rest of us always did. He would sit next
> to us and listen and the ideas would go in, as everything
> else did and everything would come out in his poetry. But
> read him. Read *A Snake Fed on the Heart of Corinth* or
> *Returning, We Hear the Larks*. Those are jewels of
> English poetry.

And what about the contemporary Rosenbergs, I asked Joseph, what about the new generations of bilingual children in our schools seeking to master English as a vital second language as he and Isaac did, what would he say to them?

> I was born abroad, in Holland, in a town called Zutphen.
> I had come to England as a boy of seven and found myself
> in Settles Street School in Stepney. I can remember the
> first occasion when the Headmaster, a man named
> Mansfield, talked to our class and I didn't understand a
> single word that he was saying. I didn't know any
> English at all. I picked it up over the space of my first
> year, I suppose.
>
> I believe in learning. I believe that everything that we
> learn is valuable. I also believe that each language gives
> a distinct flavour to life and learning, that it gives an
> added richness to what you teach and learn through it,
> that it makes for greater individuality. So people should
> be multi-lingual, particularly if their mother language is
> a part of their heartsblood, a part of their soul. This lan-
> guage, its words are something that have been born
> within and need to be brought out, otherwise they will
> lay like a heavy load on the chest, giving us nothing but
> just weighing us down. I always knew that the language

I was born into must be used, must be polished, must be heart-spoken, must contribute to a great all-round wealth of culture.

As I was leaving he gave me a signed copy of his poems, *Along the Years*, and it is still one of my most precious books. On the tube back to Stepney Green I was glowing — I had met Isaac's best friend, the man he had walked with, talked with, confided in had also talked to me, I thought, in a way of friendship, and as I read one or two random poems from his book, I suddenly came across:

> I saw an old man in a Stepney park.
> The sun was setting, it was growing dark.
> And in the darkness it seemed to me
> That the old man was a broken tree.

This poem seemed to come straight from *Stepney Words*. I thought, and I remembered:

> There was a man in the street,
> So old and cold he could not speak.
> With eyes of blue and hair of grey
> He walked, and walked by, did not speak.

Or Karen's lines about an old woman, living alone:

> The house and her make a good pair.
> She smokes her pipe
> And wears hair nets,
> She's by her own
> In a world of her own.
> She does things her way
> Lives her way.

And passing through Aldgate East and Whitechapel, the doors opened and dozens of children, coming home from school, got off the train, laughing, fooling, speaking Bengali, and Joseph's words came ringing back to me. Yes, for a few hours, I thought, I had been in Isaac's world, and then coming back here, I knew I had never left it.

1975 seemed to be a key year for those who loved Isaac and his poetry. Three biographies of him were published, almost simultaneously. As well as Jean Liddiard's book

287

there was another by an American scholar from Tulane University in New Orleans, Joseph Cohen, called *Journey to the Trenches*, and a third by the English critic, Jean Moorcroft Wilson called *Isaac Rosenberg: Poet and Painter*. In the midst of all this sudden critical attention upon Isaac, from the Basement we decided to organise a celebratory event at the Half Moon Theatre, which being an ex-local synagogue in constant use during Isaac's life in Stepney, was a thoroughly apt venue. Alan designed an evocative poster (I am looking at it, framed above my fireplace) of a portrait of Isaac set against a silhouette of trench soldiers. We invited the three biographers, all of whom responded enthusiastically and gave presentations, and also the Yiddish poet, now very old, Avram Stencl (1897–1983) who read his poem *Shakespeare and Whitechapel* in his own first language in a setting which he could remember as a busy place of worship. As he read I could only guess at the meanings of his words and I wondered about Isaac. He

Isaac Rosenberg

A CELEBRATION OF HIS POETRY.

SUNDAY
26th OCTOBER

7.30

HALF MOON THEATRE.
27 Alie Street, E.1.
tube: aldgate east

must have come here, I thought, probably as a boy with his family when they lived at 47 Cable Street, literally just down the road. Where would he have sat? What had he been thinking? Did he pray? Did he sing? What pictures were in his mind? What words of Stepney were forming in his boyish imagination? Later, I found a translation of Stencl's poem, written after his 1936 escape from Berlin, where he had been arrested and tortured by the Gestapo, to England and a new home in Whitechapel.

> The name Shakespeare drew me to London
> When I was a hunted Jew.
> A sea-mew in a thick fog,
> Into the Thames I flew.
>
> A sea-mew in a thick fog,
> I flew into London town.
> And I found my way to Whitechapel,
> Which had become my own.
>
> Flying through the thick fog
> I saw a door opening here,
> And a Jewish *shtetl*
> Like my home-town appear.
>
> I stretched out my arms,
> Everything became clear.
> Thank you Whitechapel,
> For all I have written here.

When the evening ended and as I put the key back through the ex-synagogue's letterbox below the weather-worn *mezuzah* on its doorframe, I felt its blessing and I remember thinking out loud: 'A pity you weren't there as you should have been mate. We did it for you. You would have loved it.' And as I walked back down Alie Street, towards Cable Street, as he and his family would have done, some seventy years before, from that place of worship, then place of drama and poetry, now demolished, I thought about his genius and that of the millions of young people that have come after him from all nations here in Stepney, speaking all languages, but living and growing and writing poetry together.

Afterword

My English class is in a cramped classroom in Wicker, Sheffield right next to the rusty River Don, near a river-bank pathway where addicts come to fill their tired veins with poison. In front of me sit Iranians, Eritreans, Iraqis, Armenians, Yemenis, Burmese, Kurds, Syrians, Congolese, Bangladeshis, Sudanese, Afghans and Russians, most of them refugees and asylum seekers fleeing something hostile and momentous in their lives. They like writing creatively and with realism, having no qualms about revealing secret oppressions they have known, and respond very willingly to the sense of release which narrative writing and poetry bring. Here is one young Afghan's story of his journey to find Sheffield.

> When I was a boy I wanted to be an engineer. I was born in Urozgan in the country of Afghanistan. My father was a farmer, he cultivated many vegetables, and I helped him.
>
> When the Taliban took power they tried to force me to become one of their soldiers. I refused and they put me in prison. I escaped from the jail by bribing a soldier and went across the frontier to Pakistan. I couldn't speak Urdu so it was very difficult for me to communicate. Then I went to Iran. I know Farsi, so it was better. Then my friends and I decided to go to Turkey.
>
> At first we went to Salmas, a border town. There are many high mountains between Iran and Turkey and the Turkish soldiers had hidden a lot of mines under the ground. Said, the guide, told us to get ready and then he said that we should climb the mountains and cross the border.
>
> It was very, very difficult and dangerous but we succeeded in reaching Turkey. We went to Istanbul. After a few weeks my friends decided to get to Italy. We paid a lot of money. There were 700 people on the ship, some from Afghanistan, others from Iraq and some other countries. The captain steered the ship to the land of Greece and the police took us — but after 10 days or so they left us alone.

Then we went to the port of Patra, from where the ships took many cars and trucks to Italy. I hid inside a truck and arrived in Italy after a voyage of 20 hours. I continued my journey to Rome and when I arrived there I had no money. I wanted to go to France, so I got into a train and hid in a WC and arrived in Paris the next day. Then I went to Calais.

I decided to go to England. One day I went to the station and hid under the train. It seemed like a normal thing to do, I wasn't afraid. The train went through the Channel Tunnel and then, at last, I was in ENGLAND.

I looked at his smiling face, so young and yet so much experience already, and learning words so fast. And sitting in front of him is Salam, a refugee from the Bush/Blair invasion of his country, who had just passed me this. He called his poem *Baghdad*, after the ruins of his city.

How long will I have to wait, lonely?
How long will I have to hear the fateful news?
There is nobody who has two hearts.
But I have
Yes, I have.
I left one in Baghdad.
It is always in a great suffering,
It is suffering from the pain
As it hears the sound of bombs instead of freedom bells.
As they said to the Iraqis
'We are going to liberate you.'
But thieves never tell the truth,
They came to Baghdad to bury the truth.
They came after decades of drought,
Trees started to dehydrate,
Widows were looking for milk,
Babies were hungry
People were living in poverty
So they prayed for rain.
People were praying for an end to the boycott
But it rained blood
As the bombs were dropped,
They made Baghdad a sea of blood
They made a Hollywood movie
But it was in Baghdad, not in Hollywood.

291

When we read English translations of Iranian women's poems, the poems of the Palestinian Mahmoud Darwish or the Turk Nazim Hikmet, the floodgates of language and the imagination open — even the English language which they are so earnestly chasing to find. We read this poem by the Pakistani Faiz Ahmed Faiz and it is as if they have found a release in words, so deeply do they love and respond to its testimony.

Speak

Speak — your lips are free.
Speak — your tongue is still yours.
This magnificent body
Is still yours.
Speak — your life is still yours.
Look inside the smithy —
Leaping flames, red hot iron.
Padlocks open wide
Their jaws.
Chains disintegrate.
Speak — there is little time
It is enough
Time enough
Before the body perishes —
Before the tongue atrophies.
Speak — truth still lives.
Say what you have
To say.

As I read Faiz's poem out loud in this Sheffield classroom, I am suddenly taken back half a lifetime to Stepney, remembering the effect when I first read my student Paul's poem in 1970:

Let it Flow Joe

Let it flow Joe
Let your feelings speak for you
Let the people know what you know.
Tell them what it's all about
Shout it out.

When you talk people come alive
People start to realise.

Words flow out of your mouth
When you talk about this earth.
Tell the people everything Joe
About what you know.

Talk to them Joe
Let them know
Let the words flow out.

But all these students are newcomers in England in the first decade of the twenty-first century and life is hard around them. Forbidden to work because of their asylum-seeking status, cramped in the most basic of housing, barely enough food, an icy Yorkshire winter for them and their children, zero status and living with the perennial fear of deportation. Faranak from Iran finds the words to remember how it was so much more difficult when she arrived, but how gradually, as she began to know and make friendships with her neighbours, life all around her became better, more comforting, warmer and more human. And as she read her first reflections, I thought, as I have done very often all through my teaching life, of Marjorie and the blessings of her 'poetic spirit'.

My Street

When I went to live in that street
The cold wind came fast
And slapped my freezing face.
My eyes were looking for something familiar
But everything was strange.
Can I find somebody to speak with?
How it looked strange, ugly and cold at that time.
Today I feel different.
I know the people and I love them.
I know the street where I live.
I know the street where I want to walk all day.

I copy and hand out some newspaper reports of the twenty-three Chinese migrant cocklepickers killed in February 2004, drowned by the incoming fast-moving seawaters on the treacherous tidal sandbanks across the Pennines in Morecambe Bay on the Lancashire coast, their need for safety ignored by their gangmasters. The

293

students recognise these men as kindred spirits and are engrossed in their reading and understanding. Their response pulsates with sorrow, anger and empathy. Arrian, an Afghan in his late thirties, writes a poem which he gives to me at the end of the class, looking directly into my eyes with a passionate stare which hit me like a praisesong to poetry. Here is what he wrote:

Death for Freedom

I drew a nice future in my view
And many hopes surrounded me,
So I left my home, my dear mum and my friends.
I said goodbye to everyone, even my fatherland,
I fled to find a place to be free.
It was exciting and so great at the start
But very soon I found myself a new slave.
I had to live in different way
But I was happy to be alive on the big beach
With my friends the cockles and the tide.
In my play, I must catch the cockles soon
A game of happy life and tragic death.
On a windy night the cockles attracted me once more,
I was chasing them and picking them in buckets,
And we were talking to each other in a friendly way,
I was happy to be sucked into the play.
But finally, it was my turn to be defeated.
The quick tide surrounded me with no escape.
The cockles cried and told the deathly tide,
'Release our friend, we wanted to play!'
But the cruel tide didn't respect them,
And I realised, it's going to kill me very soon —
In that moment I was happy, but very sad.
I was happy I could feel I was free,
But sad to say goodbye to everyone, even in my life.
I decided to phone my parents,
So I found my phone and called home.
'Hi Mum, I have to fly in the sky
Pray for me to be free, goodbye, goodbye!'
I cut the phone and shouted loud at the cruel tide,
'I'm ready! Swallow me, swallow me-e-e!'

As I read Arrian's words I knew again that from all over the world, where there are people there is poetry, a truth that has been told me a million times all through my life

294

in the most surprising of situations, in the most amazing of places, in the most unpromising of contexts. Long live the poets in all of us, the words and human messages that we harbour and express, and thank you Isaac for telling me this countless, countless times. From the slaughterlands of Ypres to the sands of Morecambe Bay, from the Great Lakes to the Rockies, from the Caribbean islands to Stepney and Sheffield and Mozambique, you have never left me: poetry, the world's first language and words we all speak.

Decolonising The Land Rover

Chris Searle

from *Labour Monthly* January/February 1978

Having read here in Mozambique[1] of the racist remarks made by the chairman of British Leyland and his subsequent resignation, I send you the enclosed poem which I hope you will publish.

Its author is anonymous, and it was printed in the weekly journal here, *Tempo*, and I have translated it. As a statement of fraternity and solidarity with the Land Rover workers of British Leyland, I think it is very forceful and moving. The chairman of British Leyland makes racist remarks about black workers in England; a worker's poet here defies any form of racism and sends his solidarity to all car-workers at the British Leyland Land Rover works at Solihull. We have many messages of support from British trade unionists for liberation movements in Africa: now here is revolutionary Africa answering to British workers and showing them how their products can help to liberate and develop the continent:

WE ARE DECOLONISING THE LAND ROVER!

No more is it the car of the collector of taxes —
We have decolonised it!
Now there is no terror when it enters a village
For the Land Rover no longer belongs to the colonial
    policeman or soldier.
Yes, it is old, and knows all the bumps and cracks in the
    roads,
This British car is certainly experienced.
Once it was the sure ally of the exploiter's whip —
But now we have decolonised it!
Through the mud and the sand

Its power and its four wheels
Will guarantee a safe arrival at the most distant
    machambas[2]
And at all the peasants' co-operatives.
It enters the village or the experimental agricultural centre
With its militant roar in the safe hands of the driver,
Faithfully obeying all his manoeuvres,
But sometimes suffering through lack of spare parts —
We are decolonising the Land Rover!

With our products
We buy the fuel it consumes,
With our intelligence
We mend any breakdowns that happen,
With our struggle
We make a friend of this enemy —
We are the decolonisers!
We are liberating the Land Rover
And now it is independent at last!
For those who served the enemy have also transformed
    themselves:
Today's militant mechanic
The re-educated deviant
The prostitute converted to our comrade —
We have decolonised her, and married her
And there will be no divorce!

From Tete to Cabo Delgado[3]
From Niassa to Gaza
From the provincial headquarters to the country posts —
This jeep passes and greets
The caterpillar, its brother,
The maker of roads who is also decolonised.
It passes the Berliot at its tasks,
That old crusher of the mines,
The little vanguard worker of the changing roads!
The first to understand and enjoy
The opposing contradictions

Between the liberating caress of our hands
And the suffocating squeeze of the oppressor, the enemy
    who you served.

The hands of the workers who made you
Are equal to the hands of the workers of our land —
Those English hands which forged you
Know that one day they will help to make their own
    revolution,
And raise the clenched fist of their solidarity!
Now this militant roars over the tracks of Zambezia
Jumps over the rough roads of Sofala
Passes through the orchards of Manica
Through the corn of Gaza
Through the palm trees of Inhambane
And into the city of Maputo, where it rests.

It carries through the country
The eyes of friendly foreigners
Who help us with our production —
We are decolonising a weapon of the enemy!
We are decolonising the Land Rover!

Those four wheels and the powerful motor,
That cab with its control dials
That shape of the chassis that was once linked with fear
    now doesn't make the people run away!
Men, women and children of the countryside
Make signals to the driver,
Ask for lifts —
We are decolonising the Land Rover!
And the people don't run away any more.

(By 'A.M.', translated from *Tempo*, July 24, 1977)

[1] Chris Searle wrote to *Labour Monthly* from Nampula,
Mozambique.
[2] Machamba — collective farm.
[3] The place names are all names of provinces in Mozambique.

Blair Peach
1946–1979

Poem for Blair Peach

His was a precious, loving life.
He built his passion with great bridges
    from the farthest islands of the southern seas
    to the mist that clears in the classrooms of Bow —
Life was too short to stand injustice,
    to stand the insults that he saw around him:
Humans used as pawns
Humans named as the blame for sorrow
    that they themselves felt and lived!
He saw and lived oppression on his pulses —
Colours to him were beauty,
    not a form of self-made blindness!
The human is a beaming jewel,
    from New Zealand to the streets of Southall
    he shone with its brilliance!

You who seek to murder beauty — understand!
It rises with the dawn of every day
It stays and glows with the moon and the stars
It screams with the lungs of every new-born child
It reasons with the truth of every thinking human —
Never forget the blood that crosses oceans,
Blair's brave heart swells to fill us all.

First published in *Red Earth*, 1980